SOLLY ZUCKERMAN

By the same author

Without Benefit of Laundry
(AUTOBIOGRAPHY)

SOLLY ZUCKERMAN

A Scientist out of the Ordinary

John Peyton

JOHN MURRAY
Albemarle Street, London

First published in 2001
by John Murray (Publishers) Ltd,
50 Albemarle Street, London W1S 4BD

The moral right of the author has been asserted

A catalogue record for this book is available from the British Library

ISBN 0-7195-6283-X

Typeset in Monotype Bembo 12/13.5
by Servis Filmsetting Ltd, Manchester

Printed and bound in Great Britain by
St Edmundsbury Press Ltd,
Bury St Edmunds, Suffolk

This book is dedicated to the memory of Joan,
Solly's wife and the heroine of his story, and to Mary,
my wife, who bore the brunt of its telling

Contents

Contents

Illustrations

The author and publisher would like to thank the following for permission to reproduce photographs: Plates 12, 13, 14, 15, 19, 23 and 26, The University of East Anglia; 21 and 23, © Zoological Society of London, supplied by The University of East Anglia; 18 and 24, Dr Deryk Darlington. The remaining plates come from the Zuckerman family archive.

Foreword

For nearly two and a half decades, from the time of Macmillan to that of Wilson, Heath and Callaghan, Solly Zuckerman exercised what was, for a scientist, a unique influence in the heart of British government, and to some considerable extent in Washington and Paris as well.

Zuckerman came to London in 1926 as a 22-year-old medical student. He quickly qualified as a doctor but never treated a patient. Instead, he became an anatomist and a zoologist, and the support of the London Zoo was one of his key causes. But he was never confined by narrow definitions. During the war he became an expert on the effects of bomb blast, and through his influence on Air Chief Marshal Tedder, Eisenhower's British deputy, he had a great impact on the choice of bombing targets during the run-up to the Normandy landings.

Zuckerman's true flowering, however, began in the late 1950s when he became the most formidable Whitehall warrior, moving through the paths of that jungle with sure-footed confidence. He became the great prism who could shed light in all directions and advise on all problems. When I asked Mountbatten to undertake an enquiry into prison escapes, he at first said he would only do so if he could have Solly as his *expert* adviser on gaol security. When the oil spewing from a wrecked tanker threatened to destroy marine life around the coast of Cornwall, Solly had to pronounce on whether detergents would mop up the oil more quickly than they would kill the fish. He was asked to, and to some extent did, apply his hand to everything.

Although not always strikingly lucid, Solly was a very clever man. He had tremendous powers of concentration and a perceptive intuition that enabled him to go with great speed to the heart of a problem. But having got there, he sometimes found it difficult to explain how he had done so. This was balanced by the determination with which he held his central ideas, and the courageous independence with which he expounded them. His heroic fight against nuclear nonsense, never unilateralist but never meekly accepting received wisdom either, was one of the great sagas of the past quarter century, continuing to his last days with those great essays in the *New York Review of Books*.

This sustained crusade illustrated another of Solly Zuckerman's paradoxes. No one, coming unknown and from far outside, ever more completely stormed and penetrated every bastion of the British establishment. No one but Solly ever invited me to a country dinner *à cinq* with the Queen and Prince Philip. As a Whitehall scientific adviser he was in the unusual – and powerful – position of knowing the great world better than almost any minister he served. But although Solly conquered the establishment, he never allowed it to conquer him. He got more radical, certainly more critically iconoclastic, as he grew older. There were few issues of current interest and controversy on which he was not firmly on the liberal side.

He was therefore a very remarkable man. I greatly admired his intellectual speed and breadth, occasionally laughed in affectionate amusement at his 'out Sollying Solly', but above all loved him as a friend. Eight years after his death he rightly deserves a perceptive biography. This, in my view, has been brilliantly provided by John Peyton who writes about his subject with skill and sympathy but above all with a discriminating insight, and sometimes a detached amusement, which make him see, and portray, the whole man.

Roy Jenkins

Preface

Writing a book about anyone's life is an uneasy business. It becomes daunting when the subject is as complex as Solly Zuckerman. Putting together a coherent account of a man whose every movement, as with a kaleidoscope, caused the picture to change, has been a baffling task. There is no shortage of information: nearly a thousand pages of autobiography tend to overwhelm and confuse; more than nine hundred boxes of letters, speeches and learned papers in an archive in the library of the University of East Anglia are anything but easy to digest. From the mass of material there emerges a man who set out to unravel and explain, but who was himself almost beyond reach of explanation.

The first half of his story, growing up in South Africa, settling in England as an academic scientist, studying the destruction of war and advising on its conduct can be told in the order it happened. In the second half, he pursued together and at the same time three careers, each of them unrelated to the others. To avoid total confusion, I have had no choice but to handle them separately. In doing so I have left the reader with the need to keep in mind that the man who was sitting in the Court of Appeal listening to a judgement about the rights of Fellows of the Zoo was the same as the one who might later in the day be chairing a committee in Whitehall, or planning the teaching programme of the Department of Anatomy at Birmingham University. Since, from 1946 until 1960, that was his principal employment and his home was in the city, I have placed Birmingham first in the postwar years. In order to avoid interrupting the account of his long involvement in the affairs of Government, I have put the Zoo next.

His work with and for Governments divides easily into three parts. Fourteen years of committee work in Whitehall showed him something of the ways of Government – he called them a stimulating tutorial. As a top-ranking civil servant during the decade or so that followed, he advised first the Ministry of Defence and later the Government as a whole on the great range of problems thrown up by advances in science and technology. Unable, in the last phase of his life, to detach himself from all that had gone before, he sought to focus attention on the two major perils which he saw confronting the world: the existence of nuclear weapons and the damage to the environment caused by the rising numbers and messy habits of the human race. To end the book I have included two chapters: 'An American Dimension' stresses the importance of America and Americans in his life. 'A Man out of the Ordinary' is an attempt at a coherent picture of a many-sided man.

From the beginning I faced two questions. First, how on earth did this young, unknown student of anatomy contrive to travel so far and to squeeze so much into the span of a single life? Secondly, what did he do that was memorable, of interest to a generation that did not even know his name? To the first question the answer is a powerful and inquiring mind, a storehouse of a memory, phenomenal energy and, when he chose to use it, legendary charm. His judgement of others and his skill in measuring their potential served to link him up at different stages in his life with people who, in their turn, recognised his worth and helped him on his way. Other facets, so much a part of him that they press to be included, were his love and knowledge of the arts and music and his huge enjoyment of the good things of life. There was another side to him. A halo would not have lodged easily on his head. He could be mean as well as generous, cruel as well as kind. Uncertain of himself, he craved reassurance and hoped, without ever doing so, to find it in positions, honours and applause. He had a tendency to intrigue, more because he enjoyed it than for anything he achieved by it, and he was inclined to value people as much for the credit he thought they brought him as for anything else. Such were the shadows, of which his critics made much; their mistake was to ignore the light which made them so easily visible. One is left at the end of the day feeling that even the great array of his talents is no complete explanation. There was something else indefinable, beyond the compass of a single word, an amalgam of power and purpose and the need to prove something to himself as well as to others.

The other question, what did he do that was memorable and of interest to those who have never even heard his name, is more difficult. Living as we do in an age of unparalleled technological advance, we have come near to regarding the past of even a decade ago as too distant – nearer to the dinosaurs than to us – to be important. There remains the possibility, however, that if we forget Solly Zuckerman, we shall be losing sight of a man who, at least as well as any of his peers, understood the significance of science and of the huge acceleration in scientific activity which has been such a feature of the last half century. Recognising both the benefits science conferred and the price it exacted, Solly sought, with some success, to persuade governments to make room for science in their thinking. It was his respect for facts, the trouble he took to establish them and his refusal ever to allow them to be obscured by guesswork, opinion or wishful thinking that gave his advice in this and in other fields its cutting edge. In contexts as widely separate as planning for the invasion of France in 1944; the unprecedented destructive power of nuclear weapons; and the impact upon the environment of mankind's growing numbers and of the processes involved in supplying their needs, he had as a result an influence upon immediate events and upon what followed to warrant him being at least remembered, with even a hint of gratitude added.

In the wartime campaign in Sicily and Italy he had learned of the importance to embattled armies of transportation and of its vulnerability to air attack. In his advice to Tedder, and through him to Eisenhower, he pointed to the French rail network. It would give to the Germans the key advantage of being able to reinforce against Allied landings on the Channel coast far more quickly than the Americans and the British would be able to support them. The latter would not only be dependent on sea communications, but, lacking port facilities, would be more than usually at the mercy of the weather. If Overlord was to succeed, it would be necessary not merely to interrupt but to paralyse the railways in the area serving the French coast. For that purpose, heavy bombers from the strategic air forces would be required. That advice, insisted upon by Eisenhower, was, after intense argument, followed, with the result that German rail traffic in the area was reduced to a fraction (less than a fifth) of its normal level. Had it not been so, the outcome of Overlord, an unprecedented and complex operation, hard fought and involving land, sea and air forces, might well have been different.

At the time that Solly joined the Ministry of Defence as its Chief Scientific Adviser, Western strategy, in the event of a Russian attack, was based on the principle of massive nuclear retaliation. NATO's response to attack was to be total and not far short of immediate. Addressing NATO's annual conference in 1961 – in the presence of the Supreme Allied Commander – he spoke of the devastation which the use of nuclear weapons would cause, of the spread and escalation of the conflict and of the fact that, within the battlefield, the first casualty would be the sensitive apparatus of communication by which the commanders controlled the operation and were informed of developments. The reaction of one of those present, General Earle Wheeler (Commander in Chief American Forces in NATO) was immediate: 'We have', he said to Solly, 'painted ourselves into a corner, how do we get out of it?' In the following year he reiterated his conclusions in a paper which Mountbatten (as Chief of the Defence Staff) sent to the Chiefs of Staff for their consideration, adding that, as matters then stood, he agreed with it. At much the same time (June 1962) McNamara moved away from the doctrine of massive nuclear retaliation – which dated back to Dulles days – to what he called 'a full options policy', or as it later became, 'flexible response'. It would seem that while others certainly shared Solly's opinions, it was his speech to NATO in 1961 that prompted a rethink and began a move back from the position in which the use of nuclear weapons would be the automatic and immediate response to any attack.

Solly's wide-ranging mind and his capacity to immerse himself in great but separate issues at the same time were a notable part of his armoury. In the same year as he delivered that address to NATO (1961), he made another important move in suggesting that the new University of East Anglia should include a School of Environmental Sciences. He had in mind the impact that population numbers, the processes involved in supplying their needs and the waste generated were having upon the balance of the planet. Forty years ago, he saw without widespread understanding of the issues, there would be little hope of agreement as to what restriction was called for and even less as to how it should be implemented. What he looked for was a broad-based approach free of artificial and unnecessary boundaries. He maintained that science and technology were the servants of society and were under a duty to make clear the hazards which faced mankind and indicate how they should be met. The School has to an extraordinary extent moved in accordance with his vision, 'long and robust', as Professor Davies has called it. It is not the least of his memorials.

In thinking and puzzling about Solly as I have over the last two or three years, I have been constantly surprised, as he was, that the beginning and the end were part of the same story, and by the quantity and variety of its content. I have come, as I have said, to regard the two volumes of his autobiography as a pantechnicon into which he loaded the contents of a capacious memory and a large accumulation of assorted material. It is a story which, though far from dull, is told in a monotone: or to vary the metaphor, it is a non-physical map, in that taking no account of peaks or troughs, it is all at one level. It is as if he did not want, or could not find the time to judge the size and weight of what he did. He stopped only when he died, too late to attempt a summing up. Certainly he never broke off from the present and what lay ahead for long enough to look back at what seem the three peaks of his career. There was his crucial advice on bombing strategy prior to Overlord; then his part in dislodging the notion that a war fought with nuclear weapons could end in anything other than devastation; and finally his vision that man's relationship with the space that surrounds him warranted patient, broad and honest study. One of them would have been notable, together they were unique.

I have digested the warning of Dr Alan Glass to anyone bold enough to attempt to understand and explain Solly. 'It is not all that fanciful to claim that here was a man who lived not one life but two or even three or more lives sometimes simultaneously, sometimes sequentially. This is a thought for future biographers to ponder and muse upon.' Nevertheless, I was reluctant to turn away and lose the chance at least to shift some of the debris with which time has already begun to cover up the memory of a man who was in good times and in bad a far-sighted and loyal servant of this, his adopted country – and of mankind.

After huge expenditure of paper, time and effort to capture something of Solly, I feel rather as I imagine Jacob did at Bethel, with this difference. Whereas he wrestled with the angel for a single night, I wrestled for nearly three years with someone who was not an angel, but rather enjoyed being an enigma.

Who was Solly Zuckerman?

'The view from my Norfolk window is so different from the
scene in which I grew up that it seems scarcely credible that
the present emerged from what went before.'
                              SZ, *From Apes to Warlords*, p. xi

'SOLLY ZUCKERMAN was unique. No scientist this century can
match him in the time-span and weight of his influence on
governments in peace and war. Embraced by the establishment, he
could yet stand aloof from it and be its severest critic.' So wrote
Lord Dainton in his obituary. Solly's whole life was lived on a
learning curve, long and often steep. It began with a study of the
development of a baboon's skull. It ended with reflections on the
menace of nuclear weapons and the threat to what Crispin Tickell
has called 'that tiny damp curved space' which is our environment.

By Solly's own account, not much was known of his antece-
dents. 'Wandering Jews were not', he explained, 'in the habit of
carrying their genealogical details with them'. They must have
emerged from that tide of unknown people flowing aimlessly
westward from Tsarist oppression in the nineteenth century. For
some reason he did not think it worth mentioning what he must
have known, that the family name was originally Daitch and that
his forebears lived near Kiev. In a cursory account of his home life,
he gives the impression of having become, by his own wish, a
stranger from his own family.

The time, the place and the circumstances of a man's birth are a
frame, large or meagre, within which he is allowed to grow. The

I

years he spent as a boy in South Africa did much, more than he ever acknowledged, to shape the man. They taught him to search, to question and to judge; they gave him time to grow; they brought him resilience and a cutting edge. They accustomed him to both being on his own and identifying those with something to teach him. Returning half a century after he had left it to the South African College School, he acknowledged for the first and the only time what he owed to the school and to South Africa. He had not been crammed with knowledge, he had been given an appetite for it; he had been 'allowed to leave it with an inquiring mind'. That restless and inquiring mind, as much a part of him as his phenomenal energy, charm and beguiling voice, made him a teacher who could lead and inspire. It made him also an adviser who, having sought out the facts, preferred them to opinion, no matter how deeply entrenched or powerfully defended.

The knowledge that he possessed such qualities and maybe the readiness of his race to wander, drove him on. England, rich, powerful and the centre of an empire, drew him like a magnet and, rather strangely, held him later when that empire had become just a volume or so on the shelves of history, gathering dust.

Meanwhile, in the open veldt of Cape Province, he came close to and wondered at the diversity and the splendour of the natural world. It was an enchantment that never left him; it caused him to write his first book, *The Social Life of Monkeys and Apes*, and his last, published after his death, *The Ape in Myth and Art*. He learned rock climbing, he became interested in anthropology, he studied the anatomy of baboons and dissection. He became aware that, in academic circles, science was regarded as inferior to the humanities. His concern with the wild and the creatures that inhabited it must have given him an interest in climate and the environment which stayed with him.

With those qualities and that background, a poor, unknown Jewish graduate from Cape Town University, who had written a paper on the development of a baboon's skull, was able to break into British institutions and society at a time when doors were not automatically opened to anyone who knocked. The war having changed the course of his life, the London Zoo, Birmingham University and Whitehall became his arena. It was the breadth of his science and his use of scientific methods that made him both unusual and important. Lord Porter, Nobel Laureate and sometime President of the Royal Society, thought 'his great strength was in the application of the scientific method to every problem that confronted him, many of them not usually seen as scientific. He was a pioneer in extending the scientific method to new problems thrown up by the war, especially the totally new problems of nuclear weapons and operational research for defence. Here he applied his scientific experience not only to the optimum deployment of the weapons themselves, but to the political problems of nuclear proliferation which followed. To many it seemed remarkable that a biologist with little previous experience in other fields should so rapidly become an expert in such a variety of different disciplines, but they all had one thing in common, they were amenable to the rigorous, logical analysis characteristic of the scientific mind. Solly was a pioneering applied scientist, who applied the methods that he first happened to learn in the biological sciences with great originality to the problems of both war and peace.' Lord Hailsham, in *The Door Wherein I Went* (1975), echoed the same thought when he wrote that one heresy which had to be scotched was that scientists were mutually intelligible to one another. It was only from time to time that 'a figure such as Zuckerman or Penney or Todd arises who can bring a truly scientific intellect to bear on the totality of scientific problems'.

In the course of a long life, Solly showed himself to be a true polymath, moving easily from one discipline to another. His knowledge of destruction, gathered from the study of countless bombing incidents, gave him an understanding of the war in the air and later of the perils of the arms race and the continued existence of nuclear weapons. His tenure of the Chair of Anatomy at Birmingham University over a period of more than twenty years gave him the opportunity to turn what was a small training school at the beginning into a substantial scientific department. His fascination with the animal world led him first to the London Zoo, which he saved as a scientific institution, and later to insist that the threats to mankind's environment brought about by themselves were a proper field for academic study. The great sweep of his mind enabled him to immerse himself in whatever caught his attention. No other scientist moved for so long or at such levels within the Government, nor did any British scientist move with the same ease in the higher reaches of the American administration.

It is hardly surprising that, looking out at the Norfolk countryside which he loved from the windows of his home in Burnham Thorpe and then pushing his mind back sixty years to the South African veldt, Solly found it 'scarcely credible that the present emerged from what went before'. Between the two landscapes, one spread out before him, the other seen in the mind, was a cascade of events which shook the world and swept him along a path which he could never have planned or even imagined. It must have been hard, as he sat down to write his story, to sort things out against the backcloth of a world in ferment; to pick out individuals in the swirling pool of memory; to recall how events followed and related to one another, to disentangle the layers of his life which, though close to one another, could only be told separately; harder still, perhaps, to recall the thoughts and hopes and the things of mind and heart which drove him on.

There is much in any man's life which is beyond reach of explanation or excuse for him even to attempt to put everything in. Solly, in telling his story, left much of himself, his beliefs, his loves and hates, his hopes and fears in shadow. Close relationships were not things he was accustomed to write about or even discuss. Through the mists of time and pretence one gets the impression of a man who, more than most, enjoyed and needed the commendation and applause of those he respected and who, despite his high profile, was at pains to resist intrusion into those areas of which he was himself unsure. Some who knew him well saw him as enjoying life to the full, emptying every cup that came his way, but too restless, too much given to searching, ever to be content.

Solly's storehouse of a memory and an archive of nearly a thousand boxes may have saved him from the fungus of wishful thinking which so often fills in memory's gaps. It led him, beyond his power to resist, to turn a story of tremendous events, of fascinating people and a great range of ideas, into a catalogue. It leaves the reader overfed, unable to digest and needing air. Concerning his inner self, his beliefs and opinions, he was reticent to the point of being secretive. Anyone curious to know more, would find himself facing a 'Keep Off The Grass' notice, indicating that beyond that point intruders were not welcome. That may have been his reason for labelling himself as an agnostic. Peter Nott, Bishop of Norwich in Solly's last years and a frequent visitor, saw him as always travelling without knowing where his journey would end: he questioned Solly's agnosticism. Colin Stephenson, when Administrator of the Shrine of Walsingham, thought that he could have made a convert of him. At no time did Solly have much to say about being a Jew. It did not seem, on the surface, to weigh with him as either a help or a hindrance, but his closeness to men like Isidor Rabi and Jerry Wiesner can be taken as a sign that he never forgot he was one.

Of his small inner family he says little, save when they are incidental to the narrative. Where one might have expected few barriers and inhibitions, in fact there were more. His wife and children were to a great extent excluded from his London life. The household, whether in Birmingham or in Burnham Thorpe, revolved round him and was organised to suit his convenience. Solly warned his young wife before he married her that with him work would always come first. In keeping her in the background, he repeatedly hurt her; yet she continued to regard him as the most interesting man she had ever met – and despite everything, to love him. While he looked on their son Paul as a potential competitor from the beginning, he was at ease with Stella, their daughter, and doted on her. Not until much later did she in turn incur her father's displeasure, when even the sight of a boyfriend was anathema to him. Both knew that they were expected to be a credit to their father. They were aware too of his concern to keep them free from his own Judaism; they understood his uncertainties, his contradictions and his volatility. Somehow both loved him yet he did not always make it easy. He has little to say of them in his autobiography. Anything more than a mention in passing might have led him to tell of things which too often he handled clumsily and without feeling.

He was interested in people who were good at whatever they did and had a sharp eye too for those who had something to teach him. He met many who played important parts in world affairs.

Those whom he thought well of were not just grandees with titles; they needed to be good at what they did. They included Mrs Bisbee, the Visiting Lecturer from Liverpool University who first ignited him; Sir Grafton Elliot Smith, head of University College Medical School and leading authority on the brain, who took him under his wing on his first arrival in England; Julian Huxley, Secretary of the Zoo, who broadened his scientific knowledge; Peter Krohn, a student of Solly's at Oxford, an original member of the Oxford Extra Mural Unit (OEMU) set up to study bombing at the end of 1940 and subsequently the scientist who, in Solly's absences, ran the Department of Anatomy at Birmingham; Anita Mandl, an endocrinologist who worked with him in Birmingham and whose loss to science he lamented, and with whom he remained friends for thirty years after his retirement; Terence Morrison-Scott, who gave him unswerving support during the troubles at the Zoo; Desmond Bernal, the scientist who first and by chance launched him into the war; e. e. cummings, the American poet, and his wife Marion, who gave him thirty years of friendship and affection, enshrined in letters of notable language.

There were those whom he wrote about as *Six Men out of the Ordinary*; two nuclear physicists, Patrick Blackett, upper-middle class son of a stockbroker, gifted, good-looking, one 'to whom thought and action were the same', and Isidor Rabi, son of poor Jewish immigrants from Poland, 'one of the most powerful minds it was my good fortune ever to enjoy and from which to learn'. Both were Nobel Laureates. Tedder – only Eisenhower called him Arthur – was the son of a civil servant. Marshal of the Royal Air Force and a Deputy Supreme Commander, he was the man who launched Solly into a new and unexpected career. Years later, watching him as an old man climbing the stairs of the Athenaeum Club, Solly commented, 'There goes the only military man whose thinking was invariably objective and intellectually honest.' Then there was 'Tooey' Spaatz, grandson of German immigrants, educated at West Point, Commander of the United States Air Force; Solly had rarely met a man who was so forthcoming in his friendship. Both were modest, unboastful men. Admiral of the Fleet Earl Mountbatten of Burma (Dickie), a grandson of Queen Victoria, Supreme Allied Commander South East Asia, Viceroy of India,

Chief of the Defence Staff, was different. Tall and good-looking, he loved uniforms, medals and ceremonial and liked to be admired. Finally, Admiral Hyman G. Rickover, 'the father of the US nuclear Navy', was the son of a Jewish immigrant who came to New York in 1899 and set up as a tailor; untidy as well as unusual, he wore uniform only when commanded to do so. Solly's selection of them shows, as doubtless he intended, his closeness to six remarkable men, and their regard for him.

For one accustomed to scientific analysis and to thinking things out, he was surprisingly ready to allow the major decisions of his life to be forced upon him by pressure either of events or other people. While it is possible that he found it hard to make up his mind on matters close to him, it seems more likely that he wanted to be sure of obtaining the best terms or that he simply enjoyed being coaxed. He could not or would not decide, both before and after the war, to accept the invitation from Birmingham University to become its Professor of Anatomy; or, having become engaged, to get married; or to leave academic life altogether and become a top-level civil servant, which he very much wanted to be. There were times when he declared himself 'unnerved' or 'taken aback' at being invited to join this or that committee, when it was obvious not only that he would be invited, but that he wanted to be. Only twice in his life did he make important decisions without doubt or apparent difficulty: first, to leave South Africa as soon as his formal education was complete, and secondly, to decline Harold Wilson's invitation to become a Minister of the Crown.

He did not relish being questioned or pressured to give answers, nor was he given to explaining. If he did so, it was in a manner that precluded further discussion. Asked why he had come to live in Norfolk, since he didn't hunt, he didn't shoot, he didn't fish, he didn't sail – what did he do there? – the reply that he went shrimping and collected pebbles left questioners puzzled and wondering, as they walked round this many-sided man, if they had understood him. No one, looking at Solly, ever saw the whole man or came away with quite the same picture. There were some who knew him best and felt that there was something within and about him which he didn't himself understand and preferred should remain in shadow. Although something of a beachcomber, picking things up because they looked interesting and dropping them if they weren't, Solly was no dilettante. He was intensely serious about anything he did. He also enjoyed it all: his work in all its forms, animals and plants, picking up stones on the beach, the arts about which he knew a great deal, food, wine, conversation and the people involved in all of them. They were all grist to his mill and from them he ground out a story and a career that was unique.

Solly's message is threefold. First, the peril of nuclear weapons has not gone away: those now available exceed by a large margin the strength and quantity required to devastate the planet and put an end to anything that could be called civilised life. They can be delivered with relative ease and accuracy to any place on earth; there is no defence against them. Some ten or a dozen nations possess them. As an extension to that, there are those now seeking to acquire them who are either mad or wicked, who would not hesitate at least to threaten the world with their use. Secondly, population growth is placing huge, intolerable pressure upon limited resources and, in doing so, poisoning the atmosphere and upsetting the climate with results likely to be calamitous. Lastly, there is his warning delivered forty years ago in California, repeated and expanded upon later. It was and it remains the scientists and the technologists 'who initiated the new developments, who created the new demands. They were the ones who, at base, were determining the social, economic, and political future of the world. Without any coherent concern for political values or goals, scientists and engineers had become the begetters of new social demand and the architects of new economic and social situations, over which those who exercised political power then had to rule. The nuclear world, with all its hazards, is the scientists' creation; it is certainly not a world that came about in response to any external demand. So, at the root, is the whole of today's environment of ever-rising material expectation. So, because of biomedical advances, is the spectre of overpopulation. So, some protest, is environmental pollution. So is the world of instant communications. So is the world of missiles. So is the unending arms-race by which we are all now threatened.' To that must be coupled the reaction and comment of Isidor Rabi, surely one of the most thoughtful and wise scientists of our time. He did not feel so confident that we have even begun to tame the atom so that it doesn't kill us ultimately. 'I far underestimated the problem; I far overestimated the rationality of human beings. I far underestimated the capacity of people to put the obvious, the fearful, out of their minds, to refuse to look at the longer distance for the sake of immediate advantage.'

As in Solly's time, so now, people are alarmed that science and technology should be taking them down roads they have not chosen, leading no one knows where, at speeds no one can control. Their alarm is intensified as they come slowly to realise that there is no authoritative, generally accepted explanation of what has already happened or what is likely to occur in the future. Nor, almost certainly, is there anyone in any government anywhere who has the breadth of scientific knowledge to attempt it. Sir Robert May, the Government's Chief Scientific Adviser at the beginning of the new millennium and the man who comes nearer than anyone else has yet done to being Solly's true successor, has this to say of him: 'I think he was an extraordinary and larger than life character who made the world a more interesting place. And in the really important things, in his role as Chief Scientific Adviser, he made the world a better place. The quirks and foibles must be seen against this larger canvas. And that is why I say in all seriousness, that in essentials he is my role model.'

Give Robert McNamara, sometime US Secretary for Defense and later President of the World Bank, the last word. Asked not long ago for his measurement of Solly, he replied, 'Oh he was huge. The real answer to the question is that he has no counterpart in your country or in mine today.'

I

'Great Things to be Savoured'

'An ordinary man-in-the-street going off to new things . . .
unabashed, unfrightened, independent . . . leaving one
country for another where the horizon was wider.'
SZ's description of himself, 1926

BORN IN Cape Town in 1904, Solly compressed the story of his life in South Africa into a single chapter of seventeen pages, entitled 'Colonial Beginnings'. Dismissive rather than informative of all that those years contained, his account gives the impression of a young man determined to leave his family and the country of his birth as soon as his education was complete and he had the means to do so. Days spent in the open, rock climbing and studying the host of creatures that had their home in the veldt of Cape Province gave him interests which lasted a lifetime.

Cape Town as Solly first knew it had a population of less than a quarter of a million, fewer than half being European; its transport consisted of horses and carts and ox-wagons – in those days only birds flew. Solly could remember the city, shrouded in purple and black, as it mourned the death of Edward VII and entered a new age. It was one which saw the human race plunging into two world wars, wresting new powers of destruction from the atom and, in its stampede to consume, disturbing the balance and the future of the planet.

Solly's parents, Moses and Rebecca Zuckerman, were as unlike each other as it is possible for a pair of human beings to be. He was a quiet, unassuming man, who ran a not very successful furniture and hardware business in Cape Town; 'a retiring character who read continuously, but with very little critical sense'. Although a Jew and interested in religion, he followed no particular faith. Somehow he imparted to his young son the notion that God was like some 'tank of spiritual liquid in the sky ready to suffuse all mankind'. When, however, that picture faded and nothing much else was on offer, Solly concluded that his father was agnostic and at least outwardly followed suit himself. Rather strangely, since he never spoke much of him, Solly, not long before he died, handed to his son Paul a brochure entitled *A Life of Jesus of Nazareth*, which his father had written and inscribed to 'my dear son Solly'. Once he had left South Africa, Solly saw his father only twice. In 1930 he returned, not for any family reunion, but to check his memories of the ways of baboons in the wild as opposed to those he had been studying on the Mappin Terraces in Regent's Park. Father and son met again and for the last time in 1939, when both his parents were briefly in London on their way back to South Africa after a visit to Palestine. 'So my picture of him is as I saw him, when he was in his mid-fifties, and although he lived for nearly thirty more years, I knew less and less what he was really like. We hardly ever corresponded.'

His mother, bustling, extrovert and handsome, devoted herself to good causes and was impatient at her husband's lack of social ambition and business sense. Her pictures show her as bearing a striking resemblance to her son. He saw her as an 'overpowering taskmaster', who set about his cultural education with intolerable vigour, requiring him to take lessons on the violin and the piano and to attend concerts, given by the new Cape Town Symphony Orchestra. Lessons in Hebrew were the last straw, 'first a penance, then a terror'. That early cultural bombardment had the effect of suppressing for the time being the interest in music it was intended to stimulate. It certainly did nothing to anchor him into the pattern of life or to a place he saw as beautiful but dull; rather it added to his resolve to go. Even in those early years, he was out of the ordinary and sought to do unusual things not within the confines of ordinary people: if birds could fly, so could he – an attempt resulted in mild concussion and stitches to a damaged head.

With the remainder of his family, an elder sister, a brother and two younger twin sisters, he had no enduring ties. When he and Jessie, his piano-playing older sister, met on her first night in London, he could hardly have been more dismissive: 'We had extraordinarily little to say to each other, and I played patience most of the time.' Similarly, when many years later he visited Israel, he showed little interest in his brother, then Harbour Master in Tel Aviv. Though he remained on slightly closer terms with the younger sisters, 'tough, courageous women', he was unable to spare them more than a pigeon-hole in his memory. Two aunts seem to have awakened a glimmer of affection: one, Aunt Dinah, an elegant woman, introduced him to novels and showed him a scrapbook she had put together of Oscar Wilde's trial. The other, Aunt Martha, he remembered fondly for telling him that he was 'the best boy of all the girls'.

While lack of interest in his father, dislike of his mother and indifference to his siblings doubtless made his departure easier, it was the sense of great things waiting to be savoured that drove him. Cape Town was small and rural; England was large, the centre of an empire. Escape from the constraints of family life was an added benefit rather than the principal motive. In later life he spoke little of his South African years. When he did so he was inclined to make much of his mother's bullying; maybe he felt the need to explain his rejection of his family.

At his first school, he contrived to detach himself from much of the day-to-day routine. Rock climbing, the wild, the creatures that inhabited it and the plants that grew there offered a welcome alternative to the tedium of organised games. While he seemed to be a loner, he showed in those early days his need of the support and encouragement of others. He was quick even then to identify and get alongside those who had something to teach him. In his boyhood he had a friend and regular climbing partner, Jackie Whitworth, whom he knew to be a far better climber than himself. 'I was willing enough to follow, never to lead. And while I would be exhausted at the end of a day's strenuous climbing, at times I was not a little frightened as we found our way to the top.' That readiness to be interested in almost anything and willingness to learn, became a part of him and stayed with him throughout his life. It brought him a broad spread of knowledge and an unusual range of friendships as diverse as it was large. His phenomenal memory enabled him to keep them.

Aged sixteen, he won a scholarship at Cape Town University; at nineteen, he took his BA degree and, in order to earn a little money, became a demonstrator at the university, his first academic post. His MA degree followed two years later, coupled with the award of the university's Senior Zoology Medal and a scholarship for overseas study. Mrs Ruth Bisbee, a visiting lecturer on exchange for a year from Liverpool, was a new experience; she stirred him and woke him up. 'For the first time in my life, I learned what it was to be lectured to in an inspired fashion and what a fascinating field of study zoology is,' he wrote. 'She transformed into an excitement what was otherwise rote learning.' So great was the impression she made upon him that, having arrived in England, he not only got in touch with her again, but even sent her for comment the draft chapters of a book he was writing on the social life of monkeys. They would come back scored through, marked with alterations and often with sarcastic comment. On one occasion, he could bear it no longer and literally wept with frustration.

In 1926, young, Jewish and unknown, Solly sailed out of Cape Town on his way to England, without a backward glance. He felt, so he said, 'no wrench at leaving, only a sense of great things waiting to be savoured. I was abandoning no loves and it did not occur to me that once I had gone, there might be someone who might miss me or whom I would miss.' He took with him a degree in anatomy, something like a hundred golden sovereigns to see him through his first few months in London, a few letters of introduction and a paper he had written on the development of a baboon's skull. His picture of himself as 'an ordinary man in the street going off to new things' is a piece of protective understatement. It is hard to believe that he ever saw himself as ordinary and 'going off to new things' seems a limp way of summing up the adventure of a lifetime, from which he had already decided not to return.

His welcome to London matched his hopes and fed his enthusiasm. While he was grateful to those who helped him, he saw no reason to explain – perhaps he could not – how he managed so quickly to get on terms with a man as eminent as Sir Grafton Elliot Smith. Head of University College Medical School and the recognised authority on the structure and evolution of the brain. Elliot Smith welcomed Solly as if his arrival was an event to which he had long looked forward. At their first meeting and on the strength of a single letter of introduction and the paper on the baboon's skull, he offered help, advice and encouragement and gave him a flying start. Solly should try for one of the School's two open exhibitions – he did so with success; he should sit for the primary examination of the Royal College of Surgeons – his knowledge of anatomy would be helpful. He passed first time. He should extend his study of baboons' skulls to include those of chimpanzees; there was a collection of skulls at the Natural History Museum at South Kensington. Elliot Smith would arrange for him to work there and would himself submit the thesis on the baboon skull to the Zoological Society of London. A young immigrant could hardly have wished for a better start in a new country. He seemed to have no difficulty in attracting the attention and interest of prominent people who he knew had much to give. When they welcomed him, as Elliot Smith did, he felt, as he himself said, he had been let in to the company of men whose disciplined minds were far more sophisticated than any he had encountered before, and who illuminated intellectual worlds of whose existence he had previously been unaware.

Solly launched himself into a crowded social life with all the eagerness of a duck finding water to land on. Here, he felt, was the life he had been yearning for. A host of new friends, a deep dive into Bloomsbury, energetic exploration of restaurants in Charlotte Street and Soho; visits to the Proms, the ballet and the House of Commons. A Tory MP showed him a darn in his shirt to illustrate how hard times were in that palace of varieties; he was unable to fit in either the National Gallery or the Tower of London for some months. Even at that time, however, when he was young and the world was packed with so many things which were new and exciting, it was work which came first and absorbed most of his attention. He quickly learned to pick out those who had something to teach him from those who had not. Of the two consultants for whom he worked, the physician he dismissed as dull. The surgeon, Wilfred Trotter, for whom he acted as dresser, was sharp and sarcastic, causing even Solly to watch his step. Addressing his regular anaesthetist in the course of an operation when the patient should have been asleep, Trotter demanded, 'If the patient can stay awake, could you try to do the same?' Examining on another occasion some X-rays of a patient on whom he was about to operate, he remarked, 'Professor Harris tells me that the trouble is at the base of the brain. That confirms my view that I shall find it at the top.' It was about that time that Solly began to think that practising medicine was not for him, a view which was later reinforced by Elliot Smith, who said, 'I don't think a surgeon', and turned him in the direction of research.

Delivering his paper on the development of the baboon skull at the London Zoo, he suggested that something once said by the great T.H. Huxley had been wrong. On returning to his place, he found a new neighbour, who said, 'My name's Huxley, I'd like to talk to you about what you have just told us.' Julian Huxley became a friend and one who, over the years continued to stretch Solly's scientific horizons. At this early stage Huxley secured for him the post of Prosector to the Zoological Society of London, to which he was appointed in 1928 for four years; the duties included ensuring that the cause of death of any animal in the collection was diagnosed and that the remains were used in the best scientific way. The Prosectorium, where dead animals were made ready for study, was at that time a primitive affair; Solly used to wonder how it was that 'those who worked there did not die a thousand deaths from some obscure infection'. He was concerned for Mrs Kelly, who cleaned up each day's mess and made tea 'in an environment of flesh, flies and specimens', and marvelled at the persistent optimism of Pincher Moss, who emptied the bins and went through the contents in the hope that in the discarded material he might find a meal. To his relief, he found that, whereas on the few occasions he attended human *post mortems* the smell had been too much for him, the more varied smells of the Prosectorium did not bother him.

For some six months while the post was vacant, he took on the duties of the Society's pathologist, and quickly became fascinated

by the problems it revealed. How was it that birds which breathed
clean air were apparently more susceptible to TB than coal miners
who did not? How should they dispose of the carcass of an elephant which had died of anthrax? Almost everything he studied in
the Prosectorium was new and exciting and every observation
cried out to be followed up. One task allotted to him by the
Curator of Reptiles, 'a woman of powerful personality', was to
relieve some giant tortoises of the constipation from which she
supposed them to be suffering. Finding themselves strung up in
tennis nets the following morning proved such a stirring experience that the enemas he had in mind were not needed. Baboons,
always near to his heart, continued to take up much of his attention; a colony of them on Monkey Hill enabled him to continue
the studies he had made in South Africa and to compare the social
life of those in captivity with that enjoyed by those in the wild.
Although the sex-ratio of the colony on Monkey Hill differed
from that of the tribes he had observed in the wild, it was clear that
in both a family group consisted of a male overlord, one or more
females and their young and a few male hangers-on. With no
room for dispersal, fights were frequent on Monkey Hill. To allow
Solly to refresh his memory of baboons in the wild, he was given,
early in 1930, three months' leave to return to South Africa.
Interestingly, in his account of that visit, while he refers to his twin
sisters who helped him with his arrangements, he makes no
mention of his parents or other members of his family.

That visit to South Africa launched him on his return into a
great outpouring of lectures and broadcasts. So carried away was
he by one paper he read to the Psychoanalytical Society that he
went on for well over an hour, with another hour or so of questions to follow. At a dinner in Cambridge of 'The Heretics' club he
became, by his own admission, 'far too excited, drank too much
and spoke too fast, too volubly and too long'. Bored by the two
dining clubs to which he already belonged, his remedy was to set
up a new one, the Tots and Quots; he borrowed the name from
Terence's '*quot homines, tot sententiae*' ('as many opinions as people').
It was also known as 'Solly's Sunday School'. Preparations for the
first dinner in 1932 exercised him greatly, so much so that he
became ill. Two friends intervened and took him almost by force

to hospital, where he was diagnosed as suffering from bronchial pneumonia. Mulishly, he refused to be diverted from his cherished purpose, and rejecting all counsel other than his own, discharged himself in time to complete the arrangements and to attend the dinner. He then succumbed and spent two weeks in hospital.

No matter how heavy his workload, he could never resist adding to it if any invitation either interesting or flattering came along. So pleased was he with his contribution to a debate in York that September on 'Primates and Early Man' that he made things worse by promising to write it up as a book. Either fatigue or trouble with a girlfriend, he could not remember which, served to stop him in his tracks and forced a return to hospital, where he was diagnosed as suffering from extrasystoles or irregular heartbeats. Medically qualified people are not as a general rule the best of patients, and on the spur of the moment, he visited a travel agent and prescribed for himself a quiet time and a short holiday in Spain. A chance meeting with two 'rowing hearties' in San Sebastian prompted him to abandon at once all thoughts of being quiet and to get very drunk, to the apparent disgust of two young American women staying in the same hotel. He must have been soon forgiven – he usually was – for one of them, the journalist and writer Martha Gellhorn, was quickly added to his collection of lifelong friends. He returned to London, cured and able to make progress with his book, *Functional Affinities of Man, Monkeys and Apes*. The irregular heartbeats never returned.

Margaret Gardiner came into Solly's life at a small party given by Lady Samuel in her flat in 1931 or 1932. With no memory for dates, Margaret still remembers the scarlet Balenciaga dress trimmed with black lace she was wearing. Someone switched on the gramophone and Solly came up and asked her to dance. She had lunch with him the next day and then spent the afternoon at the Zoo, helping him to complete the record of polar bear births – they always happen in November. Encouraged by his praise and moved by the warmth of his thanks, she drifted into becoming, as she describes it, a 'kind of secretary to him'. She has clear memories of the time, and of him: walking one evening with him in the Zoo and a jealous female ape screaming at her; taking down in longhand to his dictation the entire text of *Functional Affinities*; his distress at being asked by an unkind publisher to pay forty pounds for amendments to the text. Since he was then very poor, she paid. She remembers the care he took with his work and how dedicated he was to it.

Her father, a distinguished Egyptologist, liked Solly, but had no wish to have him as a son-in-law; her mother, Viennese and a dog lover, was annoyed by his insistence that dogs did not have souls and looked on him with disapproval. Since they loved each other, Margaret saw no point in arguing about money; they both accepted that she had more of that useful commodity than Solly did. On one occasion he stretched her tolerance too far. Having asked her out to dinner, he declared when the meal was over that he had no money, and she would have to pay. Since she had none either, she was left with no option but to surrender the cherished golden sovereign which she always carried. Years later, she reminded him of that evening, how angry she had been and how badly he had behaved: 'Yes,' he replied, 'but wasn't I charming?'

Annoying he may have been from time to time, but he was light-hearted, amusing and fun. He was fond of telling Jewish stories; there was one of a family about to be photographed and the father saying to his son, 'Stop fidgeting, can't you see he is trying to focus?' 'What, all of us?' asked the boy, evidently unfamiliar with the word and impressed by what he thought he had said. There was a line which he was fond of humming, 'Shit, said Solly, mit a Pongo Bolly'. Margaret remembers going to exhibitions of work by Barbara Hepworth and Ben Nicholson, being introduced to them by Solly, his rapid judgement of the items on show and his discerning comments. Finding that both artists were hard up at the time, Margaret bought some of their work, and later that of some of their friends in St Ives, whenever she could afford to do so. Since her son rather surprisingly told her he did not want it, she gave her by that time valuable collection to Orkney, where it is still to be seen in the Pier Museum.

When Solly went to America in 1934, she wanted to go with him, but a friend told her, 'If you love him, let him go.' She did, and they remained friends until the day he died. She remembers asking him, 'Solly, do you ever think of me?' and his reply, 'Every day of my life', leaving her no wiser. At the age of ninety-five, she manages wonderfully to keep the years at bay; no great effort is required to imagine what a source of light and joy she must have been to a young man finding his way. In a letter to her of 27 August 1980, almost fifty years after their first meeting, he wrote, 'Without your persistence and generosity, there would have been nothing in the Orkneys . . . I am glad I brought Barbara and Ben into your life.'

Early in 1933, Solly set sail for New York, having fitted in what he described as 'a final and rigorous round of social whirl', and equipped with a letter of introduction from J.B.S. Haldane to 'a blonde who was a journalist and not bad company'. His journey was in response to an invitation from John Fulton, head of the Physiology Department of Yale, to visit the University. The plan was that after spending some days with Professor Yerkes in New Haven, he should then accompany him to the Anthropoid Experimental Station at Orange Park in Florida where the Professor had a colony of great apes which he was studying. If all went well, Solly would be offered the post of Residential Director. On arrival at New Haven, he telephoned to Yerkes, who said he would come and pick him up; how should he recognise him? Solly's reply that that would be easy, since he would be the only man in America carrying an umbrella, seemed innocuous, but it sufficed to disturb the serious Yerkes, who took it as being somehow a reflection upon American manhood.

His first night as a guest in the Yerkes household in New Haven brought a series of shocks: no alcohol, by his host's choice rather than as a consequence of Prohibition, raw eggs for breakfast and complaints about the noise he made stropping his razor. Life was even worse when they got to Orange Park. They sat all day in a hide, watching the animals and making notes, a process which, so far as Solly could see, had no scientific purpose. 'A severely simple dinner', with pumpkin pie as the main dish, was not to Solly's taste. When Professor Yerkes asked him if he would enjoy hearing Mrs Yerkes read aloud, he replied with some firmness that he would not. After that, there was nothing for it but to go to bed as soon as the meal was over. Later he learned that it was Mrs Yerkes's custom always to read aloud after dinner. The book of the moment was Aldous Huxley's *Point Counter Point*, with those bits

Mrs Yerkes deemed distasteful, omitted. Dog racing, though not a normal pastime of Solly's, proved a preferable alternative.

The relief of getting away from pumpkin pie and back to New Haven was welcome. What made life seem better was John Fulton, whose 'indefatigable devotion to scholarship never seemed to be a brake on his zest for good living'. Regular weekends in New York and a number of interesting visits elsewhere made for further improvement. At the Brigham Hospital in Boston, Solly had the chance of comparing the methods of Harvey Cushing, who had revolutionised brain surgery, with those less sophisticated which he had seen practised in London. Invited back to Boston to lecture to a special audience, he spoke for an hour and was then told by his host, Professor Hooton, Head of Anthropology at Harvard, that he had an hour in which to prepare another lecture on another subject to another audience. With that second lecture, as he thought, successfully delivered, he was somewhat surprised when the Professor said that while they had enjoyed his lecture, it had not been on the subject that they expected, so would he continue for, say, three-quarters of an hour, a full hour might be asking too much, on that other topic. The Professor's appetite and Solly's readiness to satisfy it were well matched. Such opportunities to display his own knowledge and learn from others were welcome. Gerritt Smith, Curator of Mammals at the Smithsonian, wished to discuss his theories about the evolutionary significance of the act of rape. Carl Hartman of the Carnegie Institution, Kurt Richter and others, all of whom were studying the influence of sex hormones on behaviour, invited him to Baltimore, which he particularly enjoyed. Discussions in Chicago with Heinrich Kluver, psychologist and student of animal behaviour, taught him much, as well as giving him his first sight of that wonderful city.

The likelihood that Professor Yerkes or Solly would wish to prolong their collaboration after the six months probationary period was small. Though both were serious scientists, Yerkes wrapped his life in an aura of earnestness wholly alien to Solly. The immediate question of what to do next was answered with the award of a Rockefeller Research Fellowship. It enabled him to carry on in New Haven for another year and to continue to explore New York. He made contact with Haldane's blonde journalist who introduced him to Tony's, a speakeasy borne of Prohibition, of which he quickly became an habitué. Life there was, as he said, very heady; he always had a taste for celebrities and that throbbing, fast-moving city had plenty on offer. He met and stayed with Ira and Lee Gershwin, and later the more famous George. Recognising his tastes, they provided him with special wines and cigars. Dorothy Parker, famous for the sharpness of her wit, crossed his path, Tallulah Bankhead, famous for different things, did rather more. Aneurin Bevan, in New York to collect money for the victims of fascism, talked disturbingly of events in Europe. Drinking brandy in the Park Avenue apartment of one of Solly's friends, Nye warned her that he was proof against what he called 'the Mayfair kiss', a process which, he explained, smart society had devised for the corruption of pure socialists.

Solly never had any difficulty anywhere in making friends, but it must be a matter of some surprise that this young unknown, who was always short of money, was able so easily to move around New York, not only in smart and fashionable circles but in those that were less so. The poet e.e. cummings and his wife Marion, determinedly un-smart and wonderfully different from almost everyone, became friends for life. Persuaded by Solly to go to a play, the poet walked out after some ten minutes of the first act, exclaiming loudly, 'Hell, don't they know we're all mad? Have they no sense of shame to expose it in public?' Solly himself was surprised, even puzzled, by their friendship; it was one which revealed another side of himself and one which was not always on show. 'It is strange that Cummings and I understood each other so well. Or did we?' A carefully preserved correspondence of more than thirty years has this as the first: 'Dear E.E. Cummings and Marion, This is the most appalling colour for notepaper I've ever met. I feel like the front of a servant-girl writing to her back, just using it. I wanted you to see it, that's why I started this note this way. We now move over to white.'

At that time, when Hitler was throwing his shadow over Europe, Solly could without doubt have remained in America, yet he felt 'nostalgic for England'. Without a job, however, on either side of the Atlantic, he was obliged to give thought to earning money. The offer of the Chair of Anatomy at the Peiping Union

Medical College at Peking was the result of efforts made on his behalf by Sir Grafton Elliot Smith, who counselled acceptance. Solly's selection for what he described as an honourable office would, he thought, put him in a class by himself and turn out to his eventual advantage. Solly, however, declined, fearful of becoming too deeply involved in speculations about man's fossil ancestry and reluctant to desert the path of true science. Controversial assertions made on flimsy evidence about the missing link in man's evolution always aroused his particular disfavour, especially if they brought fame and fortune to those who made them. He believed that it was impossible with even a pretence of certainty, to point to a creature and declare, 'There stood the animal to whose evolutionary adventure man owes his presence on earth today'. Subsequent exposure of the Piltdown Man hoax appeared to justify his caution.

He was saved from his dilemma by the award of a Beit Research Fellowship and a Demonstratorship in the Department of Anatomy in Oxford, secured for him by friends, one of whom, Philip Hart, wrote, 'You sound awfully hard up. Enclosed a cheque. Please do not be too proud . . . the hell you will. It's to be put on our long-distance debt, that is for when I am starving as a consultant in Gower Street and you are an academic king.' Solly was not too proud and accepted gladly.

Never short of charm or unwilling to use it, Solly contrived even to make taxmen human. The official from whom he was obliged to seek clearance before he was free to leave America, first advised how Solly should fill in his return so that his liability to tax would be reduced to nil and then came out into the street with him, shook his hand and said, 'Please come again – you'll always be welcome'. President Kennedy used similar words thirty years later. Americans seemed always to welcome him; they enjoyed his enjoyment of their country, welcomed his spontaneity, and found his advice helpful, free as it was of stuffiness. His interest in everyone and everything and his extraordinary energy were like a bunch of keys which, in his hand, could open many doors.

2

Oxford, Marriage and War

'Are you ashamed to be marrying my daughter?'
Lord Reading

EARLY ON in Solly's life, before he ever arrived there, England acquired a meaning for him which it never lost. Even in 1934, having taken and hugely enjoyed his first, deep draught of America, when he might at least have explored what was on offer there, he felt (so he wrote half a century later) mounting excitement at the prospect of once again being in London. Having got back, he lost no time, but plunged into a vigorous social round, refreshing old friendships and sustaining those he had made in America. Tallulah Bankhead had rented a house near to the Zoo, where she held court and where Solly 'whiled away pleasant hours with a heterogenous collection of stage celebrities, a writer or two, a new Wimbledon champion and even politicians'.

In September 1934, he moved to Oxford to take up his Fellowship; he was at the same time appointed a University Lecturer. A rented house in Museum Road with Elizabeth (Mrs Boyd) in charge of housekeeping presented Solly with the opportunity to collect and entertain people he found interesting and wished to know: academics, actors, artists, authors, bishops, economists, painters, politicians and, of course, fellow scientists flowed through that small house in a steady stream. A recital of all their names would read like a slice of *Who's Who* and mean little, for today's memories are short and yesterday's glamour quickly fades.

Some names, however, survive. Isaiah Berlin and Freddie Ayer seen with Solly as comprising 'Oxford's three brilliant Jews' were seen to be 'much in demand'. Frederick Lindemann, later Lord Cherwell, bachelor, high Tory and scientist, long-time friend of Churchill and his influential wartime adviser, made his first appearance in Solly's life. Charles Laughton, a particular favourite of Mrs Boyd's, brought with him a huge voice, a bottle of whisky, no luggage and a load of emotional problems about which his wife, Elsa Lanchester, later wrote a book. The house in Museum Road gave Solly the chance to display his pictures by Ben Nicholson and John Armstrong and his Barbara Hepworth carvings and drawings. The Duke of Wellington, an undergraduate at the time, remembers taking Frances Day, a lively and glamorous blonde singer, to see Solly after lunch. Needless to say, he welcomed her warmly, bombarding her with all manner of intimate questions concerning reproductive physiology, the subject which was engaging his attention at the time.

Mrs Boyd, being an excellent cook, had her mind on things of a higher order than paying bills. She put them away in a drawer, where they stayed, leaving her free to look after the food and the visitors. Not until 1939 did the extent and gravity of the accumulated problem become clear. The patience of Oxford wine merchants was, like Hitler's at that time, exhausted and none were willing to supply. The matter was left to his new wife after their marriage later that year. Membership of Christ Church, which carried the right to dine at High Table and use the Senior Common Room, was a valuable prop to Solly's social life.

Although it was the centrepiece of his life, Oxford was a base of operations rather than a place of confinement. Like a river in flood, Solly's life streamed along, following several courses at the same time; one in Oxford, another in London, with a third, very much taken for granted, on the continent for frequent holidays. Life must have been fun, but it was also earnest; his pre-war Oxford days were 'a period of intense productive work'. A shared bed–sit flat in Paddington made it easy to attend scientific meetings and read papers. Weekends were spent away with Lord and Lady

Wimborne in Northamptonshire, where he met the composer William Walton; in Bedfordshire with Henry and Gwen Melchett, where Professor Lindemann or H.G. Wells might be fellow guests; at Buscot Park with Lord Faringdon, whose weekend parties became increasingly political, with a leftward slant, and Ellen Wilkinson (a Member of Parliament and an important figure in the Labour Party), Nye Bevan and Jennie Lee as guests. He managed frequent trips to France and Italy; a month in Austria with the Melchetts, and another with them on their yacht in the Mediterranean. He proved an indifferent navigator; given the night watch and told to steer towards the shadow of Mount Parnassus, he became confused, aimed at the wrong shadow and took them a long way off course, though without disaster.

According to his pupils, Solly was a wonderfully successful and inspiring teacher. He was not the first to discover that the easiest way to capture and hold the interest of undergraduates was to face them with his own problems. A small operating theatre and a room for monkeys enabled him to make progress with his work on the hormonal conditions which underlie the human reproductive cycle. He studied the factors which might cause the enlargement of the human prostate and the reaction of female tissue to treatment with male hormones. The five years 1934 to 1939 gave rise to some ninety scientific papers and monographs. It is hard not to feel some sympathy with Sir Wilfrid Le Gros Clark, who, as head of the Anatomy department, was required to advise on and approve the volume of work which this hugely energetic newcomer was throwing up for his approval: his advice understandably was that Solly should write less; also understandably, it had no effect. Gloomy and resentful by nature, he must have found Solly's bounce a considerable irritant.

Bertrand Russell, whose practice was to think first what he wanted to say and so make his first draft also his final one, advised Solly to do the same and not to waste 'both time and paper finding out what it is you think', a counsel of perfection which Solly and many others have found hard to follow. In order to gain space for his considerable output, he agreed, in 1938, to edit a *Bulletin on Animal Behaviour* (subsequently *Animal Behaviour*) and, to gain yet another outlet, shared in the launch of the *Journal of Endocrinology* which, after the war, he edited for some ten years. His aim was to give scientists the quick and sure publication which they needed; his problem was to beat off takeover bids from established houses and always to have available a sufficient supply of papers to keep up a constant output. Such problems, however, soon gave way to others, larger and more grave.

Neville Chamberlain's agreement, reached with Hitler on 29 September 1938, brought relief that did not last and shame that nothing since has ever quite rubbed out. In a letter written a week earlier to Joan Rufus Isaacs, to whom he was by that time engaged to be married, Solly wrote that he had been playing patience for hours. He felt as if he had been doing it for days. Ever since it became certain that the Czechs were going to be forced to accept the AF (Anglo-French) proposals, it hadn't seemed worth while doing very much else. 'There seems absolutely no reason for hope . . . and if you can tell me how we can find a path between Hitler accepted peacefully as a god of the world and Hitler opposed by world war, tell me.' He had yet to meet someone who did not believe that 'our Chamberlain in his infinite wisdom just chucked the game away'. War, so long unthinkable, began to look inevitable. The chance remark of a colleague to that effect and the suggestion that no one was giving much thought to the role of scientists in war caused Solly to see the future in a different light. He sought out J.D. Bernal, one of the more colourful and unusual people in Solly's life. A crystallographer of brilliance, an eccentric and of the far Left, he has been well described by Max Perutz: 'a flamboyant Irishman with a mane of fair hair, crumpled flannel trousers and a tweed jacket . . . We' (his students) 'called him Sage, because he knew everything, from physics to the history of art. Knowledge poured from him as from a fountain, unselfconsciously, vividly, without showing off on any subject under the sun. His enthusiasm for science was unbounded.' Solly, who thought Bernal should have at least shared in a Nobel Prize in the early 1930s, was impressed by his ability to discourse learnedly on any subject, his enormous head, his shock of hair and his habit of travelling light – the clothes he stood up in and briefcase with slide rule, a razor and the papers he was working on. With the problem of civil defence beginning to emerge from the shadows and acquiring, not before time, some importance, Solly and Bernal became involved in talks first with Sir Arthur Salter, then MP for Oxford University, and later with Sir John Anderson, the Lord Privy Seal, and Dr Reginald Stradling, his Chief Scientific Adviser. Bernal, whose suspected 'red' leanings were a source of official concern, was deemed acceptable – he could, in the view of Sir John Anderson, be 'as red as the flames of hell'; all that mattered was that he could help.

Meanwhile Solly, to whom work was then, as always, totally absorbing, faced a problem as to his next move. Having been offered the Chair of Anatomy at Birmingham University and knowing full well that acceptance would mean leaving his work at Oxford, his comfortable house and Mrs Boyd's cooking, he prevaricated to a point which must have severely tested the patience of the university authorities. Moreover, he had another problem of an altogether different nature; he wished to marry Lady Joan Rufus Isaacs, grand daughter of the first Marquess of Reading who, as Rufus Isaacs, had been Attorney-General, Lord Chief Justice, Viceroy of India and Foreign Secretary. Her other grandfather was Alfred Mond, the founder of ICI, who became the first Lord Melchett. After the fashion of the time, she had attended finishing schools in Paris and Rome and done a season in London as a debutante. She could well have married one of those eligible, though not necessarily interesting, young men whom she met in the course of that elaborate and somewhat weird launching process. Instead she accepted the proposal of an Oxford don fourteen years her senior, dedicated to his work and cherishing the comforts of a well organised bachelor life. To Joan's father, by then the second Lord Reading, the idea of his daughter marrying into the male-dominated academic society of pre-war Oxford was most unwelcome. She was young, inexperienced and would be neither comfortable nor happy in such an alien world. Support for the match came from the formidable Stella Reading, widow of Rufus Isaacs and founder of the Women's Voluntary Service; the Melchetts were also in favour. Lady Reading, Joan's mother, who was becoming exasperated by Solly's dithering, delivered an ultimatum: he must either marry the girl or get out. Her husband also was stung to protest, when Solly said he saw no need for any formal announcement. 'Are you ashamed to be marrying my daughter?' Joan's own determination to marry the man she thought the most interesting she had ever met was decisive so far as her family was concerned. His mother's ultimatum and the outbreak of war forced Solly to make up his mind.

Such worries as Solly had at that time were as nothing compared with those which faced his new wife. She accompanied him to Birmingham when he went there for a final discussion concerning the Chair of Anatomy: lunch with Dr Raymond Priestley, the Vice-Chancellor, who had been with both Scott and Shackleton to the Antarctic, and with members of the Council and their wives – 'all those elderly ladies with their fur tippets' – was a novel and somewhat disturbing occasion. Solly's account gives the impression that he was not too much concerned, even slightly amused, at her discomfort. The jolt of that introduction to the academic world at the age of twenty-one was intensified when, back in Oxford that evening, she met for the first time Freddie Ayer and Isaiah Berlin: 'I've never met people like that before; they might have come from a different planet.' Solly's half-comment, half-excuse, was to the effect that they were his friends and would soon become hers. 'Oxford was,' he added with more than a trace of smugness, 'a very different place from a debutante's London.' His suggestion, unnecessary and patronising, that Joan was no more than a debutante at the time took no account of the fact that she was already a serious art student and also engaged in working with child refugees from Germany.

In a letter to Joan, undated but probably written early in 1939, when they were on the brink of marriage, he mentions a visit they made together to look at a small house by a canal in London, where there was a possibility of a Chair. 'Will there, oh will there be another little house on another canal. Will there Joan? I feel there will, I know there must be. And now I am busily making a virtue out of necessity, and can see 1,000s [*sic*] of reasons why another canal, not one in London, would be preferable to the one there. Can you see any?' Later in the same letter: 'It is easier to say these things than explain to you those other difficulties. And that I haven't done. If you were to realise them fully (and that I shall see you do) and if you were then to brush them aside – in full understanding – then things will be much easier and there won't be any clouds. Please, darling Joan, be a little patient with me. I am probably not as maddening as the general bloodiness might make me appear.' He could hardly have written a letter more revealing of himself. It was not simply that he wanted to get his own way; he always found it hard to see that there could be another. What he found uncomfortable to explain now, he would 'return to later and the clouds would then go away'. He did not, of course, do so and the clouds remained.

It was a letter which was written in the knowledge that the young woman he was about to marry was generous and monumentally patient. Of that he took full advantage, expecting her to adjust the contours of her life to his, to leave her friends and to replace them with his. At that stage he ignored altogether the fact that she enjoyed painting and possessed considerable talent. To add oppressiveness to mere unreason, he laid down curious terms: there would be no children; that, given the war and the German attitudes towards Jews, was not as unreasonable as it seemed. She would wear only grey or black; when she bought a green dress, she was obliged to take it back to the shop. She would make no changes to the décor, nor was she to interfere with the running of the house in Museum Road. Since she loved him, she was content to accept for the moment and slowly to wear away his conditions. She accepted too his brusque insistence that with him work would always come first and was unshaken by his ensuing challenge: 'Can you cope?' Drawing on great reserves of skill, patience and infinite understanding, she showed that she could.

The Second World War arrived quietly. In a voice so dry that the words seemed to crackle like frozen grass trodden underfoot, Neville Chamberlain stated that as from eleven o'clock that morning Britain was in a state of war with Germany. Ration books, gas masks, slow trains and uniforms told of the abnormal situation. There was a feeling of being somewhere in the neighbourhood of a precipice, without knowing quite where it was. Everything seemed stuck somewhere between the familiar world to which there could be no returning and another, unseen, unreal, but full of menace. Solly's early contributions to the war effort consisted of filling sandbags, heaping them round the windows of laboratories in Oxford and, as a qualified doctor, albeit one who had never practised, putting undergraduates through their medicals prior to their joining the forces. The instructions he was given were simple: 'Make sure they all pass, unless they have flat feet.'

It took time for war, so unreal both in prospect and beginning, to envelop everything, reaching down with long giants' fingers into the core of people's lives, leaving almost nobody and nothing untouched. Just as war lifted Solly out of the cloistered life of a science researcher and teacher, so it gathered men and women in their millions from the small meandering streams of everyday life, sweeping them along in its flow, absorbing their energy, using their skills, testing their courage. The common purpose pushed them in the direction of uniformity, if not equality, and it demanded of them unaccustomed levels of compliance and obedience. People didn't retire, they didn't take holidays, their alternatives vanished; they applied themselves in countless ways to producing ever more powerful means of destruction and to using them. That drive to destroy took up so much of the reserves of human energy that little was left over to keep the civilised world on its hinges.

Solly had two principal anxieties: first to reassure the cherished Mrs Boyd that she need not be worried about his marriage and that Joan, his newly wedded wife, would not interfere with her running of the house. His next was to finish a monograph concerning 'the histogenesis of the tissues which react by cell division when stimulated by the female oestrogenic sex hormone'. Beyond those cares, however, he began to find room for a concern, far from unique, that what would now be called the scientific establishment was not being sufficiently active 'in mobilising the country's scientific resources in the fight against Hitler's Germany'. Seeking a platform from which to express such views, he and a few others, including Desmond Bernal, revived the old Tots and Quots dining club which, during his absence in America, had gone into limbo. The club, resurrected, burst into new life and also into print. It was agreed that if the members would put together a resumé of one evening's discussion, Penguin Books would publish it as a paperback. Intended as a protest that scientists in general were not being sufficiently drawn into the war effort, the promised paperback, *Science in War*, duly appeared. Julian Huxley commended it as 'a tract for the times which every scientific worker should read'. Noting that it was conceived, written, printed and published in less than a month, he observed, 'This abbreviated gestation, more characteristic of a rodent than of a human being or book, though very remarkable, has had certain unavoidable defects.' Despite the concerns expressed in the book, scientists were meanwhile being absorbed quite quickly into the war effort.

It is hard now, even for those old enough to remember, to make the journey back to a time of innocence, when little was known about bombing and its effects, the hurt to people, the damage to buildings and generally what it would do to the elaborate but brittle structure of twentieth-century living. More particularly, almost nothing was known about blast, though some rather exaggerated notions, originating in the Spanish Civil War, were in circulation. Cyril Joad, a philosopher for whom Solly had scant respect, dismissing him as 'a radio propagandist', thought that a single bomb – and in those days they were all small – could flatten a square mile of a city. The Ministry of Home Security at Princes Risborough, wanting to know more, asked Bernal, who was working for the Ministry at the time, to investigate and report; the particular concern being to know whether shock waves from an explosion nearby would cause concussion to people in an underground shelter. Bernal, aware that Solly was not far away in Oxford and that he had some monkeys, replied that, while he could deal with the 'physical parameters', he would need 'Zuckerman and his monkeys'. The monkeys positioned in a nearby trench were unaffected by the explosions; so too were Solly and Bernal when they took their turn.

They concluded, contrary to the established wisdom, that lung injuries from blast were of the same order as blows from a flat object and were certainly not, as had been supposed, caused by the entry of shock waves through the mouth and nose. Looking at wounds from high-velocity fragments, they were able to show that the speed at which a projectile travelled was the major factor in the gravity of the injury. In that too they were in conflict with the firm established opinions of the Medical Research Council (MRC). Intruding into the territory of such an august institution is like taking a walk in a minefield; explosions follow. The MRC responded sharply; that if a government department required advice in such matters, the Council was the proper body to provide it. Its expert on statistics was sufficiently upset to circulate a note suggesting that laboratory experimentation would shed no light on the matter, adding majestically that from the public point of view, 'ignorance is bliss'. Ignorance there certainly was. Solly collected together all the written work he could lay his hands on concerning wounds and how they were caused. It showed that at that time, 'We knew practically nothing'.

Since the matter clearly required further study, Solly was authorised by the Ministry to put together a small investigative team whose name, the 'Oxford Extra-Mural Unit' (OEMU), intentionally or not, told nothing about its function. Peter Krohn, an ex-pupil of Solly's, was its first recruit; Angele Vidal-Hall, who had worked in the Bursar's Office of Magdalen College, was enlisted as Solly's PA to look after administration. She has memories of him at that time. Few people, she said, were neutral in their reaction to Solly Zuckerman. They tended either to be captivated by his intelligence, his fearlessness, both moral and physical, his vitality, his enthusiasm, his human warmth, or to be alienated by his often overbearing manner and merciless attacks on those of whom he disapproved, especially on those he considered to be fools. No doubt envy of his achievements underlay some of the antagonism. She saw a great deal of him and his method of working in that first year, and realised that only careful selection of the relevant data and rigorous accuracy in analysis could have enabled him to make the leap from endocrinology to the patho-physiological and economic effects of bombing. She saw how much his clearly-expressed conviction that he was right infuriated his opponents, but at the same time gave a real sense of purpose to those working with him.

Solly's vitality astonished her. After a day of meetings and discussions in London, he would drive back to Oxford, have supper, get her round to do some work with him and after that do some experimental work in the endocrinology laboratory in order to relax. There was, she said, no side about him; if the typists could not cope with a load of work, he would sit down and bang away on his rather primitive typewriter. He asked no more of others, rather less in fact, than he was prepared to put in himself. He communicated his enthusiasm and shared it with the rest as new avenues of research opened up. He had the outstanding virtue of a chief in that he was ready to trust, to delegate and, if something went wrong, to help sort it out. He was, she found, a loyal and generous friend; he attracted people with his warmth and sense of fun. Far from being a hard man, he showed, despite his autocratic manner, an understanding of other people's problems, and was outstandingly patient and kind to anyone with a special trouble who needed encouragement.

The diversion of the Luftwaffe in the autumn of 1940 from attacking and destroying the airfields of Britain and the fighter aircraft dependent upon them may not, at the time, have seemed to be the turning point that it was. The Germans let slip and never recovered the opportunity to mount a successful invasion which, in putting Britain out of the war, would have completed their domination of Western Europe. They resorted instead to a strategy of bombarding from the air the towns and cities of Britain and destroying with their U-boats the shipping upon which survival depended. As the German attack focussed on the civil population, so caring for the injured and the homeless, disposing of the dead, clearing away the debris and keeping the shipping lanes open became the hard, grinding tasks. A Bomb Census was set up alongside a Casualty Survey run by Solly and centred on Guy's Hospital; it had a flying squad to investigate incidents and an analytical section in Oxford. In October 1940, a lone German aircraft bombed Banbury, hitting, among other things, a small single-storey building in the railway station and causing casualties. Solly, informed of the occurrence, hurried over and carried out a thorough examination. From that first incident and others which followed, he learned that 'a coherent story could be distilled from the debris of destruction.'

Over the next twelve months detailed examinations carried out by the unit of more than a hundred incidents brought about a different pattern of thinking. Painful experience of the effects of bombing brought with it new thoughts as to how they should be handled. Instead of broken bodies and shattered buildings, people began to think in terms of 'the standard casualty rate' or 'the vulnerable area' of an explosion. They acquired, as a result, a clearer idea of what they could expect to happen and how to cope when it did. Most casualties were not the direct result of explosions, but were caused by the collapse of buildings, falling masonry or flying debris. There would be five times as many people in shelters at night as in daytime. While the standard casualty rate varied with the size of the bomb, measured ton for ton 50kg bombs produced significantly more casualties than 250kg or 500kg bombs. The biggest, Solly came to understand, was not necessarily most effective in the irrational world where bombs play their part. The threshold of blast pressure, which was likely to be lethal, would not be experienced except in the immediate area of an explosion. Such facts, now proven and obvious, were new then, and their discovery helped people to come to terms with what was going on.

A report entitled '*The Field Study of Air Raid Casualties*', which Bernal and Solly put together, embodied all that they had learned in that first year. It became the standard work of reference on the subject and it marked the end of their apprenticeship in what Solly called 'the macabre science of destruction'. It established their reputation as the possessors of unrivalled knowledge of a subject previously unexplored. Time moved on and, as it did so, the horizons of the war widened. There had been no invasion. German bombing had not, despite Hitler's noisy boasts, brought Britain to her knees. The Russians had not been knocked out of the war by that first tremendous German onslaught. Above all, America was in. The growing strength of the RAF made it possible to begin to think in terms of attack. Those who had had the anguish of seeing their homes destroyed welcomed the prospect of the Germans being shown what their leaders' war did to ordinary people. Those whose business was to plan operations began to reflect upon what bombing might achieve. Some, including Lord Cherwell, believed that bombing enemy towns and cities would so damage the economy and break the morale of the people that Germany would be unable to remain at war. So, with the hope that bombing might bring victory without the need for an invasion, the Cabinet in 1942 issued its directive that unrestricted attacks should be launched on Germany. No one at that time knew that the much heavier bombing that followed would not have that effect.

Even at the time, however, there were those who believed that a strategy which assumed that bombing could bring victory was mistaken. Costly in terms of aircrew, planes lost and the time needed to replace them, it would absorb huge resources, needed elsewhere. There was, after all, a battle to be won in the Atlantic if the sea lanes were to be kept open. Moreover, the claims made for the strategy exaggerated the effectiveness of bombing by a wide margin and the weight of bombs said to be required far exceeded the RAF's capacity at that time to deliver them. Inaccuracy of bombing was also a limiting factor.

Cherwell was concerned that such arguments, if not answered, might undermine the strategy of which he was a staunch supporter. He therefore welcomed a suggestion of Solly's that careful examination of the effects of German bombing of Birmingham and Hull might provide useful guidance as to the effectiveness of British bombing strategy. So strong was Cherwell's belief that it caused him to take for granted that Solly and Bernal, who were to conduct the inquiry, were of the same opinion. He also expected that it would provide guidance as to the weight of bombs required to crush a particular city; it did not do so, nor could it have done.

The inquiry that Solly and Bernal set up was wide enough to include physical damage, lost production, absenteeism, health, casualties and morale. Aware of the importance Cherwell attached to their report and the eagerness with which he awaited it, Solly kept him informed of progress. It may be that, in doing so, he caused 'the Prof' to fear that the report might not match up to his hopes, Cherwell decided not to wait. Instead he set out his own views in a minute to the Prime Minister on 30 March 1942, noting that he did not wish to anticipate the report itself – but in Solly's view doing exactly that. Moreover, in one important respect what Cherwell wrote, using information provided to him by Solly, directly conflicted with the conclusions of the report published only a week after he had written his minute. In it he had said that in Hull 'signs of strain were evident, though only one tenth of the houses were destroyed'. He went on to say that he had little doubt that if ten times as much damage were inflicted upon fifty-eight principal German towns and cities, 'it would break the spirit of the people'. Whereas the report made it clear that there was no evidence that German attacks on Birmingham and Hull had come anywhere near to breaking the morale of the people, Cherwell was suggesting, on the strength of evidence gathered by Solly and Bernal, that British bombing of Germany could, even would, have that effect. The doubts of both Sir Henry Tizard, Chief Adviser to the Chief of the Air Staff, and Patrick Blackett, a chief scientist at the Admiralty, were directed not to the ethics of area bombing, but to its effectiveness. Blackett also thought that Cherwell's views greatly exaggerated the RAF's capability, by as much as 600 percent.

At that time, of course, no one was able to foresee that the seven million tons of bombs dropped during the Vietnam war – three times the total of all British, American and German bombs dropped on European soil in the Second World War – brought no victory, only death and destruction. Forty years or so after the event, when he came to write his autobiography, Solly took the view that Cherwell's minute to the Prime Minister and the strong support it gave to the strategy of Bomber Command was crucial. 'The outcome would', he thought, 'have been very different if the Prof had not been there to put the weight of his authority, and his influence on Churchill, behind a bombing policy.' Blackett is on record as believing that Bomber Command's policy of area bombing was 'the worst strategic mistake of the war'.

Those two reports, the *Field Study of Air Raid Casualties* and the one on Birmingham and Hull, both told of the effects of German bombing of English towns and cities. Their purposes were however different. Whereas the first aimed to give guidance as to how those effects could be diminished and people protected from them, the second was to measure the usefulness of bombing as a means of securing the defeat of Germany. During the four months that separated them, the mind of Britain was moving from thoughts of defence to the possibility of attack. Solly and Bernal moved with that change. Lord Mountbatten, then Head of Combined Operations, became intrigued with the idea that those who knew most about the effects of bombing might have a role in planning the strategy. He invited both men to join his HQ.

Solly's first allotted task, to estimate on how many nights in a month conditions were suitable for a small cross-Channel raid, led to a mass of paperwork and to the answer that there were none.

Ration packs for the Commandos, how to make a tough bunch of Marines tougher, and planning a seaborne attack on Alderney were other problems that came his way. George Jellicoe, in the Commandos at the time, came to tell him about a raid: 'I hadn't expected him to listen to me, he did. I took to him at once.' Lack of inflatable dinghies in one raid had obliged them to use captured German ones which leaked. Some two years later, long after there had ceased to be a requirement, a whole load of Jellicoe Mk I inflatable life rafts made their appearance. To their chagrin, neither Solly nor Bernal were allowed by Mountbatten to accompany the Dieppe raid as observers, though both were concerned with the *post mortem*. Bernal looked at the damage to the naval and support craft, Solly at the wounded who returned. From the examination, in which he had the help of Peter Krohn and his Oxford unit, Solly learned little of any worth, though the memory remained. Years afterwards, on a holiday in Dieppe, he stood under the cliffs where so many had died and remembered the study he had made.

3

The Mediterranean

'I am a lifelong admirer of Zuck.'

Lord Scarman

FOLLOWING THE victory of El Alamein, Bernal and Solly were despatched by HQ Combined Ops to Cairo, to study Army/Air co-operation and the use of fragmentation weapons. They were together to advise on bombing; Bernal would take the strategy, Solly the effects and the casualties. Their partnership ended, however, when soon after their arrival in the Middle East, Bernal was required urgently in Canada to do a presentation to Roosevelt and the American Chiefs of Staff on Habbakuk, the code-name of a weird project for a giant aircraft carrier built of reinforced ice known as Pykrete after Geoffrey Pyke, its pioneer. It was half a mile long, with a hull thirty feet thick, unsinkable by torpedo and able to launch any known aircraft. The project did not, in the event, find favour with the Americans and was dropped.

Bernal's departure left Solly saddled with the strategy side of their joint role as well as his own. He was, he said, appalled to find himself on his own without support and with no one with whom to share thoughts on war in the desert – and Solly always needed to talk. Sandy Thomson, a Major in the 8th Army RAMC, bored with working on chemical warfare which wasn't going to happen, who had contrived to attach himself to Bernal and Zuckerman when they first arrived in Tripoli, now stepped into the breach. On his first day he had turned up with his Brigadier's car which he had borrowed. Although he could not replace Bernal, he was able to take much of the routine work of examining and reporting off Solly's shoulders. For good measure he proved skilful in handling the attentions of the intrusive bureaucrats of Middle East HQ. Professor Zuckerman could have an army car; Thomson, being only a Major, could not in his absence use it and there were problems about his office accommodation. The Army Operational Research Section in Cairo, not wanting to be left out, decided to do a study of their own, duplicating Solly's, on the effectiveness of weapons. A senior officer in the RAMC, hearing of Solly's casualty survey, wanted to produce one himself and to grab Thomson to do the work. Somehow or other, between them they managed to cope with the fungus of officialdom which, once the fighting was over, reasserted itself and recovered its hold upon everyone. Thomson quickly became proficient in the detailed work of house-to-house and casualty studies which Solly always required. He subsequently stayed with Solly through the operations in Pantelleria, Sicily, Italy and Northern Europe and, when the war was over, joined him again in Birmingham.

The ostensible purpose of Solly's mission to the Middle East was to study the effects of bombing; he had also to report how and why so many of Rommel's troops had got away after El Alamein. Tripoli, attacked continuously over a period of two years by RAF bombers, offered a mass of information. RAF operational orders and the debriefing reports of air crews presented a picture which in many respects was in sharp contrast to the detailed Italian records of the dates and times of air raids, the planes engaged, the bombs dropped, and the casualties and damage caused . Ships half-sunk in the harbour, damaged quaysides and a hospital full of wounded Italian prisoners of war gave him a wealth of additional material. Overall, the information available gave a new and not very encouraging indication of the accuracy of RAF bombing at that time. Although the majority of the thousand or so RAF aircraft which had attacked Tripoli in night raids claimed to have reached their primary target, less than 10 percent of their bombs had fallen within two miles of the point at which they were aimed.

As earlier at home in England, so now in North Africa, Solly was the first to apply his mind to the effects of bombing as opposed to the methods. He concluded that taking weight for weight, British bombing in North Africa had been less effective than either American or German and that the RAF set their fuses wrongly; he argued that they should be set to explode a fraction of a second after impact instead of immediately, thus giving time for penetration of the target. He learned too, since at that time accuracy of aim could not be counted on, that plastering an area was effective; pinpointing targets was a waste of time; and that despite the publicity given to blockbuster bombs, larger numbers of smaller bombs were more effective. Solly and Sandy Thomson between them somehow contrived to collect and examine a huge amount of evidence, achieving this under the difficult circumstances of a damaged and recently captured city, with a largely Arab population which had no interest in the war.

On 15 March 1943, Solly, having completed all the work for which he had time, went on to Algiers, where he was due to meet Air Chief Marshal Tedder, later Marshal of the RAF Lord Tedder, then commanding, under Eisenhower, all Allied Air Forces in North Africa. At that point he moved to an altogether different level of the war. On his first night there he found himself for the first time face to face with the Americans at war, and from the start he found them easy to get on with: 'They were men who were learning, as I was learning, and unlike some professional military people whom I had already met, there was no assumption of superior knowledge and no assurance that they knew how Germany was going to be defeated.' That attitude made it possible for him to get on easy terms with the Americans, whether scientists, soldiers or politicians, and for them to do so with him.

On the following day he met Tedder, also for the first time. Quiet, reserved and, as Solly described him, 'intellectually concerned by the far-reaching political and technological events that were transforming the world', Tedder had originally been picked out by Lord Trenchard as having 'a great gift for getting his priorities right'. Solly's initial report on Tripoli and a copy of what he had written to Air Chief Marshal Sir Sholto Douglas, Commander in Chief Middle East, in Cairo on the air war in the desert, were his introduction. The two men spent the whole of an afternoon together, for most of the time alone, and without the interruption of a single telephone call. Tedder had two particular concerns which he expressed to Solly: first, 'Tunis was going to be Germany's Dunkirk and they must not escape as we had done.' Secondly, 'the air must win its own battle before it could help fight the Army's or the Navy's, neither of which could help the air.' It was an extraordinary meeting between two remarkable men; one can only guess what it was that touched off such immediate mutual recognition of each other's worth and what in particular caused Tedder, with other things on his mind, to set aside so much time to this scientist he had never previously met.

That meeting saw the beginning of a relationship of trust and friendship, tested in Pantelleria, and developed in Sicily, Italy, in the preliminaries for Overlord (codename for the cross-Channel invasion in 1944), and in the operations that followed. Tedder was one of a very small number of men in Solly's life in whom he found no fault; he was also one of his *Six Men Out of the Ordinary*. Tedder showed him 'new horizons of experience' and made him learn the ways of the world. He directed what Solly interestingly described as 'the finishing school of the first phase of my life'. He taught him that while there could be no compromise about what is the best available truth in new scientific knowledge, compromise was unavoidable in dealing with the titans who bore the direct responsibility of command in the war. 'Command turned simple men into prima donnas. Tedder knew this and I did not.'

Two months in London were largely taken up with preparing the final version of his Tripoli report and answering questions as to the effectiveness of bombing, but on 10 May Solly was bidden to return to North Africa as soon as possible. Before obeying that urgent summons, he was required to settle an important item of business. Someone somewhere in the great creaking machine of government came up with the fact that he had failed to account in detail for the £102.10s.0d. which he had received to cover two months subsistence in Cairo and Tripoli. Unable to say what he had done with £21.5s.0d, he sent 'them' a cheque for that amount and was given a receipt. He was also given an RAF uniform and the honorary rank of Group-Captain to indicate his respectability and explain as required how he came to be wandering around in places where civilians had no right to be.

'You're late', was Tedder's greeting on Solly's return from London; then, pointing to the files stacked on the table, 'Tell me what we've done wrong while you've been away.' A quarter of a million Axis troops, trapped in Tunisia with no means of exit, had surrendered and been taken prisoner. The files, dim shadows of large events, told him little and Tedder would say nothing as to the reason for his sudden recall; he would hear that in Constantine the next day from General Spaatz, Commanding General of the North West African Air Forces. He should then study what was proposed and within forty-eight hours telephone to Tedder and say, in as few words as possible, whether it could be done. 'It' turned out to be the capture of Pantelleria, a small, rocky island between Sicily and Tunisia, heavily fortified and judged by Mussolini to be impregnable.

Eisenhower, then in overall command of Allied forces in the Mediterranean, believed its capture to be an essential prerequisite to a successful invasion of Sicily. Solly's first task was to judge whether or not it would be possible to reduce the island by bombing and thus avert the need for a seaborne landing which was planned to take place in fifteen days' time; such a landing was certain to be costly in terms of casualties. His next was to produce a plan, showing how it should be done and estimating the number and weight of bombs required to silence the defending batteries. Having spent two days examining the aerial photographs of the island's gun emplacements, for which he had asked and which the Americans had supplied, he telephoned to Tedder in Algiers the cryptic verdict, 'It is on provided Mary is in'. Mary was Air Marshal Maori Coningham, the New Zealand born Commander of the North West African Tactical Air Force. The message meant that in Solly's opinion Pantelleria could be eliminated by bombing, so long as the necessary complement of bombers were available. Up to that time, Solly, apart from Sandy Thomson, had been a one man band; now Barney Campion, a sergeant in the RAF, was assigned to him as secretary. Campion stayed with Solly for the remainder of the war and thereafter worked for him in Birmingham until his eventual retirement, a total of thirty years.

Solly's plan was based on what he called 'the vulnerable area of a gun', i.e. the area round a gun within which the burst of a bomb could make it unserviceable. A high density of strike, a thousand tons per square mile, would be necessary. Individual batteries were to be the aiming points, four to six batteries per day. Detailed analyses of results should be produced each evening and targets for the following day selected in the light of that information. He estimated that something between fifty and sixty bursts of 500lb or 1000lb bombs per area of 150 square yards would be needed with bombs fused, as he had come to prefer, to go off a split second after impact. The island's surrender on the fourth morning, as the landing operation was about to begin, was something of a triumph for him. He took note, however, of Tedder's warning that not too much should be learned from an operation the features of which were unlikely to be repeated; no enemy air presence and a very limited objective made possible a massive concentration of force on a small target. Ten out of the fifteen batteries attacked were out of action and at least three of the remainder had suffered significant damage. The subsequent *post mortem* showed, among other things, that something short of direct destruction of the guns was enough to bring about substantial reduction in fire power. 'A hundred bombs falling within a hundred yards of a six gun battery might fail to secure a single direct hit; yet their secondary effects might be completely to neutralise its guns. Bombs not only damaged the ground and the material and units which make up a battery; they also demoralised, and demoralisation may play as big a part in silencing a battery as any other single factor.'

His reputation soared; there cannot have been many similar instances in the history of modern war of a virtually unknown civilian scientist even being asked so large a question, let alone of one coming up with an answer within days which, accepted by military commanders, then succeeded. Eisenhower himself in his despatch wrote, 'Professor Zuckerman's exhaustive report on the subject might prove of as much value in the fight against the Axis as the capture of the island.' Solly was, as he said, 'bathed in praise', not least by the one from whom he probably valued it most – Tedder: 'I had complete confidence in Zuckerman's knowledge and judgement. It was a fortunate day when he was sent to the

Mediterranean. His services were of incalculable value.' With Sicily next on the Allied list, Solly's advice was to attack the nodal points of the railway system on the island itself and in Southern Italy. The destruction and damage to rolling stock and repair facilities proved crucial, and largely because of them 'the Sicilian and Southern Italian rail systems had become practically paralysed by the end of July 1943'. The efficiency of a railway system, he observed, 'appears to fall very rapidly when bombing simultaneously leads to an increase in the calls upon and a decrease in the capacity of repair facilities'.

Once Sicily was taken, he had the task of examining in detail the results of the bombing: for that, he needed staff. It was, as he pointed out to the Air Ministry, 'somewhat of a strain for one person both to help create the debris and then to crawl over it'. His memories of Palermo were of the general air of misery which hung over the captured city and of 'doorways where mothers sat picking lice from their children's hair'. His proposed bombing targets, mostly railways, in Southern Italy were examined by Tedder and closely questioned before being accepted. A short visit to London enabled Solly to gather together the staff he needed for the Bombing Survey Unit. Cherwell, a long-time believer in the merits of night bombing, gave Solly a message to deliver to Spaatz to the effect that the Americans' daylight bombing was both ineffectual and costly: it was not well received.

One interesting comment on those days was made by Lord Scarman in a letter to Joan following Solly's death some fifty years later:

> I want to tell you simply that I am a life-long admirer of 'Zuck' – as we called him in 1943 when he came to the Mediterranean to devise the bombing strategy which enabled us to invade Sicily and southern Italy and to clear the Germans out of that theatre of war.

4

Letters from the Middle East

'Do you want me back?'
Solly to Joan, 1943

WAR THROWS people about, unties their relationships and loosens the bolts of the structures which are the base of their lives. They find themselves wondering in the surrounding turbulence what can survive the storm. So it was with Solly, despatched suddenly in 1943 to the Middle East. Distance, separation and the uncertainties of war caused him, in a series of wartime letters to Joan, to take another look at the world outside the window, and at her, and even to wonder if she would want him back.

Joan, suddenly left on her own in wartime Oxford, took refuge in the library of the Ashmolean Museum and began to study what was for her a gap in the history of art between the Greek and Roman and Giotto. So completely did she immerse herself, that she left Solly behind on the surface of her life and even let slip from her mind the thought that she should write to him. Absorbed in the war, he would not be interested in what went on in her small world; he would not, she thought, need letters which told him nothing he did not know. Always on the move and for most of the time engrossed in examining the debris of war, Solly became conscious of Joan's disappearance from his life and a need to be reassured that she would at some time return to it. Meanwhile, he needed very much to know what she was doing, how she was and what she felt for him. She kept all the letters he wrote to her during his absences in North Africa, Sicily and Italy and they still survive.

The first came from Government Rest House, Lagos, days after leaving England. He was excited to be back in what he called his old country – Africa. He adored the smell of it all.

Almost everybody smiling and showing their teeth, women in vast shawls and strange coiffures, poorer women in rags and babies on their backs, and flat breasts. Our own people, almost all in uniform, and very superior. Even the one white woman of the station, beautiful as an advertisement and I am sure the subject of more dreams than she could count. It was just the same as a lot of other memories that came back. Except for the fact that the blacks had a strange decayed Arab Mohammedan culture and one man I saw about an hour or two before sunset was doing the usual stuff on a grass rug, bowing his head onto the ground and all that, and with an agonised expression on his face.

Back in the air later and looking at the earth below him, he wrote,

It's night and a wonderful moon is tracing the rivers and swamps of Africa which lies very black below me. Every now and then an isolated light can be seen or two or three together, but I can't imagine who the black people are sitting beside them. And yet they're there all right, black, very black, shining and naked, wrapped in old rags and happy. Even happy as they puzzle out the incredible ways of the white man. Happy in those endless forests and swamps and by the sides of their wide shining rivers. We're so madly ignorant about them and I think so very backward at the problem of fitting them into the world. But it's not a problem that can be ignored for ever. Poor wretches, they themselves don't even know that they have to be fitted in sooner or later.

I wish I could tell you just how lovely it all is through the small window at the side of which I am writing. So lovely, and as it has always been, so mysterious. Heaven knows how little of Africa is known – but it's very little really. Those myriads of rivers, those mazes of swamps, who really has walked by them and seen their birds, their monkeys, their crocodiles.

He told of asking a black boy about the birds that lived there and how he had had to be content with the answer that there were parrots and big birds and small birds. He went on,

One could spend weeks looking at the birds alone – and yet no-one there gives a damn. There were no monkeys nearer than 50 miles this morning – but I'll see some tomorrow. Oh I wish you were here. We'll come one day to these parts.

From Cairo early in February, he wrote of how Khartoum was like a holiday at the sea. There was more to look at, per square yard, in the Sudan than anywhere else he had been. He would love to come back. It would be nice, didn't she think, it could be their first holiday, but no, that was already to be in New York. The whole experience was so strange that it was difficult to tell her anything, but he made a considerable effort to do so.

This strange city compounded of ancient Arab and Jew dwellings mixed with the grand pompous modern Italian. A civilian population of whites who haven't quite gathered their wits together. Arabs, Jews, whom one can't tell from one another, and the latter of whom probably have no blood relationship with Jews elsewhere – apparently quite undisturbed. Wandering parties of Bedouin – or whatever they are – on their camels with big rope mesh bags moving like scissors with the movement of their beasts, and others on foot, wherever one goes in the country. Road signs in German and Italian, a million relics they've left behind, tons of their records and letters lying everywhere, so many bits of their broken aircraft etc that we haven't even had time to pull the stuff together in dumps, the Mediterranean outside the Hotel, Spring and the bees – it's beyond me to put it all together in a letter. The Hotel I'm staying in is a memory of glorious pre-war luxury where one now eats out of the tinned rations one brings in. It's made of a series of lovely two storied patios, each with a gay garden, and with – you can tell me I'm wrong when I get back – bougainvillia growing on the walls and everything else green.

Rather patronisingly he asked her if she knew anything about General Gordon and the Mahdi and the Khalifa and General Kitchener's battle of Omdurman, and then gave her a brief rundown on the subject. A week later he was writing from Tripoli a forlorn and different note. 'It's very bad being away from you so long. I don't even know if you're well or happy or what. What are you? Do you want me back?'

On 13 July, from HQ North African Air Forces (Advanced), after Pantelleria, he sent an aerograph asking, 'How are you darling? I am looking forward so much to hearing from you. All my love, S. P.S. Pantelleria went very well didn't it?' His next letter told of how yesterday, as he walked down the hill from where he was staying, he saw some people dressing the carcass of a sheep on the roof of a small block of flats.

Tonight as I came up from work there was a party going on – the sheep, strange exotic Arab music and strange dancing, all in the light of a brilliant moon which showed up every detail of the lovely landscape, hills and valleys and all. I can hear the music from where I am writing, and I wish you were here to listen to it with me.

He still hoped to get back in a couple of weeks, if only for a spell, but things were busy and he was kept busy with them, flying here, there and everywhere. At the moment, he was completing a vast report, but that should be done in a day or two, after which he hoped to return home – this time without a load of work.

Towards the end of July, he wrote for the first time as 'Professor S. Zuckerman, Scientific Adviser North African Air Forces' c/o General Spaatz. He was getting desperate, as the prospect of his return continued to recede. He was beginning to find the spinning-out of this fortnight more and more unbearable. He couldn't tell her how much he missed her and how much further away 3 Museum Road became every day this trip was prolonged. He kept hoping that events would clear sufficiently to allow him to leave tomorrow, the day after and so on. But instead every day brought new excitements – into all of which he was now drawn. Mussolini's going was the latest; if only Italy wouldn't prolong her agony. He had been over in Sicily a few days ago and would be returning there before leaving for home in order to organise his survey of effects. He had got her a straw hat, but little else. When he returned it wouldn't be like last time with lots of work. They were going to have a holiday. 'So darling, just expect me any day now. I want to see you more than I can say.'

A week later, with, quite unusually, time on his hands, he was bored and wished 'to be finished with the job and home back with you'. It was hot, he was sunburned, he had bought her all the straw hats he could find and there was nothing else to buy. He was returning in two days to Sicily; then he would come back to her. He went on to complain about the bites from mosquitoes, flies and other crawlies. He would see he was deloused before coming back to her.

Having been back in England for a while, he wrote on 27 October saying how he had been moving in a whirl around Algiers, Tunis, Brindisi, Bari, Foggia and Naples. A trip into the line, a look down Vesuvius and another down Etna, days in Palermo, Africa again and back; the data he wanted were, he explained, very scattered. There followed a question and more than a hint of complaint, 'Is all well with you? So far I've not had any word from you?' On 7 November, Joan's first letter after his visit to England had arrived. It told how she had again become ill the moment he left. It was the third time that the first letter from her after one of his visits home had contained such news. His Italian was progressing, but the Sicilian failure to enunciate like the true Italians was holding him back. He did not think he would reach drawing-room standard. He told of how his party now numbered seventy. Sometimes it was fun, sometimes it was not; there was still any amount of material and 'glorious big problems to see a way through'. Joan's letter of 6 November had just come when he wrote, 'I can't tell you how much I miss you. This kind of living just isn't real, however absorbing it is. I hate to think of you eating alone and I hate having to eat at the head of my mess-table.' There followed a tale he had heard from an American Air Staff Officer. One of his aircraft was lost in bad weather over Taranto Bay. The pilot of another plane, flying over the area and observing a dinghy, went down to explore. There he recognised the man in the raft and on his return reported, 'Say, what's Pinky doing in a dinghy in Taranto Bay – Sure I saw him there.' A boat was sent out and fetched Pinky in. Their easy and casual way of doing things appealed to Solly.

Disappointed not to be getting back for Christmas himself, he sent some earrings and a ring to Joan via Air Commodore Elliot. They were late-nineteenth-century Sicilian, and he had acquired them from a collection which was being broken up. He was being held prisoner and wouldn't get away for another couple of weeks. Signals from Mountbatten bidding Solly to come and join him in Delhi were intercepted by Tedder who replied saying he could not. All Solly wanted was to go home and stay there. It would have been easier, he wrote to Joan if he hadn't struck 'a bit of a gold-mine of very useful information out here'. On 22 December he couldn't work for thinking of her and it was madness for every hour he didn't work put off his departure by that amount of time. He was so worried her last letter was dated 15 November, there were four before that. 'You are well, aren't you?' See that the flat is empty by Jan 1 and that you are free to be with me. I'm longing for you'. The last letter was dated Christmas Day 1943:

It won't be many days before I see you, thank God . . . Not having heard from you for so long has started me off on an agony that overrides in importance everything. And it's there all the time. Not very useful at a moment when I'm completing a *most* important !! report. I'll be able to laugh in a few days, but not before.'

Joan kept and cherished those letters. They reminded her of things that Solly thought and wrote when she was not there, but which, when she was, he could neither show nor say.

5

Overlord

'What's the point of circulating minutes? There will never be
a true history of what's happening'.

Air Chief Marshal Tedder

B Y THE end of 1943, the epicentre of the war was moving from
the Mediterranean to Northern Europe; Eisenhower was to
be Supreme Allied Commander for the cross Channel invasion
codenamed Overlord, with Tedder as his Deputy. Returning
home from Italy at the end of December, Solly brought with him a
sealed letter from Tedder to Air Chief Marshal Sir Charles Portal,
the Chief of the Air Staff; on arrival, he was taken straight to the
Air Ministry. In his letter, Tedder set out the lessons of the
Mediterranean and his own conclusions. Portal's immediate
response was to arrange for Solly to see first Air Chief Marshal Sir
Trafford Leigh-Mallory, Commander in Chief Allied Expeditionary Force (AEAF) and then Air Chief Marshal Sir Arthur
Harris, Commander-in-Chief Bomber Command.

At Leigh-Mallory's suggestion, Solly was shown the plan for the
period prior to D-day. The air section struck him as thin, 'no more
than an expression of hope'. Its aim, to interrupt the French
railway system by bombing twenty key points in an arc 50 to 60
miles away from the invasion, fell far short of what he thought was
required. He also doubted whether Leigh-Mallory would have
available the aircraft necessary even for that limited objective. He
was concerned too that no allowance had been made for the

uncertain Channel weather and the likelihood of flying being interrupted. He undertook to produce an alternative plan.

Twenty-four hours later, he met Harris for the first time in his house at High Wycombe, and spent the night there. Harris conveyed 'a sense of power and determination'; Solly found him more remote, more self-contained, than any of the senior airmen he had met and, surprisingly, a keen cook, who prepared the Eggs Benedictine himself. Expecting his host to show at least some interest in the air war in the Mediterranean, Solly was surprised instead to be treated to a monologue on the activities of Bomber Command. Harris regretted the choice of Spaatz to command all the American Air Forces in Europe; he stressed the importance of the strategic bombing of Germany, which he thought Spaatz appreciated not at all. His collection of pictures of devastated towns in Germany reinforced his belief in the effectiveness of his strategy, even though intelligence sources at the time indicated that war production in the Reich was still increasing. For Solly it was an unusual experience to be obliged to remain silent and for so long. Not until the following morning did Harris ask for his opinion on anything; he then demanded a straight answer to the single question, could heavy bombers be used against coastal defences? Solly's reply, that they could, was not what Harris wished to hear and they had no further talk.

In putting together the alternative plan he had promised to Leigh-Mallory, Solly recalled the lessons learned in Sicily and Italy that an army's communications were both vital and vulnerable. Accordingly, he concluded that the paralysis of the rail network in north-west France should be a top priority. The success of Overlord required that the Germans should be denied the massive advantage of being able to reinforce against a cross-Channel landing far more quickly than the Americans and British, dependent on sea communications, would be able to support it. His plan, codenamed Transportation, required the destruction by bombing of some seventy-six nodal points in the network. The aim was not simply to cut at selected points as the original plan had stipulated, but to destroy the 'means of maintaining the railway system in operation' and so prevent the movement by rail of major reserves in the direction of the Channel. This, he recognised, would involve the diversion of heavy bombers from their missions within Germany – rather more than half the capacity of the American Strategic Air Force and rather less than half that of Bomber Command.

The new plan ran into immediate difficulties. First, if it did not actually contradict Pointblank, it came very close to doing so. Pointblank was a directive of the Combined Chiefs of Staff which laid it down that priority should be given to targets which contributed to the destruction of the Luftwaffe; it gave no place to communications. Secondly, the so-called Air Barons, Spaatz and Harris, were unhappy at the idea of losing, even temporarily, a large part of their capacity. Harris particularly was hostile to the plan and completely disavowed all responsibility for its consequences. He had done much to build up the force he commanded, he had a mission to bomb Germany out of the war and men with missions are not easily persuaded to change course. He thought that the diversion of his heavy bombers to a secondary role in Overlord, for which they were neither equipped nor trained, would be wrong. Ever since Anzio, he had had little confidence in seaborne invasions and he firmly believed that it would be possible to win the war by bombing. A whole year was to pass before the attacks on Dresden brought second thoughts as to the wisdom and effectiveness of the area bombing strategy. Spaatz was rather less vehement. His principal anxieties stemmed mostly from the chilly relations which existed between him and Leigh-Mallory. The one thing he wished to avoid was that he or any part of his force should come under the latter's command. Later, after being well dined by Solly in Christ Church, he made his position clear: 'I'm not against the [AEAF] plan, I believe you are right. But what worries me is that Harris is being allowed to get off scot-free. He'll go on bombing Germany and will be given a chance of defeating her before the invasion, while I am put under Leigh-Mallory's command.' Thirdly, in drawing up his plan, Solly was unaware that Portal, as Chief of the Air Staff, had called a meeting to seek a compromise between those who favoured German towns and cities as targets and those who favoured communications; Solly thus appeared to be speaking out of turn. Lastly, the British Government and particularly Churchill, on the advice of

Cherwell, supported strongly the existing strategy of Bomber Command. A further problem was the identification of key targets in the French rail network. The military planners knew little of railway working and nothing at all of the French system, whereas those who knew about railways were at least as ignorant when it came to bombing strategy.

It was in this context that the visit of M. Pierre Moreau was most helpful. Spirited out of France, he landed one night in the early months of 1944 at Manston airfield in a Lysander aircraft. He was a French railway official of some standing; he brought with him his heavily pregnant wife and an up-to-date manual of the workings of the French railway system. He also knew how the Germans planned to use the French railways in the event of an invasion. Solly called on him the next day at Brown's Hotel to make arrangements for him to work at the Railway Research Service, which was then looking at the question. Progress was somewhat interrupted when Madame Moreau produced a son. As M. Moreau had come to England at the behest of the British Government and was working for it, he thought it not unreasonable that MI6, which had made the arrangements, should pay the obstetrician's account. When the comparatively minor difficulties that MI6 had no official existence and therefore no money had been overcome, there remained the question of who should pay the charge for the baby's circumcision. MI6 would go no further and M. Moreau was unwilling to resume work until the matter had been settled. When the impasse finally reached the Air Council, Sir Charles Portal, as Chief of the Air Staff, put half a crown on the table as his contribution and others followed suit, with the result that the matter was settled and M. Moreau resumed work. He became, however, increasingly concerned as, in accordance with the Transportation plan, attacks on the French railways proceeded. He is reported as having stopped work altogether when on 23 May 1944 he heard Radio Paris reporting that the French railway system was in complete chaos, that whole marshalling yards had been pulverised into rubble, that countless engines had been destroyed and scores of railways stations made unusable. The rest of the destructive work which could not be done by Allied pilots had been accomplished by experienced squads of saboteurs. It is impossible not to sympathise with M. Moreau, whose advice must have been invaluable, in the difficulties he encountered later when he came to claim his pension. The French railway authorities insisted that his time in England represented broken service.

Solly's abiding worry throughout this period was that so many of those in powerful positions, including Cherwell, 'preferred *a priori* belief to disciplined observation'. They saw the AEAF plan as a threat to the independence of the Strategic Air Forces, which should for that reason be opposed. In retrospect, and reflecting upon what was at stake in Overlord, it seems strange that the so-called Air Barons should ever have acquired such unfettered control over the powerful arm they commanded but could not be said to own. Eisenhower, who warmly supported the plan which he considered crucial for the fate of the huge venture which he commanded, appealed to the British Chiefs of Staff to bring the heavy bombers into action against the railway centres, while at the same time the US Air Forces made the conflicting proposal that transportation should only be targets of last resort. Portal, invited to re-examine the whole issue, called a meeting of all the commanders and intelligence staffs concerned. Such was the animosity at that time directed against Solly by opponents of the AEAF plan that Tedder, whose support for him had been constant, nevertheless decided that it would be better if he did not attend. He did, however, have a hand in drafting the paper which supported the plan and in it suggested that 'since the railway system was the one common denominator of the whole enemy war effort, it may well be that systematic attack on it will prove to be the final straw'.

The upshot of that vital meeting was a proposal by Portal and Eisenhower that top priority be given to the AEAF plan, and the Combined Chiefs of Staff then decided that the control of all the Air Forces, including the strategic bombers, should pass to Eisenhower until September. Despite his previously negative attitude to the plan, Harris's response was, in Solly's view, 'all that could have been asked for'. At other levels, however, the argument went on, with the result that three more weeks passed before Eisenhower was able to direct the bomber forces that their mission was to destroy the Luftwaffe and the facilities on which it depended, and 'to disrupt the enemy's rail communications, particularly those affecting the enemy's movement towards the Overlord lodgement area'. Astonishingly, even that was not the end of the matter; the bombing of French railway targets would, it was suggested, cause high civilian casualties. On 5 April the War Cabinet's Defence Committee met in the underground War Rooms to consider the Allied Expeditionary Air Forces plan for the first time. By any standards and for anyone, no matter how inured to the ways of Government or to the vagaries of human behaviour, the occasion was an unusual one: for Solly, it was a revelation. He found himself on one side of the table with Portal and Tedder on his left and Sir Archibald Sinclair (Secretary of State for Air) on his right. Opposite them was the formidable figure of the Prime Minister, who, clad in siren suit, armed with a whisky and soda and supported by Cherwell, opened the meeting.

It had, he said, been called to discuss the plan to use the strategic bombers in preparation for Overlord. The plan was the brainchild of a biologist who happened to be passing through the Mediterranean. Portal interrupted to say that that was grossly unfair and that Solly had done more than anyone else to analyse the effects of air operations. Tedder, when asked by the Prime Minister whether the plan had his backing, replied that it had. A brusque dialogue ensued: PM: 'You don't know a better plan?' Tedder: 'There is no better plan.' PM: 'I'll show you a better plan.' He did not do so. Portal, asked for his views, favoured the plan, saying that it was vital to the success of the whole invasion that it should be properly executed. Cherwell, unmoved by the clearly stated opinions of Portal, the Chief of the Air Staff, and Tedder, as Deputy Supreme Commander, echoed the oft-repeated arguments of the plan's opponents. It was essential, as he had all along been advising the Prime Minister that the strategy of Bomber Command should be supported.

The meeting ended in the small hours of the morning without a decision. Tedder, near to despair, dropped Solly at his flat and left with the comment, 'This, I suppose, might be the end. I wonder how much it would cost to set up as a tomato grower.' Solly, on seeing the minutes of the meeting, was surprised that they were neither full nor accurate. He was minded to protest but, on the advice of Portal – with his greater experience of such occasions –

refrained. Further meetings followed on 13, 19 and 26 April, but still the Prime Minister was unwilling to give the plan more than a qualified go-ahead. Solly's comment on the last of those meetings was simple: 'Winston's menacing power could be overwhelming.'

Eventually, at a meeting of the War Cabinet on 27 April, the Prime Minister announced that he would convey to Eisenhower their grave misgivings about the whole plan – and the French civilian casualties it would involve – and invite him to reconsider. Eisenhower replied that he was totally committed to it. On 3 May a further meeting of the Defence Committee endorsed the plan, subject to the unenforceable, face-saving condition that casualties should not exceed ten thousand. Still rumbling with discontent, Churchill asked Roosevelt to intervene. This the President declined to do; he was unprepared 'to impose from this distance any restriction on military action by the responsible Commanders that in their opinion might militate against the success of Overlord'. In the circumstances, it must have been a source of relief and even surprise that by D-Day all of the designated railway targets had been bombed. The Intelligence Staffs, however, still entrenched in their previously expressed opinions, declined to change their position and sought to minimise the effects of bombing the railway network, despite the fact that both Eisenhower and Tedder, to whom they were answerable, were publicly declaring the opposite. There were, however, those in intelligence circles who took a very different view. Noel Annan believed Solly to have been totally right in his insistence that transportation should be a prime target. Derek Ezra, as a Major in intelligence stationed in Versailles, acquired a series of German charts of rail movements for the first half of 1944. These showed that, as a result of the bombing, rail movements had dropped by the time of the invasion to a mere 13 percent of what they had been earlier. His belief was and still is that Solly was fully justified in the advice he gave that bombing should be concentrated upon movement of troops and military supplies and the means of such movement, in other words, upon the North French rail network. The conclusion reached by the US Government Agency after the war was that 'the transportation was on the point of collapse'.

At the heart of the argument were two scientists, Cherwell and

Zuckerman. There were, as Churchill wrote in his history of the Second World War, 'no doubt greater scientists than Frederick Lindemann, but he could decipher the signals from the experts on the horizons and explain to me in lucid and homely terms what the issues were'; he had been 'my trusted friend and confidant for thirty years'. Once Cherwell had convinced himself that Germany could be bombed out of the war, and he had done so a long time back, no argument could shift him. He had little liking for either opinions or facts which suggested that he might be wrong. As the Prime Minister's scientific adviser he had the inside track. The Prof, as he was widely known, was loved and hated with equal fervour. On his death more than ten years after the war, Solly wrote to Cherwell's close friend and executor, Robert Blake, to say how sorry he had been to miss the funeral. However much his views and those of others had clashed with the Prof's, Solly would always remember his kindness when he first joined the House (Christ Church). Even when he took an opposite line, his sense of personal loyalty was never affected. Blake regarded the Prof and Solly as being generally on terms of mutual respect and admiration, even if from time to time they edged towards armed neutrality, as a result of having been on opposite sides in the argument about wartime strategic bombing of Germany. Having at the time had no strong views on the bombing issue, Blake had come to think, in the light of all the evidence which later became available, that the wartime strategy of Bomber Command had been mistaken.

Solly by contrast, even if he had by 1944 ceased to be an outsider, remained one whom a stranger would not expect to find participating in the top level councils of the war. In the months of argument prior to Overlord, he never lost sight of the need to deprive the Germans of the advantage which the availability of the French rail network could confer on them. The argument ebbed and flowed and it was not until mid-April that Eisenhower was free to direct attacks upon the seventy-six nodal points in the rail network which Solly had selected. It is relevant now to ask what would have been the outcome, if he had not given that advice and persisted in it. Another layer to the question is what would have occurred if the Deputy Supreme Allied Commander had been someone other than Tedder, unaware of Solly's worth. The conclusion reached by Webster and Frankland in their official history of the war and quoted by Solly seems abundantly justified: 'The immense power of the strategic forces was not used in the attack on communications in such a manner as to produce the most rapid end to the resistance of the enemy'.

By July 1944, what had seemed for an age to be no more than a dream had been achieved: a huge force, the largest ever assembled to cross the English Channel, had broken through Hitler's Atlantic wall, secured a lodgement on the north-west coast of France and then broken out into the occupied countries and towards the Rhine and Germany itself. It is a recurrent feature of human affairs that, as soon as one set of obstacles is removed, others arise. So it came about that with victory assured, other factors began to assert themselves: the size and diversity of the force; the rivalry and mutual recrimination between its commanders; the usual fallibility of plans; the difficult terrain of northern France; and, not least, the abominable weather. The combination sufficed at least to slow down the progress towards victory. The determination of the Air Barons to do it in their way – 'Don't count on us to be with you after D-Day' was the message to the Army from the Combined Strategic Targets Committee – did not make things easier.

Confusion and muddle are endemic to human affairs; order and tidiness, being the exception, are usually short-lived. Even when things are running smoothly, someone, particularly in large organisations, will contrive to slip in some supposed improvement which will restore the supremacy of muddle. In 1944, when Allied air power was supreme, in order to settle differences of opinion as to which were prime targets for attack, there was born 'the Combined Strategic Targets Committee'. 'The fact', wrote Tedder as Deputy Supreme Commander, 'that the operations of the immense Strategic Air Forces are supposed to be conducted by a committee advised by a series of sub-committees, is so remarkable and constitutes such a unique method of conducting military operations that there is no risk of it being forgotten.' To Solly it was like using 'a hazy crystal ball'. It was a classic instance of what was intended as a solution making things worse. A persistent difficulty lay in the absence of agreement as to what was strategic and what was tactical. In practice and by some unwritten law, the term 'strategic' implied specified and distant targets which were deemed appropriate for heavy bombers. Targets which were near at hand and in which ground troops were involved, came to be regarded as tactical and so inappropriate.

That argument about the choice of targets has lingered on, though the weight of evidence has been in Solly's favour. Lord Scarman, in the letter already quoted of April 1993, wrote, 'In 1944 I saw him day in and day out as he advised Arthur Tedder on the bombing strategy which destroyed the capacity of the German forces to hold Western Europe against our invasion and liberation. The Tedder/Zuckerman partnership was, in very truth, a war winner.' Field Marshal Lord Bramall has no doubts as to the worth and importance of the so-called interdiction bombing,

> The air battle in all its depth and aspects was perhaps the critical strategic and tactical factor in Overlord's success. Without the Luftwaffe being kept off their backs throughout, without the complex interdiction programme before D-Day and during the bridgehead battle, and without the power of air bombardment at the appropriate place and time, there was no way the land forces were going to get ashore, hold their bridgeheads against fierce counterattacks and indeed break out to Paris and the Seine. Without the air forces, the staggering victory in Normandy, culminating in the Falaise pocket, could not have happened as it did and as one of those on the ground who benefited, I salute them.

Some German thoughts on the matter are revealing, even perhaps conclusive. Albert Speer, Hitler's Minister of Munitions, in a speech in November 1944, admitted that there was 'now clever and far reaching planning' behind the attacks on the German railway system. 'Germany had,' he said, 'been lucky that the enemy had not made use of this detailed planning earlier.' He made it clear to Hitler that it was the attacks on the rail network that 'throttled traffic and made transportation the greatest bottleneck in our war economy'. In another letter, written at the same time to Borman, Speer rammed home the point, 'The systematic attacks on railway installations are largely responsible for the critical situation. . . . The disruption of our communications may well lead to a production crisis which will gravely jeopardise our capacity to carry on the war.' The official history of the American Forces delivered a similar verdict. It was clear toward the end of the war that the transportation campaign had paralysed Germany. The attack on transportation had been the decisive blow that completely disorganised the German economy. For a long time Bomber Command stuck to the view that the best and indeed the only support it could give to Overlord was to intensify the attacks against suitable industrial targets in Germany. The Air Staff judgement of 28 June, on the other hand, was to the effect that generally speaking the conclusions of the Bomber Command memorandum had been proved entirely incorrect and that the support which it had given had played an outstanding part in the establishment of the bridgehead.

Solly's account of the battle which followed Overlord, 'Glimpses of Normandy', is a fragmentary tale, reflecting his own considerable travels and the fact that no one ever knows everything about anything, particularly in the movement and confusion of battle. His personal objective was to reach the scene of destruction as quickly as possible after the event and there learn what he could. His constant anxiety and preoccupation was that the attack on transportation targets was not accorded the priority which he believed to be necessary and hindsight showed would have been appropriate. It seems unlikely that Field Marshal von Rundstedt would have been able to bring together a force of some 70 German divisions, 15 of them armoured, launch his huge attack on the weak Allied centre and achieve the deep penetration which he did, had the German railway system not been able to move the troops required. The Chiefs of Staff had agreed that in September the Strategic Bomber forces should be returned from Eisenhower to their own commanders, thus freeing Spaatz and Harris to continue their own wars against Germany without too much concern for what was happening on the ground. There was a failure to recognise that transportation was the one vulnerable link which bound all others together; consistent attacks against that link stopped, or would have stopped, the movement between them of materials and products, and of troops.

The relationship between Eisenhower and Tedder has to be seen as one of crucial importance from North Africa onwards until the final German surrender. In Solly's view, it was the quality of goodness which people saw in Eisenhower which made him realise Tedder's virtues. In *From Apes to Warlords*, Solly mentions only two occasions on which he found himself face to face with Eisenhower, though there must have been others. His selection of them is puzzling. The first took place at the time of the first landings in Sicily. Tedder and Solly were discussing possible bombing targets in the former's caravan, when Eisenhower walked in, saying that he hoped he was not interrupting. Tedder replied that they had only been talking about the history of warfare in the Mediterranean. The conversation then moved on to something which Eisenhower called 'indeterminate probability'. It ended with Solly promising to provide an algebraic equation proving that Eisenhower was wrong in what he had been saying: he duly sent it on and seemed surprised to receive no reply. The other occasion, again related by Solly, was when, on Tedder's advice, he went to say goodbye to the Supreme Allied Commander after the German surrender. Eisenhower, with his eyes already on the Presidency, was talking of the need to preserve democracy; Solly interrupted, saying that he reminded him of one of Low's cartoons, in which one half naked old Colonel was saying to another in the Turkish baths, 'Gad Sir, Lord Beaverbrook's right; the Tory Party must save the Empire if it has to strangle it in the attempt.' With the somewhat laboured comment that Eisenhower was saying much the same thing, but with Democracy taking the place of the Empire, Solly scored no points. Again Eisenhower was not amused, and one is left to wonder why Solly, who greatly respected him, should have so mishandled what was their last meeting.

It is at least arguable that Eisenhower has never received sufficient credit for the way in which he persuaded a diverse collection of individuals, talented and determined, each with his own role to perform and each with his own view of how the war should be won, to come together as a team. He had at the same time to digest a stream of instruction and advice from the Chiefs of Staff and from two Governments. Expectations that sensible relationships will always, or even usually, exist between people at or near the top, be they military commanders or politicians, are likely to be disappointed. The nearer the top, the sharper the rivalry, suspicion and mistrust are likely to be. The Americans were not the only ones who found Montgomery difficult and the total lack of trust, respect or liking which separated Leigh-Mallory from Spaatz was always going to be a source of problems in any plan requiring their co-operation. The extent to which personalities tend to overshadow arguments and obscure the facts is sometimes, quite often, forgotten.

Solly was always watchful, quick to fasten on to whoever or whatever held interest for him. There were two men in his life who showed Solly things he had not seen before, taught him lessons he never forgot and for whom he had total respect. The first was Tedder. In his autobiography, Solly recalls Tedder in France not long after the invasion asking, 'What's the point of circulating minutes, there never will be a true history of what's happened'. That Tedder said it and Solly remembered and quoted it is a sign of the respect which both men had for facts and how little either cared for varnish. The other was Isidor Rabi, the son of poor Jewish immigrants, who in due course became Chairman of President Eisenhower's Science Advisory Committee. He was the man who, Solly wrote, 'was to reveal himself as a statesman, who as much as anyone I knew had a realistic view of what scientists could do in the promotion of international understanding and world peace'.

The war in Europe ended in May 1945 with Hitler dead by his own hand in his bunker, the German capital in ruins around him; five years had passed since he launched his armies upon Belgium, Holland and France. Three months later, two atomic bombs brought Japan also to its knees. It took time before the relief and joy that the war was over faded and people came gradually to perceive the enormity of the event.

6

Peace and the Department of Anatomy

'My years in Birmingham could not have proved more
rewarding.'

SZ, *Monkeys, Men and Missiles*, p.5

THE CLOUD that mushroomed up over Hiroshima and Nagasaki in the early days of August 1945 signalled that the awful drama of the Second World War was over. It also marked the arrival of a new age. The descendants of Adam had eaten once more of the fruit of the Tree of Knowledge and had acquired the option of destroying themselves. The curtain fell; the heroes – and in those days we were allowed to have some – took their bows and departed; the huge supporting cast and the massive audience, each a part of the other, followed them and dispersed into the flat, low-lying lands of peace. The scenery and props of war, now drained of meaning, were replaced with others reflecting the changes wrought on Britain by the long struggle to survive. Rich and powerful in 1939, centre of a great empire, six years later it was on the verge of bankruptcy, with a shaky currency and a battered and outdated industrial infrastructure. Efforts to massage the nation's self-esteem with thoughts of empire and talk of a special relationship with America were of little avail; the empire was crumbling visibly and no one wants a special relationship with a beggar. There were daily reminders of the cost of winning; towns and cities bombed and unrepaired, shortages of almost everything, the mockery of an eight-penny meat ration, an inedible fish called Snoek waiting to make its appearance, with over all an undertaker's shroud of gloom. Without the imperatives of the struggle, first to survive and then to win, it was as if the mainspring of a clock had been removed and it had ceased to work. A vague desire to get back to something called normality achieved nothing; no one anyway had any clear idea where or what normality was.

In those early postwar years, for lack of both vehicles and fuel, traffic jams were rare; there was, however, a feeling of being stuck in one with no means of escape. To go back whence we had come was unthinkable as well as impossible; yet a world which contrived at the same time to be both stale and strange was hardly enticing. The absence of signposts in many places symbolised the fact that even those who knew where they wanted to go could not find out how to get there. We were, as Matthew Arnold wrote in *The Grande Chartreuse*,

> Wandering between two worlds, one dead,
> The other powerless to be born.

For a decade and more, Britain sought to get back to the dead one.

The war churned up the lives of millions. Solly's it recast entirely, opening to him endless opportunities. The Government, knowing almost nothing about the effects of bombing, needed as a matter of urgency to learn about wounded people, shattered buildings, disrupted services and their impact upon morale. Solly, by chance in the right place and at the right time in the first year of the German Blitz, had been able through the study of countless incidents to build up such a body of knowledge that the procedures he laid down were adopted as standard practice. Later, as the war moved on, his concern widened from the damage caused by enemy bombs and came to embrace the whole strategy of bombing and the contribution it could make to winning. As an acknowledged expert in destruction, which he called the currency of war, his advice was sought and taken by both military commanders and their political masters. The return of peace might well have sent him back to a full-time academic career; but a combination of the Cold War, the arms race, nuclear weapons and that own unrivalled knowledge he had acquired of destruction, combined to keep him near the centre of things for a further forty years before an astonishing career finally ended.

With the return of peace, that flow of opportunities provided by war dried up, leaving Solly on his own, facing the need to decide for himself what his next step should be. In name at least, he was committed to Birmingham University as Sands Cox Professor of Anatomy; but perhaps because of the past it did not appeal. When, back in 1938, he had first been told by the Board of the Faculty of Medicine that they intended to recommend his appointment for the Chair, he had at once begun to wobble. He was, he said, taken aback, he was honoured, it was all so sudden, he still had work to do in Oxford. He wondered, moreover, if the Department would be adequately equipped for the kind of work he would be doing. No successful applicant for an academic post had ever developed such cold feet so quickly.

A Faculty minute of 13 January 1939 noted the Senate's approval of his appointment and at the same time recorded a resolution asking that the Senate reconsider the matter, since 'it would not be easy to find the extra funds required by Dr Zuckerman for his researches on top of £300 per annum already approved'. The Faculty was later informed that 'Dr Zuckerman had agreed to his appointment being deferred pending further negotiations regarding the necessary funds'. Another minute of 18 May reported that 'Dr Zuckerman had not yet definitely accepted the appointment but had again visited the school and inspected sites for animal houses'. 'Capital expenditure on his special requirements would be limited to £2,000 and that at present the Council could not see its way to provide more than £500 per annum towards the cost of the special research which Dr Zuckerman had in hand and proposed to continue.'

A further minute dated 13 October reported another visit by Dr Zuckerman, who had seen the accommodation already provided for animals. The Faculty noted his suggestion that due to important work on behalf of the Government and his work at Oxford, he might come to Birmingham on a part-time basis; they even agreed, with commendable patience, to recommend it to the Senate. Finally, yet another Minute of 10 November 1939 reported that 'in the event of Professor Zuckerman being unable to undertake the duties of the Chair, in these circumstances his taking office should be deferred until the end of the war or until he shall notify the University that he is freed from Government work, whichever date is the earlier'. Such skill in delaying tactics matched that of Fabius Cunctator, the Roman General accorded the title by reason of the skill with which he avoided engagement with Hannibal in a battle which Rome would have surely lost.

Although formally named in 1943 as the University's Professor of Anatomy, when the war ended he still hankered after Oxford. There, however, Le Gros Clark, head of the Anatomy Department, effectively blocked his way. He wrote to Solly, as early as 1944, to say that if he were to return to Oxford, the space that had been available to him and to his research students in pre-war days would be required for other purposes. He doubtless recalled Solly's energy and ebullience, his disturbing way of generating additional work and the disturbing habit of putting in papers which he was then himself obliged to read and forward. Subject himself to fits of depression, he must have found the prospect of Solly's return anything but welcome. Moreover, he disapproved of the long wartime absences and looked with disfavour, tinged perhaps with envy, upon the wide-ranging friendships and elaborate social life. There were other possibilities for Solly: one in Oxford, away from anatomy, another in London, but both came to nothing. An invitation to go to the Air Ministry with Tedder, the new Chief of the Air Staff, as his scientific adviser, had its attractions; but, warned that it might lead to him becoming a civil servant for the rest of his life, he turned it down.

Although he remained reluctant to go to Birmingham, fate, reinforced by the lack of an alternative, seemed determined that he should. In retrospect, his dithering and uncertainty seemed foolish for, as he came to recognise, the years spent in Birmingham 'could not have proved more rewarding'. Not only was he given splendid premises and every encouragement by the University to make something of the Department, he was also allowed four new lectureships and space for his own research. As an unlooked-for bonus, he was free to spend half the week in London. Fate again was helpful in steering him into a situation which, far from seeking, he almost rejected. He had the opportunity to achieve as an academic scientist, to be useful without being dependent in Whitehall and to learn at the same time the who and the what and the how of Government. Above all, he had the intense interest and energy which enabled him to seize every opportunity that came his way. He had also had the luck to stumble into a situation which allowed him to have his cake and eat it.

The next step was to acquire a house. Number 6 Carpenter Road provided Solly and Joan with a home they could share, as opposed to a place where a bachelor could be comfortable, which was all that could be claimed for Solly's small house in Oxford. Their son Paul was one year old when they moved, their daughter Stella was born a year later. The second half of Solly's long learning curve lay ahead; it proved to be at least as steep as the first. For the time being at least, building up his new Department from a small beginning, and embarking upon what turned out to be a fourteen-year apprenticeship learning the ways of Government, were all that he could manage and far more than any normal mortal would think of shouldering.

As Professor of Anatomy at Birmingham University, his task was to build up the Department almost from scratch and to set out and oversee complex teaching and research programmes. Although he thought and spoke of himself as having full executive authority over the Department, his role was more that of a chairman, from whom ideas flowed. He was particularly adept at finding people with the executive skills that were required to carry them out. A talent he possessed in unusual measure lay in identifying an individual well fitted to perform a particular role and then almost throwing it at them, leaving them to get on with it. Maybe it was that which lay at the root of his success in building up a degree of *esprit de corps* which those who experienced it found unique and unforgettable. Everyone was involved – scientists, technicians, secretaries, cleaners, the lot; there were no boundaries, they were to a very real extent a family and the ties lingered on into retirement. Birmingham was perhaps the single period and place in his working life when and where, being surrounded by those who admired, even loved him, he was relaxed; he had no need to make an impression, he had made one already.

Leaders and managers who make a habit of absenting themselves from the scene of action normally end up in trouble. Solly was able somehow to meet the demands of both Birmingham and Whitehall. He contrived without any apparent difficulty to keep them separate and to deploy in turn the very different skills which each required. He was himself convinced that the university, far from losing as a result of his other commitment, actually gained from it. Although jokes were made from time to time about his 'rare visits to Birmingham', there were few complaints. When in 1960 he accepted the appointment of Chief Scientific Adviser to the Ministry of Defence, he did so on terms that he remained – without salary – in charge of his Department in Birmingham. The Vice-Chancellor, Sir Robert Aitken, though he recognised that the arrangement was unusual in that Solly would be doing two full-time jobs, accepted on the ground that Solly was so different he could make a success of both.

One important change, to which he devoted much thought and effort, was the establishment of a novel BSc Honours course which would involve each year a small number of specially selected students who would be absorbed into various research projects within the Department. Each had his own tutor, at the beginning either Solly himself or Peter Krohn or Anita Mandl, both of them leading lights. Those chosen had to work hard – seven days a week – and were at the end required to put the results together in a bound thesis and then face a lengthy examination by professors from other universities. The success of such an innovation depended not only on the dedication of students, but on the willing co-operation of tutors; and it was here, as Peter Krohn has pointed out, that Solly's 'inspirational leadership' showed itself. Over time more than a hundred students benefited: 'Results showed', as Solly said, 'that undergraduates in the right environment and properly cared for can do good research work.'

What Solly looked for were those capable of excellence, who would be a credit to the Department – and, of course, to himself. Those lucky enough to be selected were put under pressure and made to give all they had; the imprint stayed with them for life. He rejoiced at their successes and was fully aware that some of the credit would spill over on to himself: he took an interest in their subsequent careers, helped them to obtain appointments and kept their names, though not always their faces, stored in his warehouse of a mind. There were of course those who, being themselves more comfortable with mediocrity, were ready to dub him and damn him as elitist, a word which now tends to be used with heavy disapproval. One of Solly's problems was that his constant pursuit of excellence brought him into sharp conflict with those who had no taste for it.

Oogenesis, anthropology and endocrinology were the fields which attracted his attention at this time. First oogenesis, or the formation of female germ cells; he came to doubt, then to challenge and finally to disprove the prevailing view that new eggs were produced in each production cycle. He was able to prove the earlier view of the German microscopist Waldeyer that the ovary was equipped with a finite number of germ cells and that as these were used, they were not replaced. He presented his conclusions at a conference of American endocrinologists in New Hampshire in 1951, to which he had been invited by Dr Carl Hartmann. Hartmann chaired the meeting, heard Solly and then declared himself to be both 'convinced and convicted' – he had, like Solly, 'uncritically fallen under the sway of the prevailing hypothesis'. Solly, not unreasonably, judged his own performance to be 'an academic triumph'. He might have mentioned, but he did not, that his confidence in proclaiming his new-found belief owed something to Anita Mandl's experimental work.

The second field which particularly attracted him was endocrinology, the science of hormones. He sought to understand 'the mechanism whereby the hormonal and nervous systems worked together in controlling the functions of the body'. Here his interest stemmed from his earlier studies in South Africa and the London Zoo of the social behaviour and the reproductive cycle of monkeys, in which he at least came near to determining the time when ovulation takes place and understanding the hormonal control of the phases of the cycle. In 1937 an American, George Corner, had at much the same time reached the same understanding as Solly in his earlier works on the control of the menstrual cycle. He was, he said, 'happy to mention that Solly Zuckerman had stated in the same year as I a conception of the antagonism of progesterone to oestrogen in the primate cycle practically identical with mine: Solly and I, then as now cordial friends, had no reason to contend for priority in this matter.'

At the same time, Solly began to look at how light affects the reproductive rhythm of so many species. For his examination, he chose the ferret and from it concluded that the eyes were 'the primary receptors in the sequence of events in the same way as the ovaries through the hormones they produce constitute the terminal reactor in the system'. Although these studies led to no clear conclusion, they were seen as having 'generated a much needed re-evaluation of the field. He was a sceptic who demanded attention.' That questioning of assumptions which seemed to him to offer too facile a way out of difficulties was the basis of his science. It enabled him, as Peter Krohn has pointed out, 'to see the shape and size of problems and decide on ways of tackling them'. Who knows what further progress he might have made, if he had been free to pursue single-mindedly, full-time, the tasks he defined? That was left to others who a decade or so later in 1977 shared a Nobel Prize.

On Solly's arrival at Birmingham in 1946, the Anatomy Department had a staff of six, half teaching, half technical. When he left twenty or so years later it was more than a hundred; nine hundred learned papers were published and no fewer than twenty of his students became heads of departments in other universities or professors on individual merit. Forty years later there are still those who readily acknowledge their debt to him. His double life, with half at least spent in London, could well have caused him to lose all hold on the Department; it did nothing of the kind. His return on Friday and his presence there at the weekend meant that while the rest of the campus was in darkness the place hummed with life and the lights stayed on well into the night. For all those who taught, learned or worked in whatever capacity in the Department, the experience of those years was unforgettable. He did not always get his own way. Change disturbs and is resisted at least as much in academic circles as elsewhere, and even the most radical of professors are not pleased when it is their idea and their plan that is put aside. His call for 'the reintegration' of the disciplines of anatomy and physiology, which had previously been combined, aroused particular opposition. Such boundary lines are greatly cherished in Britain, where they are seen as useful barriers against change. The fact that Solly had a major task on his hands did not stop him from relishing it. 'The transformation of the Department was not', he wrote, 'just a case of making the desert bloom, it was more like a seismic upheaval.'

In 1961, a new guide to dissection appeared, entitled *A New System of Anatomy* by Solly Zuckerman. It took eight years to produce and drew heavily on the hard work of many others. As he acknowledged, it particularly taxed the good nature, patience and tolerance of Bill Pardoe and Tom Spence, who together provided the photographs and the specimens. The book, which went through a number of impressions to a second edition in 1981, formed the basis of his claim to have reduced the drudgery of dissection. In future students would spend only three terms there instead of five. They would also be spared lectures on the structure of the body, which he regarded as conventional and unnecessary.

Solly's success in building the new Department and breathing life and vigour into it depended on his skill in recognising people's capacity, fitting them with a task he, sometimes better than they, knew they could do and leaving them to get on with it; he was a very good picker. Those who worked in the Department in Solly's time all spoke of the way in which everyone joined together in a single unit and felt that they belonged. Over many years Peter Krohn was never far distant from Solly's life; his pupil at Oxford, he was the first to join the rather oddly named Oxford Extra-Mural Unit at the beginning of the war. Krohn worked with Solly in Sicily, Italy, Australia (Maralinga), New Mexico (Albuquerque) and finally in Birmingham. Quite often there occur in Solly's autobiography sentences beginning, 'with Peter Krohn's help'. That long partnership and their deep mutual regard says much for both and is something for Solly's detractors to reflect upon. Peter Krohn is one of those rare men who are content to achieve, but who neither boast nor seek the applause of others; he speaks of science as 'an edifice so large that people disappear into it, only a few getting their name on a brick'. Election as a Fellow of the Royal Society in 1963 was a distinction based on merit which gave him, as it must all those so honoured, great satisfaction. His role in

Birmingham was to take overall charge in Solly's absence, to share in the important work of overseeing the BSc students and, above and beyond all, to provide, in his own words, 'a shoulder for everyone to cry on when things went wrong'. Although he was the obvious successor when Solly left Birmingham in 1968, he opted instead for retirement: 'I won't follow in Solly's footsteps, I never could.'

After Solly's death, Peter was the man to whom the Royal Society turned to get a measurement of him. He put together, in the obituary he wrote, the thoughts of a score or so of men and women, most of whom were with him in Birmingham, some of them quoted later in this chapter. In the course of assembling the material for it, Peter wrote to Anita Mandl, saying that he wanted 'to get over his [Solly's] charisma'. Having first pointed out that what he said was capable of two quite different meanings, she went on to say she had met few people who were 'blessed with such charisma'. 'One blamed him at times', she went on, 'for switching on his charm and then switching it off when the "need" had gone. One could forgive all that because when the charm was "on", he made you feel good, your work was worth doing, you were a valued member of his team, and there was always more to come.'

A rather surprising appointment at a later stage was Sir Francis Knowles, who joined the team from Marlborough College, where he taught biology. Although, as Solly admitted, Knowles knew nothing of human anatomy and had done little research, Solly's instinct that he would fit in was justified: Knowles's knowledge of the recently introduced electron microscope enabled him to make a valuable contribution and he became a welcome member of a close-knit team. He too became an FRS while at Birmingham. Anita Mandl might well have made a third, but when in 1963 Solly told her of his intention to propose her, she said that she would prefer him not to do so, as she would be leaving to get married and would therefore be abandoning her scientific career, which she did two years later. Misleadingly, she speaks of herself as having been only a small cog in a large machine, a description which few of her colleagues accept. Solly seriously questioned whether her own happiness made up for the loss British science suffered. She first joined him in Birmingham in 1948 at the age of twenty-one, her job at the London Hospital having come to an abrupt end. A row, well above her level, brought about the dismemberment of the unit of which she was the most junior member, and as such she was the first to go. The unfairness of her situation got around and led to a meeting with Solly. Having told her that he was not going to ask what exactly had happened at the London, he added, 'That kind of thing is not going to happen here'.

He then discussed her future prospects of ovarian research, teaching students and a possible lectureship. Here, she thought, was 'someone with vision, energy, full of human warmth and wide interests'. Discerning rather than lavish in bestowing praise, she admired him and, while perceiving the warts, was a faithful correspondent for more than thirty years after her retirement. 'I always thought', she wrote, 'there was one half to him which couldn't take the other half seriously, that's what endeared him to me.' Almost certainly she helped more than she knew; she was one of a quite small handful of people who came near to seeing the whole man, even catching a glimpse from time to time of what he usually left in shadow. A final quote from Anita gives an angle which some, who thought they knew him, would have found surprising: 'He somehow managed to muck in, share a coffee out of a chipped mug and be interested in you, you or you.'

There were others in that disparate collection who might not have enjoyed working together without Solly's unifying force. Peter Eckstein who, strangely, receives no mention in Solly's autobiography, ran his monkey colony; indeed, much of the credit for sustaining it during the war years must go to him. He did his share of formal teaching and had some involvement with the BSc students. Unlike most of his colleagues, he welcomed paperwork, editing at one time the *Journal of Endocrinology* and being, with Anita, an assistant editor of *The Ovary*. He was a great stickler for detail, with which Anita did not always find it easy to be on the best of terms; she was driven mad by his 'passion for semi-colons and other fusspottery'.

Sandy Thomson was an unlikely colleague. As a Major in the Eighth Army Medical Corps in Tripoli in 1943, Thomson had heard of Solly, having read something he had written, thought working for him would be interesting and attached himself to him.

He proceeded to take over from Solly the detailed work involved in his bombing and casualty surveys and proved skilled in keeping the bureaucrats of Middle East Headquarters in Cairo at bay. Sandy Thomson seemed to have been born to help Solly. After that first meeting in Tripoli, he stayed with him through Sicily and Italy and then rejoined him in Birmingham. He saw what was needed and did it, even including the paperwork at Birmingham which others would not touch.

Eric Ashton, one of Solly's first BSc students, was another who idolised him; a hard worker and willing slave, he would toil through the night to provide Solly with a set of figures which he said he required for the next morning. He was also just the type of man Solly knew how to use but often forgot to thank. Rather surprisingly, though head of anthropology, a subject of interest to Solly, he received only scant attention; 'I was helped by Eric Ashton' and 'Ashton died in 1985' are Solly's only mentions of him. Apparently he did most of the work in an investigation carried out by Solly to find whether dogs could be trained to detect non-metallic anti-personnel mines, a somewhat fatuous exercise which achieved no positive result.

Peter Dallas Ross, who took over the supervision of routine teaching, had never met Solly when in 1951 he arrived in Birmingham. He was at first afraid of his formidable head of department. His father told him, 'You are exploited by that man.' Asked if he would have gone to the stake for him, Dallas Ross's answer was 'Yes, I think I would.' When on one occasion he was a candidate for a lectureship, Solly told him to draft a letter of recommendation to the Dean which Solly would then sign, thus saving himself the trouble of writing; Dallas Ross's draft recommending himself in modest terms achieved its purpose in securing the post. Solly's appointment in 1960 as Chief Scientific Adviser to the Ministry of Defence meant inevitably that his absences from the Department would be considerably longer than before and would involve someone standing in for him. 'I want you to take care of the Department while I am away,' he said to Peter. 'But Solly, there are five senior lecturers above me, what will they think?' 'That's your problem.' It was solved by splitting the Department into five and putting each in charge of his own section.

Alan Glass joined the Anatomy Department as a BSc student in 1951. Having left it to do a spell of hospital doctoring for a year, he returned and remained there until his retirement. Solly impressed him as one who got to the heart of a problem with amazing speed, whose concentration on a problem was such as to shut out all else from his mind, who helped and encouraged students, reading, commenting on and approving their papers for publication. But for Solly, Alan himself would have followed his father into general practice. With Solly's guidance, he was led into neuro-anatomy or brain research – the study of brain waves by means of electrodes fixed directly in brain tissue – which had always fascinated him.

His critics took pleasure in dubbing Solly a snob and a name-dropper and, to an extent, he was. He could, however, with equal accuracy be described as a collector of interesting people. He stretched his net much wider than any snob would think worth his while. Into it there swam a great variety of people from a large range of backgrounds and occupations who, important or not, he found interesting. Among them, F. P. Reagan, an American-born embryologist and 'a superb micro dissector and illustrator', was as unpredictable as he was eccentric. Arriving late one night and naked in the students' laboratory, where he planned to have a bath, he found, to his surprise and dismay, Eric Ashton at work. Having tipped the jug of water he was carrying over the wretched Ashton, he departed without a word. He lived in the Department; he taught in the dissecting room, even on occasion taking a bath there. He cooked and ate in his own room which he kept locked; and since he liked to sleep as close to the ceiling as possible, had his bed mounted on tables.

Bill Pardoe, the Head Technician and Photographer of the Department, was a willing horse whom Solly liked, found useful and did not hesitate to exploit. Tom Spence, not long out of the RAF, impressed Solly with his desire to learn. He was unusual in that having left school aged fourteen without the equivalent of even one 'O' level, not only did he overcome what in those days was an almost insuperable obstacle, but obtained his BSc, published a book and numerous scientific papers. More unusual still, in due course he broke through the barrier between the technician and the teacher, ending up as a senior lecturer. It was, as Solly said, 'a remarkable achievement'. Spence was devoted to Solly, who, he said, 'never looked down on me, he always treated me as a social equal'. 'One paper of his represented more effort than did ten from the academic staff', was Solly's perceptive comment; 'Tom was a lovely man' was a view which the whole team shared.

Ernie Sims, wounded and twice mentioned in despatches in the First World War, was 'a considerable character and a perfectionist in the preparation of bodies for dissection' who was said to resemble Boris Karloff. Following a particularly grisly murder when a woman was killed and cut up with some skill, police in the course of their inquiries interviewed Sims as one who was known to be skilled in dissection. He was at such pains to tell the police exactly how he would have cut her up, and his explanation so closely corresponded with what the killer had done, that he had some difficulty in establishing his innocence. Barney Campion, as a Sergeant in the RAF, was first seconded to Solly in North Africa to look after his rapidly accumulating clerical problems. He then joined the Bombing Survey Unit when it was first set up in Sicily and ultimately followed Solly to Birmingham, where he ended up as a chief technician and a much-valued member of the team. Last but by no means least, there was Mrs Ford, the cleaning lady and a particular devotee of Solly. By his decree she and no one else was to do his room; she could be relied on never to disturb his papers. White coats were her particular province; she distributed them in a manner which reflected the rank and importance of the wearer. Those lower down collected their own; the Professor had his hung in his room with the starched sleeves already pushed out for him and the buttons fixed just as he wished. She stayed on by his special dispensation until she was eighty and, by Anita's account, found retirement turned life into an empty space.

Solly, in common with most of the human race, sought to show of himself only what he wished others to see. It is helpful to take a look at him behind the screen and see him through the eyes of students who endured his pressures and were shaped by him. Their comments form a garland which any teacher would be proud to have conferred on him by his pupils. Charles Oxnard, Professor of Anatomy, University of Western Australia: 'That incredibly prolific man produced an exodus from Birmingham Anatomy that has taken individuals to every continent, filled many Chairs in Britain and around the world and formed a Zuckerman mafia that has had an incredible influence in each of his areas of biological research . . . The students and staff who were touched by Solly carry with them a scientific education second to none.' Joe Herbert, MRC Cambridge Centre for Brain Repair: 'Working with him was unforgettable. He seemed to know everybody – scientists, politicians, writers, businessmen. He radiated intellectual energy and power; his students learned the rigour of the scientific method and the importance of questioning accepted dogma . . . After talking to him, I felt I was walking on air, a foot above the ground.'

Gabriel Horn, Master of Sidney Sussex College, Cambridge: 'With the enormous pressures upon him, he could have filled in the time with me in many more important ways, but he chose not to do so. Instead he talked about a career in Anatomy, the future of the subject and the likelihood of a Chair becoming available and helped me to an appointment.' Professor J.W. Moore: 'The years spent in Solly's Department with all the excitement and clear sense of purpose were the most enjoyable, if stressful, of my academic life.' William A. Cushman, Emeritus Professor of Neuro Psychiatry, Institute of Psychiatry: 'When the examinations were over, he would call in at the students' laboratory and tell us all with a delighted smile that we had done well.' Sir Colin Dollery – Physiology: 'His staff used to joke that he was the first scientist to turn a female baboon on heat upside down and write about what he saw.' Professor J.T. Eayrs, student and later his successor in the Chair of Anatomy: 'I, along with so many others, owe him a tremendous debt in the formulation and forwarding of my career. He owed much to his rapid grasp of facts and figures and his amazing ability to pick out what was important from a mass of verbiage.' Professor Arie Zuckerman (no relation of Solly's), Dean of the Medical School of the Royal Free Hospital: 'I owe everything to him; I would not be where I am today were it not for Solly.'

One unusual post-graduate student who sat at Solly's feet in the late 1950s was Gathorne Gathorne-Hardy, later Lord Cranbrook. He arrived in Birmingham University from Borneo, where he had been studying cave swiftlets – small birds which build their nests in caves from their own saliva. Solly, who was at that time concentrating on hormonal control of the reproductive cycle, was immediately interested – for other and better reasons than that Gathorne-Hardy was the heir to a title – and persuaded the authorities to allow him to complete his PhD course in two years; Solly himself became his supervisor. Since time was never a commodity of which Solly had much to spare, his new pupil had to grab such half-hour fragments as were available over breakfast at the Athenaeum, or in Solly's office at the MoD. He was impressed by the succession of people coming in with papers, handing them over to the great man, waiting until he had dealt with them and then departing with them. He noted particularly the absence of anything in the nature of an in-tray or an out-tray.

Gathorne's choice of sparrows as the birds whose reproductive systems he would study was dismissed by Julian Huxley as ridiculous. Everyone knew that sparrows did not take kindly to captivity and were therefore not suitable for research work. His second choice of pigeons eventually won him a newspaper headline which read 'Peer Proves Pigeons Won't Sit on Pointed Eggs'. One day he was on the roof with Solly to choose a suitable site for a bird loft. Passing a tank on the roof, Solly casually opened the lid, saw two pickled orang-utans inside, exclaimed 'Oh my God' and shut it quickly. In Gathorne's maiden speech in the House of Lords as Lord Cranbrook some twenty years later, he spoke of his time as a graduate research student 'under the benign, stimulating supervision of Lord Zuckerman, who at that time', he added, 'held three jobs any one of which would have fully occupied a normal man'. Lord Shackleton, who followed, put him right: he had never known Lord Zuckerman when he was not doing twelve jobs.

Others who had contact with the Anatomy Department at Birmingham from time to time were Sir Gordon Wolstenholme, sometime Director of the Ciba Foundation: 'No one could compare with him in concentrating the full power of his intellect on the problems before him and bringing all the salient points into brilliant focus', and Sir Richard Harrison, FRS, sometime President of the Anatomical Society: 'He appointed me or got me involved in almost everything I have really enjoyed in my life.' One visitor, who came as an external examiner, was Emmanuel

Cyprian Amoroso, known as 'Amo', the first West Indian ever to be made a Fellow of the Royal Society and a remarkable personality. Warm-hearted, outgoing, and with a good understanding of students, he captivated, and was loved and respected by everyone. 'I love that feller,' was his verdict on Solly.

During those years in Birmingham, while enjoying prodigious success as head of an important Department, Solly was also responsible for some notable scientific work. Supported by a talented staff and admiring students, he was probably happier, less stricken with doubts about himself; less concerned to seek what he would never find than at any other time in his life. It must be a matter of some surprise that the last man to hide his light, should in nearly a thousand pages of autobiography have devoted fewer than fifty pages – and a third of those concerned his social life – to a period of which he had every right to be proud. As Peter Krohn commented, 'he hardly gave it breathing space'. It is not that he was untouched by it, indeed in later years he spoke with affection of 'the old gang'; he remembered them, kept in touch with them and came as near as he ever did to allowing his heart to catch up with his head. Some twenty years after he had left Birmingham, he wrote to Anita saying how marvellous it was that she managed to keep in touch with 'our extended family'. He was never either so much at home or so generally liked in Whitehall. In the more combative and contentious atmosphere of the latter, there was always someone whom he needed to impress or to challenge.

In 1955 Solly added gratuitously to the complexity of his life by taking on the Secretaryship of the Zoological Society of London and the London Zoo. It gave him a position which he wanted, burdens which he could have done without and nothing in the way of a financial reward. Five years later, he accepted appointment as Chief Scientific Adviser to the Ministry of Defence, where he faced a truly formidable agenda: the unification of the three Service Departments within a single Ministry of Defence and the backbreaking cost of the arms race which, pursued for long enough, could only lead to financial ruin – it smashed the Russian economy – or annihilation.

His appointment in 1966 as Chief Scientific Adviser to the Government brought the curtain down on his Birmingham years and on his academic career. There were two farewell dinners, one given by the Faculty of Medicine in the Great Hall, with the Chancellor of the University, Anthony Eden, by that time Earl of Avon, presiding. The other was a warmer and happier occasion given by the Department; he was presented with a silver snuff-box and a bound set of his own research reports. He wrote afterwards to Anita,

> I was terribly touched by the way in which so many past and present members of the Department joined together to commemorate my time in Birmingham. Thank you very much indeed for the magnificent snuff box and the splendidly bound volumes of my research reports. I shall treasure them both. Yours ever, SZ
>
> PS [in long hand] Please don't forget me.

When Solly left Birmingham in 1969, Professor John Eayrs, one of his first BSc students, was persuaded to return to Birmingham from London University in order to succeed him. On Eayrs's retirement, he was followed by Professor J.J. Owen, an immunologist from Newcastle University, with altogether different interests from Solly. From the moment of his arrival he showed scant respect for Solly or his work and embarked on expunging all traces of Zuckerman. The Zuckerman Room became the Library and the head of Solly sculpted some years before by Anita Mandl, vanished. Survivors from the previous regime such as Eric Ashton, who had a personal Chair, and Deryk Darlington, the Executive Dean, were ignored. This stripping-out process seems to have been altogether more drastic than what would ordinarily follow the arrival of a new incumbent.

Solly, hearing of what was going on, wrote rather sadly to Anita. He had information about the Department from one or two of their old colleagues, who did not seem to be enjoying what was happening – or what was in prospect – one little bit. He had not, he wrote, been consulted about anything, and he suspected that his name was scarcely music in the ears of the University authorities. The idea of appointing an immunologist as head of the Department of Anatomy would have been excellent twenty years ago, but the way things had turned out made it less than sensible. He wondered how long it would be before the 'Z. Reading Room disappears?'

As quite often happens, one man's success promotes the unease and envy of others and is followed by a new order, dismissive, contemptuous of its predecessors and deliberately trampling over what they had built. What hurt Solly particularly was the dumping of two collections he had built up and of which he was proud, one of reprints, the other of skulls; the latter he managed to salvage. He regarded the dispersal of his monkey colony as being just another blow aimed at him, without, moreover, any regard for the distress caused to the monkeys. Alan Glass heard Solly say to Professor Owen, 'You can promote your own work without destroying other people's.' Owen, who evidently had small regard and less affection for Solly and all his works, did not feel called upon to reply. 'All is changed,' wrote one member of the previous regime to Anita, 'and not for the better in my view. Our Department has virtually disappeared.' As Professor Owen's secretary put it, 'Life was as if Solly had never been.' Certainly there are few traces of him to be seen there now. A famous university such as Birmingham could perhaps be expected to have a greater regard for its own history and for those who had a part in it.

Happier altogether were the memories of Solly, cherished by those he had worked with in the Department over many years. In 1974 and 1984 there were reunion dinners in Cambridge to celebrate his seventieth and eightieth birthdays – arranged by Joe Herbert – which people who loved and admired him came, some of them great distances, such as Charles Oxnard from Australia. Solly wrote to Anita asking tentatively about another for his ninetieth. She replied cautiously; she was unsure, there would sadly be a lot of missing faces. In the event, his own would have been amongst them for he died in the year before his ninetieth birthday.

After his death, Sir Robert Aitken, who as Vice-Chancellor had always given him unstinted support, wrote to Joan about Solly's great career, 'With half-blind eyes and half-paralysed hands, I can't write you a proper letter, but I must send you a word of sympathy, that your long life together, like ours, has come to its end, leaving you lonely, and a word of congratulation on the unique, great career, which – not without your help – Solly achieved.'

Pam Warwick (as she then was) was his secretary in Birmingham for eleven years from 1958 to 1969. It was a time when the children were growing up and she became almost a member of the family. Since she handled some of his Cabinet Office and Zoo work, she was something of a bridge between his different lives. Within the Department she was one of the team he created and which revolved round him; she was therefore as well placed as any to have a picture of him at that time. Looking back, she sees her work for him as the best education she could have had.

He was good at explaining the background of all the matters we were handling. This made my task interesting and me able to handle his business more easily . . . The atmosphere he created was tense and not easy. One could not ignore him; there were no shades of grey, only black and white, love and hate. This feeling ran right through the Department, everyone was aware of the change of atmosphere when he was there, and most, of the mood he was in . . . The spirit of the Department was extraordinary, it took over our lives . . . The Department was his pride and joy and I think he was happier and more relaxed there than anywhere.

There was, as she learned, the harder, more steely side to him; his motivation was, she thought, power. 'He gave 100 percent and expected the same from those around him. No excuses, no bad days were tolerated.' Bad days did, however, occur. Having struggled reluctantly to work on a day when she had a bad cold, she found herself not thanked but challenged, 'Why should I be exposed to your germs?' On another occasion, returning from London in a bad mood, without a voice and frustrated by his inability to communicate, he wrote something on a piece of paper and passed it to her: 'I am going to kill you,' she read. That was altogether too much for her; she fled to Nottingham and telephoned to say that she was not coming back. Two months later, however, he apologised; she came back and stayed. People could be furious with Solly and even hate him at moments, but he had a magnetism about him which brought them back. Paradox could well have been his middle name: he could be generous and mean, warm and heartless, kindly and brutal; in return he was both loved and hated, admired and rejected.

One of his many talents was the ability to persuade people that it was only sensible to do what he wanted; he took it for granted that they wanted very much to help him and were waiting for the opportunity to do so. Whether it was born in him or cultivated does not greatly matter, it worked wonders. Pam, well aware of his skill at getting his way, was not surprised to find herself taking two or three York paving stones in the boot of her car each time she went to Norfolk; he had bought them in Birmingham for use at The Shooting Box, his newly-acquired home in Burnham Thorpe. His explanation was that the added load would make for safe driving: 'It will hold the car on the road.' While, of course, she knew it to be nonsense, she was still willing to perform a tiresome chore. He had a way of making those who worked for him aware of the importance of what he was doing, that in helping they were themselves doing something that mattered.

There is a picture of Solly walking on the seashore in Norfolk, in one hand a shrimping net – no ordinary shrimping net, but one made for him in France to meet his special requirements – in the other some kind of container. That chance snapshot shows, without the need for words, how he faced life: interested, inquiring, exploring, collecting and ready, as Noel Annan found, to explain and to talk of what he had seen. 'To go for a walk with Solly on the beach was an education in itself; he would go with his shrimping net over his shoulder, trousers rolled up, "See that stone there," and he would immediately give you a little lecture, absolutely fascinating . . . He was a natural teacher without ever being a bore.' Solly's son Paul remembers how they used to collect cornelians and how his father, competitive always, was keen to find more and bigger ones than anyone else to be added to his cherished collection. Finding one day an unusually good one, he was surprised when his father insisted on buying it from him for a pound. He remembers too his father at Stella's funeral, taking from his pocket two or three of these stones and throwing them on to her coffin, as it was lowered into the grave; a small, barely observed incident, a side of him he would have wished to keep hidden.

The man in the photograph, picking up, studying and storing away whatever caught his eye, was the same one who, attending an international conference or a Whitehall committee, looked for the people and the items of interest and remembered them. While it would be fanciful to suggest that Whitehall generally had much in common with Nature, Solly found things in both which fascinated him and demanded his attention. He could learn something from almost anything: the contents of a Whitehall in-tray or those of a pool of seawater left by the receding tide, the fragments of an exploded bomb or a piece of Victorian ironwork, were all things of interest, which engrossed his attention.

7

'Dear Brum'

'I have seldom spent fuller or happier hours than I did in
dear Brum under your and Solly's roof.'

John Betjeman

A SMALL house in Museum Road, Oxford, essentially a bachelor
establishment, designed for the comfort of one man, cannot
have been for Joan more than a step in the direction of married
life. The war, however, and the total liquidity of Solly's plans when
it was over, effectively prevented them from even looking for an
alternative until he found himself destined beyond doubt for
Birmingham. In 1946 they acquired number 6 Carpenter Road,
Birmingham. In contrast with that house in Museum Road, it was
a large, elegant family house of early Victorian vintage in the smart
and peaceful suburb of Edgbaston, set apart from but still very
much a part of Birmingham. The process of moving, in the teeth
of a freezing winter with minimal coal rations and builder's men in
and out of the house, could hardly have been more uncomfortable.
Maybe it was the memory of that winter which prompted Solly, in
writing to e.e. cummings, to say, 'Your letter reached us, buried
beneath the ice-cap of the Truman/Stalin period in human affairs'.

It is strange how little the rest of England knows about its
second city, the wealth created there and its culture. London is too
busy being a capital, the seat of government; too engrossed in politics and international affairs, too busy with high finance; too full
of people who count things, too few who make them, too many

86

accountants, too few engineers. The nuts and bolts of life come from Birmingham, and Birmingham is rightly proud of the fact. History made it different. A town of no great importance in the seventeenth century and more than five miles away from any city, town corporate or borough, it was not covered by the Five Mile Act. It thus escaped the provisions of the Clarendon Code, which restricted the right of dissenters and non-conformists to set up their own places of worship. Likewise, at that time the right to trade in all major cities was restricted. Traders were required to belong to guilds and to observe their rules in the conduct of business. In Birmingham, they were free to change their practices as they thought fit. The outcome, of course, was that, free of such shackles, the city became, in religious matters, a centre of dissent and in trade, of innovation. The city prospered with banks, iron-making, chocolate. The Chamberlains, the Darbys, the Cadburys, the Martineaus, the latter being Huguenots driven from France, were all people who sought freedom and worked hard to keep it. It was natural that Solly should have felt comfortable and at home in this city, with its tradition of dissent and innovation.

Their children grew up in Birmingham; Paul was a year old when they arrived, and Stella was born there. Joan, who grew to love it, wrote a book with Geoffrey Eley about the city, its history and its people and the way it has always welcomed the new. 'It is deep in the Birmingham character to be ready to try something new.' First among her memories of their new life are of Solly's anguish, when together they took Stella to hospital, a young baby and very ill. They feared she would die. Though they lived well in a large and comfortable house, and had lovely Italian girls to look after the house and do the cooking, money was always tight. Since neither governments nor universities are particularly generous pay-masters, it was only when he retired that he was able to earn what others felt his advice was worth. The existence of any unfilled space in Solly's life was always a source of unease. Not only did it mean wasted time, but it made room for unwelcome doubts about himself and uncertainty as to his place in the scheme of things. A good defence against such worries was a social life well filled with interesting people. At that point in his autobiography, there occur such phrases as 'entertained an ever widening social circle', 'people started dropping in', 'parties for staff and BSc students' and house guests every weekend.

Birmingham was a rich source from which he could draw, and No. 6 Carpenter Road provided him with an ideal base. One unusual addition who gave him great delight was Ivan Shortt. A prominent member of the Jewish community, a magistrate and a prison visitor, he was also the country's greatest expert on old silver plate. His firm owned a substantial number of the old dies used by Matthew Boulton in the second half of the eighteenth century, and even the special cupboard he stored them in. Such a man, with his knowledge and his collection of objects, was meat and drink to Solly. Here was an opportunity to learn from a master and, as such, irresistible. He became a friend as well as a pupil and began to talk of his 'fascinating new world of Sheffield Plate'. John Betjeman, whom he took with him on a visit to the works, was entranced by a glimpse of the graces and skills of the past. He also took with him a special favourite, 'the exquisite' Rosamund Lehmann. Professor Garner, one of the University's engineers, had other sides to him which attracted Solly; he had written a learned treatise on English Delftware, and was also an authority on Cromwell's Protectorate, which, far from being sterile, he judged to be as creative as any other age. Thomas Bodkin, the University's Professor of Fine Art, presided over the Barber Institute, a building of his own design which housed a valuable collection of pictures, many of which Bodkin had bought himself. It was a condition that a collection of portraits of Dame Martha Barber should be hung there. Since to have done this would have lowered the standard of the exhibits, the ingenious Professor Bodkin, whom Solly described as immensely entertaining and 'great fun at dinner parties', instructed the architect that a narrow corridor of space should be left between two walls in which the pictures could be hung but not seen – or seen only by guests who were allowed after dinner to share the joke.

Although he does mention Professor Ellis Waterhouse, Bodkin's successor, he makes no reference to a speech he made, welcoming the Anatomical Society to Birmingham on behalf of the university on the occasion of its annual conference. 'I don't know anything about anatomy, but I know what I like', won him considerable applause. When he followed it up with 'as my friend Solly Zuckerman said to me on one of his RARE visits to this university', the applause was much greater, though Solly is said not to have joined in. Lancelot Hogben, whom Solly knew to be 'a stimulating teacher and a brilliant experimental zoologist', was appointed to the Chair of Zoology on his suggestion. He had a tiresome habit of inventing enemies wherever he went and he tended to drink too much; one night when drunk, he rang up and delivered a confused version of Churchill's famous 'We shall fight them on the beaches' speech. Peter Medawar, who succeeded Hogben as Professor of Zoology, was another recruit of Solly's and a particularly distinguished one; he became a Nobel Laureate and President of the British Association for the Advancement of Science. John Squire, the third of his recruits, became Birmingham's Professor of Pathology. The three together added to the number of like-minded friends in the University.

There were visitors too from the outside world. Admiral Rickover, known as the father of the American nuclear navy, was the last of Solly's Six Men. The son of poor Jewish immigrants, he carried a sizeable chip on his shoulder and was famous for his devastating rudeness, particularly to his superiors. He came to Birmingham to receive the honorary degree which Solly proposed should be conferred on him. Urged by Solly, he agreed to wear for the celebratory dinner the cross and insignia of the CBE, conferred on him for his wartime services to the Royal Navy. It didn't stop him exclaiming, when he saw the assembled company all covered with medals, from exclaiming loudly, 'Jesus, a nation of heroes'. The Admiral had a formidable wife to match himself and to correct anyone who rashly overlooked his merits.

In January 1961, John Betjeman stayed with the Zuckermans at 6 Carpenter Road. He wrote to Joan afterwards, 'I have seldom spent fuller or happier hours than I did in dear Brum under your and Solly's roof'. The letter is an outpouring of thanks, checked only by an uncertainty as to what he had enjoyed most: 'the claret at lunch, the '49 of a dim but superlative chateau, with the sweet Climens after on Sunday'. 'The Lafittes on Saturday' were much appreciated; there followed a paean of praise for Brum and the people and things it contained. 'The Van Dyck, the Rubens landscape, Archbishop

Robinson, the Gainsborough wagon, the Murillo of Cana of Galilee and the battledore and shuttlecock in that non-smoking very Brum hall; the Sung Mass in the broad Brum chancel of St. James . . . Mr Short [sic] and that marvellous Boulton plate in the jewellers' quarter on a silent Sunday morning, the visit to the Bishop and his family and then that tour of the Pre Raphs – I say what a feast of joy . . . Oft may I return to Brum and see you again and listen to you and Solly and talk a lot myself.' The letter shows Betjeman overflowing with enjoyment; it tells too of the delight that both Zuckermans had in Brum and how well versed they were in the wealth and variety it offers.

Gladwyn Jebb, sometime British Ambassador in Paris, and his wife came to stay for the Jewellers' dinner. Joan was fascinated to hear him calling to Solly when they were dressing to know if any of his neighbours had a KCMG star which he could borrow, since he had left his behind. She and Solly were also amused when Lady Jebb remarked to her neighbour at dinner that she had never imagined Solly and Joan having such a delightful house in the middle of Manchester – and she did say Manchester.

Solly's social habits made him an easy target for name-dropping accusations; sometimes apparently unable to refrain from sprinkling his conversation with titled or famous names, he needed, so it seemed, to impress himself as well as others. The unknown Jewish immigrant was always at his elbow on smart occasions to remind him of the man he had once been and whom he had never left far behind. He knew and enjoyed interesting people, indeed, he collected them and liked to talk about them. If some had titles, that was no reason for leaving them out, but it was the people themselves and their emergence from the ruck that interested him. Politicians, mainly those who represented neighbouring constituencies, came on the scene: Patrick Gordon Walker, a colleague in Oxford days and MP for Smethwick; Roy Jenkins from Stechford, who became a lifelong friend and gave an address at his Memorial Service: 'I always found him a loyal friend and ally, although I could see that it was easier to feel affectionate towards him if he was on one's side rather than against one.'

Hugh Gaitskell from Leeds, Nye Bevan and his wife Jennie Lee (MP for Cannock) were all guests in his house from time to time, though for the sake of tranquillity, the Gaitskells and the Bevans did not stay at the same time. Solly, coming to know and understand the political world, was careful at all times not to become too entangled in it. Hugh Fraser from Stafford was the only regular Tory visitor. Bevan, interested in Solly's work, used to inquire as to what his study of the reproductive systems of monkeys had taught him about the problem of human population. While in a predominantly industrial area such as the Midlands Labour MPs could be expected to outnumber Conservatives, that can only be a partial explanation of why his friends came from the Left rather than the Right of politics; a better one is that, as a persistent questioner, he was more at home with the party which at least seemed to be the source of challenge and innovation.

He did not, however, allow himself to be drawn into the fractious business of party politics. Harold Macmillan and Roy Jenkins were probably the two politicians he respected most. When invited by Harold Wilson to join the new Labour Government in 1964, he showed no hesitation in turning it down. If he could not continue to serve the new administration as he had served its predecessor, he would, he told the Prime Minister, leave Whitehall. He saw his role as that of a man of ideas, an adviser, not as an executive; he understood that his advice, to be of worth, must remain free of the twists and turns of party manoeuvres. Political parties, he could not have failed to notice, had a way of absorbing people, and saving them the trouble of thinking for themselves.

It was while Solly and Joan were still living in Birmingham and Bernal was their guest, that these two old friends and collaborators finally parted. Bernal, a brilliant scientist whom Solly credited with having played 'a critical part in elucidating the structure of the first ovarian hormones,' was insisting, with all the naivety to which brilliant men are sometimes prone, that there was no alternative to a Marxist society. Solly, never greatly concerned about other people's politics so long as they were not forced upon him, became quite heated, leapt to his feet and proclaimed that he wasn't prepared to fall in with some pre-designed framework which instructed him as to what was right and wrong. In a letter to Margaret Gardiner, he described the incident and how he had said to Bernal, 'I do not give a damn what you believe in or think is right, but I am not going to allow you or anyone else to deprive me of the privilege of being wrong.' Suggestions that Solly was a serious left-winger and even a member of the Communist Party hardly ring true; he laughed too easily and questioned too readily.

It was Solly's way always to have an eye open for people, incidents and things which interested and amused him. Pam Warwick, his secretary, recalls a day when, driving him to the station in Birmingham, they passed through a street which was undergoing the process which the authorities like to describe as 'improvement'. This, they saw, involved the removal of a splendid piece of Victorian ironwork, which was delicately known as a 'Home of Iron Convenience'. He told her to stop the car so that he could get out and have a look at it; he then instructed her to negotiate its purchase. In due course the iron convenience was delivered to his home in Burnham Thorpe where, promoted from its earlier role, it is now an unusual, even majestic, summer-house.

The Cadbury family, of chocolate fame, became friends from early days in Birmingham. On one occasion when he was with Hugh Fraser, the MP for Stafford, waiting on the station platform for a train, a man in an untidy mackintosh came up and asked if he could lend him a pound. Solly handed it over. 'Who was that shifty character?' Hugh asked. It was Laurence Cadbury, head of the firm at that time and, as Solly pointed out, a member of the Board of the Bank of England. When he finally retired from the Civil Service in 1972, Solly was invited to join the Board of Cadbury Schweppes. Initially he preferred to be a consultant while he learned about the business. Adrian Cadbury remembers Solly telling the Board that, while their products were good, they did not understand, as they should, their own processes, particularly the cultivation and treatment of cocoa.

Before he retired from the Board, the company paid him the considerable tribute of naming their new Research Centre in Reading after him. Solly, delighted, wrote to Adrian Cadbury, 'The fact that you have attached my name to the Research Centre fills me with more pride than any honour I have ever received.' Samuel Goldblith, a Vice President of the Massachusetts Institute of Technology, in a letter of 22 December 1981 to Adrian Cadbury, wrote,

I enjoyed very much the remarks you made on the occasion of the dedication of the Lord Zuckerman Research Center. In particular, I am delighted that you pointed out the standard of excellence that was typical of Solly. I know Solly was deeply moved and deeply touched by the fact that the building was really dedicated to him and it finally struck him that he was indeed having the Zuckerman name linked with that of Reading. His closing comments were no simple afterthought. I know they were well thought out and developed, and, in the car going back with him to London, I know how deeply moved he was.

Solly's integrity, his respect as a scientist for facts, did not enable him to resist the temptation to garnish a story for the sake of a laugh. He enjoyed telling people that the Cadbury family bought their wine at the Co-op, while he knew them to be members of the Wine Society, a co-operative organisation but hardly the same as the Co-op. As a Director, he was accustomed from time to time to attend dinners given by the company, after which he used to be driven home by one of the company's employees, known as Irish Tom. Rather oddly, Solly always insisted on stopping for a cup of coffee on the way. Since he never had ready money on him, Irish Tom was left to settle the bill. While it is unlikely that Solly ever troubled to repay him, he did in the end present him with his overcoat; Irish Tom was said to be pleased with the settlement.

8

The Zoo

'Isn't it wonderful to see something positive one's done – in
three dimensions. It's the main pleasure I get from the Zoo,
all those buildings that wouldn't have been there if I hadn't
tried.'

SZ, letter to Margaret Gardiner, 27 August 1980

FOUNDED IN 1826 under Royal Charter by Stamford Raffles,
the Zoological Society of London's purpose was declared to be
'The advancement of zoology and physiology and the introduction of new and curious subjects of the animal kingdom'. Despite
that rather grand start in life and the privilege of having its home
in Regent's Park, it did not then receive, nor has it since, any
regular support from public funds. Solly's repeated and heartfelt
lament was that in this respect it differed not only from all other
national zoos in the world, but also from similar English institutions such as the Botanical Gardens at Kew and the Natural
History Museum at South Kensington. The live flora and the dead
fauna were thought worthy of support; the live fauna were left out.
Nor, and this was at the heart of the problem Solly faced, did it
ever enjoy the benefit of a substantial endowment fund to secure
its future needs. An offer by the Government at some time towards
the end of the nineteenth century to put the Zoo on a footing
similar to that enjoyed by like institutions was unwisely rejected
out of hand; a decision which, after the privations of two world
wars, was seen to have been a mistake. It is not one, however,
which any Government since has been minded to put right.

By 1945 the neglect of the interwar period and the shortages of the war had taken their toll. The gardens had become vegetable plots; fear of escapes during air raids, food shortages and financial difficulties had caused the collection to be much reduced; the reptile house was 'depopulated'; bombs had left their mark and repairs of buildings had been postponed. For the staff, many of whom had been away in the armed forces, there was neither a career structure, nor any adequate pension scheme. In 1943, a Dr Sheffield Neave, an entomologist, pointed out that in paying its Secretary or Chief Executive a salary, the Society was in breach of its own Charter and bylaws. As a result, Julian Huxley was obliged to resign and Dr Neave was appointed in his place; Dr Neave got what he wanted, but the Society lost the man it needed. The loss of someone of the stature of Julian Huxley added to the difficulties of the time. The change reflected a long-cherished British belief that good public servants can be had, if not for nothing, at least on the cheap.

The fact that from its beginning the Society had two faces was the source of some confusion. Primarily a scientific institution, it was also a club for the well-to-do, whose members alone had access to the collection. Only after some years and on weekdays was the public admitted as a means of increasing income; on Sundays admission was limited to Fellows. As recently as the 1930s, the Secretary, Sir Peter Chalmers-Mitchell, wrote to the Ministry of Agriculture, making the Society's position clear: 'I am afraid that the opening of the Gardens [on Sundays] to the public would have to be resisted to the last extremity.' The war, however, and the prospect of lower attendances, led the Council to have second thoughts. It relaxed the rule and admitted members of the armed forces all day on Sunday, the general public in the afternoon. With the return of peace, Sunday mornings were once again for Fellows only, despite the fact that by that time their subscriptions amounted to only 6 percent of the Zoo's income.

Solly's first employment was with the Zoological Society of London – so too was his last. In 1928 he was appointed as the Society's Prosector or research anatomist, a job which lasted for four years. In 1955 he became Secretary and in 1975 President until he retired in 1984. During those years, whatever the rule book said, he ran both the Zoo and the Society, and saved them from terminal decline. His concerns were first for the creatures collected together in Regent's Park, that they should be well cared for and properly housed. Secondly, he recognised, as his predecessors did not, that the staff should be well trained, have a career structure and a secure pension scheme. Thirdly and, it must be admitted, last, he had some residuary concern for the public who paid to come in. That concern did not, however, always stretch to the general appearance of the place, the explanations offered concerning the animals or the catering, which left much to be desired.

It was Solly's strength that he saw the role of the Society as a mixture of the scientific and the educational. Scientifically, its role was to continue to add to the great body of knowledge already built up concerning the natural world. Educationally, its role was to make that knowledge readily available and thereby to increase mankind's awareness of the immense diversity of creatures with which it shares the planet and to warn that with the right to enjoy is coupled a duty to protect and conserve. Solly, while accepting that the Zoo had a role in educating, did not accept that entertainment was an important factor in getting people there in the first place. Both he and the Society should have given more thought to the provision of an amenity which the public would be willing to sustain.

'Zoos exist because the number of people who want them to do so vastly outnumber those who want to see them suppressed.' That terse and unarguable proposition* was Solly's curtain raiser to a declaration as to what should be required of anyone wishing to manage a zoo and to handle what he always referred to as exotic animals. First, they should 'show that they are just as humane in their attitude to wild animals as those who are opposed to zoos'. Secondly, they must be able 'to demonstrate and to demonstrate publicly that they are trying to abide by the standards set by the best zoos'. Thirdly, they must show that 'they treat their public educational standards seriously'. Fourthly, the 'keeper staff has to be properly trained'. Fifthly, they must be able 'to demonstrate, not to the world of amateurs who write about zoos, but to the scientific world, that they are seriously concerned with research of the

---

* *Great Zoos of the World*, 1979

quality and kind which yields knowledge that is not only relevant to the health and breeding of wild animals, but also to man's own wellbeing'. Finally, 'they should be able to show that they have a contribution to make to the preservation of species which have either become extinct in the wild or which are now endangered'.

Such were Solly's imperatives to be observed by all who were running a zoo; they were to be followed not at some future date when it became convenient, but from the beginning. The thoughts behind them were those of his youth in the veldt of Cape Province, when he first encountered monkeys and succumbed to their spell. A well-managed zoo provided the opportunity to study at close quarters the needs of the same animals, their health and breeding and how they might be conserved from the encroach-ment of man upon their natural home. He was anxious lest in the cramped circumstances of Regent's Park the research activities of the Learned Society and the Institute of Zoology would be over-looked, and that visitors would not understand that it was the Society which owned the Zoo, and not the other way round. He favoured moving the Zoo to Whipsnade, where in the greater space available – several hundred acres as opposed to forty in Regent's Park – paddocks could take the place of cages and the confinement aspect would at least be diminished. Whereas the Society owned Whipsnade and had the rights of a landlord, in Regent's Park it was not only a mere tenant, but was subject to the restrictions of a Royal Park, and from the transport aspect on the wrong side of it. It was also in an area where space was at a premium and where at least some of the locals made no secret of the fact that they did not like the Zoo as a neighbour. The Zoo itself was saddled with as many as nine or ten listed buildings. Those who handle the listing process have little knowledge of the animals that live in them; it is not their concern that they are locking the institution into the past and imposing upon animals conditions which could be improved. It was as if not only a hospi-tal was being listed, but its operating theatres as well.

The Elephant House is an example. In designing it, the archi-tects certainly had the majestic beasts it was to house very much in mind, so much so that they produced a building which reflected brilliantly their majesty and power, but did little to meet their needs. While it was still under construction, some of the Keepers asked how the animals were going to get in without a bridge over the moat, and if they were to use the same entrance as the public. The response of the architects' staff was to ask that the Zoo staff should refrain from such questioning, which demoralised and depressed the contractors' men. Caroline Cranbrook, working for Solly at the Zoo at the time, recalls how on being installed the elephants expressed their displeasure by pushing each other into the moat. It is strange that Solly, who raised the funds and loved the animals, should have been more interested in buildings which impressed the onlooker, rather than those which were comfortable for the occupier. Whether the elephants like it or not, the building is listed and is likely to be there for ever. The same failure to give second thoughts to the structure of the buildings caused him to lose sight of the problems of repair.

Solly's normally good relations with the staff are also said to have suffered a jolt on the occasion of the Keepers' annual Christmas Party. Held on a men only basis, it was the custom, in order to prevent them becoming too serious, to invite a group of ladies from nearby Camden Town. It fell to Solly to judge a beauty contest in which all took part; he awarded the prize to the wrong contestant and was loudly booed for his error.

There are, of course, many who think it wrong to keep wild animals in captivity. Solly's concern was that such people not only made no distinction between good and bad zoos, but that they overlooked entirely the importance of the knowledge of health and breeding gathered there over many years and the role of zoos in conservation. They ignored too their function in informing and educating the public of the great wealth of Nature; without them, most people would never see the animals or understand their need to be protected. Those who thought 'the wild' a safe place often forgot how the constant encroachments of the human race endangered the habitat and threatened the survival of many species.

Anxious as he was to leave South Africa, those early years in the veldt fashioned him, framed his thoughts and focussed his attention on the natural world. Apes and monkeys were the subjects of his first two books, *The Social Life of Monkeys and Apes* and *The Functional Affinities of Man, Monkeys and Apes*; also of his last, *The*

Ape in Myth and Art, which was published after his death. At one time he kept a baby baboon, Chastity, as a pet in his London flat. His paper on the development of a baboon's skull, written in Cape Town, was his passport to English scientific circles. Paul Zuckerman remembers seeing his father with his baboons in Birmingham, the strange clicking noises he made to them and the way they responded to him; Noel Annan recalled the female baboons, clearly in love with him, crawling all over him and licking his face.

In those early postwar years, the Zoo still had something of a hold on the public imagination and there were few competing amenities. Animal births, for example that of Brumas, the polar bear cub, were news and helped to bring about record attendances. Lacking both funds and staff, the management had little opportunity to do more than rest on its somewhat faded laurels and hope, like Micawber, that something would turn up. Little or no effort was made to attract visitors or improve accommodation for the animals. Lord Alanbrooke, having been persuaded to take office as President, found himself heading an institution which, far from being trouble-free, was crumbling with discontent and decay. Endless disputes and rows in the Council of the Society and between the Council and the Fellowship, well aired in the press, made things that much worse. After four years he resigned, and was succeeded by Sir Landsborough Thomson, Second Secretary of the Medical Research Council, described by Solly as 'a somewhat staid character'.

Flattered to be invited in 1953 by the Secretary, Lord Chaplin, to join the Council, Solly accepted, on the basis that attendance at monthly meetings was all that would be expected of him and even that was not obligatory. Without any grounds for doing so, he assumed that the Council was as it had been during his time as Prosector, some twenty years before, a gathering of 'distinguished elders of biological science, together with a few wealthy amateur naturalists'. He saw, as he said at the time, 'no reason to suppose that its prestige had dwindled'. In 1955, he went further and accepted Lord Chaplin's invitation to succeed him as Secretary. In doing so, he relied upon assurances that the post was a sinecure and would add little to what had been expected of him as a member of the Council. Moreover, according to Lord Chaplin, the Society and the Zoo were 'back on the rails'. It is not possible to believe that after two years as a member of the Council, Solly had learned so little of the Society's affairs that he was able to accept without question or challenge such unfounded statements. What is much more likely, and a great deal easier to believe, is that he accepted the post because he wanted it and that he did so with his eyes wide open and a very clear idea of the problems he would face.

While he may not have foreseen quite how rough and time-absorbing the row with the Fellows would be, there is little doubt that he entered it with relish, determined to win, and that he even enjoyed the process. The fact that he remained in the post for twenty-two years and thereafter was President for a further seven, suggests that from the moment he was offered the post, he had no thought but to accept. Solly's moments of indecision occurred on occasions when he did not know what he himself wanted. When, as on the particular occasion, he was clear in his mind, he gave little thought to possible difficulties. Two instances of his extraordinary concentration come to mind. Waiting on a platform for a tube train, he dropped his pipe on to the line; his one thought was to get down on the line and recover it, which he did, greatly to the alarm of others on the platform, who realised that the arrival of a train was imminent. In Normandy, with his mind on bombs, he failed to notice a German fighter flying low up the road. When he did, he stayed and watched it, and found himself for a split second looking into the face of the pilot who, though firing all the while, somehow missed him.

Whether or not he knew what faced him, in 1955 at the age of fifty Solly took upon himself executive responsibility for sustaining the Society as a scientific institution, managing the Zoo, looking after the collection of mammals, reptiles, birds, fishes and insects, caring for the staff, providing an attractive amenity for visitors and finding the resources which, as always, were in short supply. For performing these tasks, though miraculous powers would be required, he would be paid nothing. His account, written in six chapters of *Monkeys, Men and Missiles*, reads as if the Society and its affairs were his sole concern at that time, whereas in fact he had to fit it in as best he could into a crowded programme of advising in Whitehall and running the Anatomy Department at Birmingham

University. Having secured the post and measured the task and understood that what he had on his hands was anything but a sine-cure, he had plenty of opportunity to learn how little control a thin management exercised: 'My education continued fast.' An invitation to lunch from a group of Fellows who styled themselves the ZSL's Pink Elephants Club, gave him a sight of an organisation which existed to ensure that its members' thirsts could be cared for regardless of the restraints of licensing hours. To them the Society was not much more than an opportunity to drink as and when they wished. Attending a President's Reception, he was struck by the liberal way in which staff literally threw bottles of champagne into the outstretched arms of departing guests; another version of this was that the staff threw the bottles to avoid being mobbed. Such things were foretastes of other more serious troubles.

What was urgently needed was reinforcement for the administration, the burden of which fell at the time on one man and his secretary, the latter having been in the Society's employment for nearly fifty years. Miss Eirwen Owen, who had been Deputy Regional Commissioner for Wales during the War, was the first find. A look in the direction of the armed forces and a talk with General Sir Hugh Stockwell, brought a confrontation with the then Chief of the Imperial General Staff, Sir Gerald Templer: 'What are you doing, trying to hijack my Military Secretary? Stop messing around, Solly, and I'll find you the right man.' General Dalton appeared a few days later, he as Controller, Eirwen Owen as administrator complemented each other perfectly. 'I began', Solly wrote, 'to wonder how I had managed without them in the previous two years.'

Disputes within the Council and with a group of Fellows began to fester. 'The stage had been reached', Solly wrote in the Society's Annual Report for 1957, 'in which the Fellowship was threatening to be a financial impediment to the discharge of the purpose of the Royal Charter and was therefore threatening the existence of the Society itself.' The President, the Treasurer (Terence Morrison-Scott), who was throughout a tower of strength, and the majority of the Council agreed with Solly that the Gardens should be open to the public on Sunday mornings as well. This meant the end of the Fellows-only Sunday lunches and was something of a death blow to a club whose members enjoyed benefits well in excess of those they paid for. There was a predictable and furious reaction from some of the Fellows. Chapman Pincher, under the heading 'Zoo's Noah Saves the Ship', wrote that 'it was like a family row inside Noah's Ark'. Although the changes had been approved by a majority of those actually voting, it was argued that what was required was a majority of the total Fellowship. To everyone's surprise and Solly's huge chagrin, the judge ruled in favour of that rather absurd notion and against the Society. It was reversed on appeal and the dissidents were ordered to pay the Society's costs, which they never did. The result was hailed as a triumph by the staff and by the press. According to a leader in *The Times* of 6 December 1958, 'So far are the diehards of privilege divorced from the realities of today that they have been vocal in objecting to having to share the Zoo on Sundays with other people.' To Solly must go the credit for his determination to sustain the true interests of the Society, and not to pay heed to the faint hearts on the Council whose support was lukewarm.

At this point, the Duke of Edinburgh agreed to become President and remained so for seventeen years. His interest in science, his known concern for wildlife, his readiness to preside at meetings, gave the Society not merely a figurehead but real leadership. His involvement served to damp down the petty disputes which have so often exacerbated the Society's problems; it also curbed Solly's autocratic ways. Prince Philip was someone for whom he felt both affection and regard and to whom he was ready to defer.

Solly, though disinclined to give way if it involved a loss of face, was quick to recognise and listen to those who he realised had something to teach him. He was at pains to seek out those who could advise him. He looked on permanent secretaries as great repositories of wisdom; Sam Way was surprised at the way he seemed to idolise them. At one time there were as many as three retired permanent secretaries serving at his invitation on the Council of the Zoo, Sam being one of them. On staff matters, he went to Sir Harold Emmerson, Permanent Secretary to the Ministry of Labour, and from him received the immortal advice, 'Accept whatever happens; why, we've even had to allow the

Beefeaters in the Tower to be unionised.' On trade union organisation, he enlisted the help of Tom Williamson, then General
Secretary of the Municipal Workers Union. On finance, he took
counsel with Michael Behrens, a friend and a merchant banker; on
staff pensions, with Lord Glenconner, then Chairman of an insu-
rance company. Concerned to find a way of electing more
influential Fellows to the Council, he took to issuing lists of candi-
dates, calling attention to how they could help the Society. Many
of them, as he said, happened to be 'friends'. Solly had some kind
of aura about him which suggested to people that if an opportunity to help him presented itself, they ought not even to think of
letting it go by.

He initiated the International Zoo Yearbook, or the Zoo Bible,
as it became known; he set up an educational programme for
London schoolchildren and established a programme of scientific
symposia to keep people informed about areas in which particular
progress was being made in zoology. All other scientific publica-
tions were looked after by Marcia Edwards, who, without showing
any sign of age or strain, stayed for nearly forty years. He pursued
all the Professors of Zoology in the country, urging them to
become scientific Fellows. In order to provide awards and prizes of
interest, he first enlisted the interest and financial support of
Sidney Bernstein. He had got to know various artists when they
were visiting the Zoo and doing studies of animals, and he
approached Henry Moore, who gave him seven of each of three
pieces. These quite soon grew in value to a point where, with the
artist's agreement, they were sold to form the basis of a fund with
which to finance the purchase of other less highly priced items. At
Henry Moore's suggestion, Elisabeth Frink produced a series of
wild boars, Jonathan Kingdon produced a series of medals,
Michael Behrens presented some sculptures of a magic bird by
Tapio Wirkkala. Solly bought a few pieces from David Wynne and
last, but far from least, he acquired bronzes of a hippopotamus by
Anita Mandl.

Above all the other problems was the need for money, and
enough of it to set up a building and repairs fund. As each item on
a long list was provided for, so others arose: a new hospital, a works
and supplies building, the Nuffield Institute of Comparative

Medicine and the Wellcome Institute for Comparative Physiology. The Ford, Nuffield, Wolfson Foundation and the Wellcome Trust all responded to Solly's pleas. Charles Clore, Jack Cotton and Michael Sobell have their memorials in Regent's Park; they are inhabited by animals and enjoyed by the public. Worried about the legal costs of fighting the Society's case in the Courts, he consulted Israel Sieff, who gave a fundraising dinner to which he invited members of his family, telling them, I'm going to give so much and you so much, and so on round the table.

A first encounter with Jack Cotton, the successful property developer, was interesting. Despite a warning from his Birmingham friends, 'Have nothing to do with the man,' Solly persisted. Having secured an appointment, he went round to see him at the Dorchester Hotel and, after a few preliminaries, was faced with the direct question, 'Now, what have you really come to see me about?' Solly took a chance and responded with equal bluntness, 'I wished to see the man who I am told is a very smart and powerful businessman who has just given £100,000 to the Royal College of Surgeons about which I assume he knows little or nothing.' As a member of the College, he went on to say that if, having made his money buying and selling land, Cotton wished to throw his money about, he should put it back into the land – there were plenty of public parks which could benefit; the Zoo in Regent's Park in which he, Solly, had an interest, was just one. 'Come and see me again,' was Cotton's response; when Solly did so, he gave him a quarter of a million pounds – the first but not the last of his gifts to the Zoo. One unusual sequel was a telephone call from Nassau, where Cotton was recovering from a heart attack. He wished Solly to talk on the telephone to a well-known American cardiologist who had been called in. To Solly's insistence that he knew nothing about Cotton's heart, had never practised medicine and was not his doctor, Cotton replied, 'I know, and so does Professor de Bakey. It would reassure me if you spoke to him and then called me back.' Why did a rich man who could afford the best advice seek to have it confirmed by someone whom he knew had no special knowledge? Solly had a way of attracting from men like Cotton their trust and admiration.

As Solly and others with similar aims for the Zoo grew older, the dreams of a building fund, let alone an all-purpose substantial endowment fund, faded, and Solly found himself being carried by the current of need in the direction of the Government. He had none of the usual preliminary difficulties. As the Government's Chief Scientific Adviser, ensconced in the Cabinet Office, he could hardly have been better placed to knock on the door. He called attention to the endemic weakness of the Society; it had suffered ever since its foundation 140 years before from a lack of capital. In his annual report for 1969, he made the point that due to that lack, 'the buildings have always been retained long after they have been outmoded'. 'The Society has carried on an entirely private basis the responsibility for the national zoological collection', he wrote. 'We know of no other country where this is so.'

Roy Jenkins, as Chancellor of the Exchequer, lent him a sympathetic ear and arranged a loan from the Bank of England guaranteed by the Government. This, though welcome, had the usual result of adding to an already burdensome interest bill. Early in 1970, further help was given: £900,000 to pay off debts, and an indexed grant of £700,000 towards building costs in the five years 1970-74; the money was accompanied by a statement from the Chancellor, 'In providing this substantial measure of support, the Government have had in mind that the Zoo has become, in fact if not in form, a national institution, that it is a major London amenity and also an important tourist attraction.' It was the first time that such an admission was ever made by a senior minister. Gifts from that most generous Ambassadors, Walter Annenberg, and from Mrs Brooke Astor, the kind of benefactress of whom one dreams and who has done wonders for the Bronx Zoo in New York, gave Solly particular joy. The Wolfson Foundation gave a further £210,000 to support the Institute of Zoology. The Lion Terraces were completed thanks to a further grant of £200,000 from Charles Clore; they were opened by the Queen to the sound of William Walton's specially written fanfare *The Roar of Lions*. It was dedicated to Solly as 'the Lion of Lions'.

In 1967, General Dalton retired as Controller and Director General, having more than matched up to the original recommendation by Sir Gerald Templer; he was replaced by Colin Rawlins as Director of Zoos, and the then Scientific Director, Harrison

Matthews, was succeeded by Dr Len Goodwin, who had first encountered Solly at Oxford. The two newcomers, with the redoubtable Eirwen Owen, formed together a triumvirate who were in constant and easy contact with Solly; he would 'dash to Regent's Park for a sandwich lunch with the three directors'; later he came to see them 'as and when it was necessary. And there was always the telephone.' Solly needed the telephone as a lame man needs a walking stick. One of his secretaries observed, 'If he went to the moon, he would be sure to find a telephone waiting for him.' With the four of them it worked, but it was manifestly not an arrangement which would survive being handed on to others.

Towards the end of the 1970s, the Duke of Edinburgh gave up the Presidency, and was succeeded by Solly; not long before, Terence Morrison-Scott, who had backed Solly through all the troubles, also retired; so too did Eirwen Owen; John Phillips came and went as Secretary. Solly himself gave notice of his intention to retire in 1984, when he would be eighty; the finances were not looking good and a storm of inflation was about to break. While Solly was determined that the Government should be brought to face what he regarded as its obligations, the new Government in 1974 was equally determined to do nothing of the kind and to wash its hands of the Zoo. A note of hope was sounded when, in 1979, Michael Heseltine, as the new Secretary of State for the Environment, advised Solly, 'Strike now, the Society will never have a more sympathetic Minister with whom to deal than myself' – fine words, which, as the saying goes, buttered exceedingly few parsnips. A few half-measures, a dose of consultants and talk of an operational plan followed, but nothing much happened.

By 1984, Solly could look back with some pride at his achievements as President and Secretary of the Society. He had saved it from disintegration and collapse and sustained its position as an institution of scientific importance. His success was the more remarkable for having been achieved at a time when he had other heavy and time-absorbing commitments. Few men would have found the will or the energy which Solly provided in abundance. An outsider could have been forgiven for concluding that it was Solly, not the Society, who owned the Zoo and that the Society was his instrument. There is no doubt that, at least in the first half of his time there, he raised money, he breathed new life into the place and he looked after the staff, he put up new buildings and he provided interesting prizes for award-winners. Royal visits, which he planned with care and particularly enjoyed, were an acknowledgement of his success. On one occasion he arranged that he would welcome the Queen under a certain tree; he changed his mind, however, when one of the senior Keepers, Joe McCorry, mentioned that the tree normally harboured a host of starlings which, disturbed by such unusual happenings in their immediate vicinity, might well give Her Majesty an unexpected form of greeting. He gave dinner parties there which caused him to claim that he had all but ruined his liver in the Society's interest, and were a source of irritation to many who would have been pleased to attend, had they been invited. Those who were will remember walking round, drink in hand, on a summer evening, and being reminded of the world's marvels.

Some at least of the Society's problems survived Solly. The substantial endowment fund which he knew to be necessary to preserve it against times of adversity was still not in place. Old buildings, some listed, were in need of repair. Limited space made improvement difficult and ruled out expansion. There remained also the anomaly, to which he drew attention in the last annual report issued under his rule, that 'the public can visit the Natural History Museum to study dead animals free of charge, but has to pay to look at the living ones in our national Zoo'. Solly's pride and joy in the Zoo, once an asset, became a handicap, in that it permitted no rivalry and made little room for successors. He was not given to admitting error, but he may perhaps have wondered whether he had stayed too long. Facing a severe bout of inflation and increasing competition, there was no one with Solly's science, energy and contacts who even looked like being a successor. His retirement left it with a barely noticeable pulse.

In 1984, a symposium was held at London Zoo to celebrate Solly's eightieth birthday. Appropriately, it focussed on conservation in the wild and in captivity; it dealt with the part played by comparative medicine and by governments. It marked his close association with the Society over more than half a century, his foundation of the Institute of Zoology and the launch of the International Zoo Yearbook. It recognised his part in introducing 'hard science into the field of animal conservation' and what he had achieved in the modernisation of the two zoos in Regent's Park and Whipsnade. The symposium was 'a small mark of our appreciation of his leadership'. That 'small mark of our appreciation' was not intended to create a great stir in the outside world and it did not do so. Had the Society been by its cast of mind more demonstrative, it might have been moved to do more and say more about the man who almost certainly saved it from extinction. Scientists, however, do not ordinarily give, nor do they seem to expect plaudits from their peers. True to its scientific character, the Zoological Society of London has neither trumpeted its own achievements nor saluted its principal servants. A visitor today will not see or hear much of Stamford Raffles, who founded it, or Solly Zuckerman, who saved it.

9

A Stimulating Tutorial

'I however became interested in almost everything.'
SZ as Chairman of the National Resources Committee

COMMITTEES ARE the digestive organs of Government; they take in, grind down, assimilate and put out a huge mass of material, much of it waste. Despite a pronounced aversion to boredom, Solly was able to switch his attention on and off like a torch; he could also pick out nuggets of interest from heaps of less appetising material. Such abilities, coupled with his liking for being in places where things happened, enabled him to describe the years of his part-time activities in Whitehall as 'a stimulating tutorial'.

In 1946, while he was in the course of deciding to go to Birmingham, Solly had on his hands sufficient unfinished business to require from time to time his presence in Whitehall. As Scientific Director of the British Bombing Survey Unit (BBSU), it fell to him to write a report on the RAF's bombing of Germany. The Air Ministry, fearing that his report would only revive arguments and open up old wounds, received it without enthusiasm. For a long time they gave it only limited circulation, giving Solly the impression that, had it not been for Tedder's influence as Chief of the Air Staff, it might have been quietly buried for all time. His second task, winding up the Oxford Extra-Mural Unit which he had put together in the early months of the war, took time but presented no major difficulty. Membership of the Science Advisory

Committee, set up in the closing months of the war by the then Minister of Works, to advise the Cabinet on matters of science, was important in that it gave him a hallmark of respectability.

The Committee sounded more significant than it was. In origin it was probably not meant to be much more than a polite nod to scientists generally, acknowledging that they had been useful in war without going so far as to admit that they might also have their uses in peace. Solly's only recorded memory was of it ranged round the new Minister of Works, George Tomlinson, for a photograph as if they were a football team and he its captain. Lacking the muscle to do more than tie up its own bootlaces, reporting to a minister low in the pecking order and offering advice to those who showed no interest in receiving it, the Committee had few friends and no admirers. It would have been a simple matter for Solly to uncouple himself and go away; he chose not to do so. Instead, bypassing Tomlinson, he wrote to the Deputy Prime Minister, Herbert Morrison, suggesting that since it cut no ice, it should be wound up and replaced with a science secretariat. Morrison's response, not unusual in such circumstances, was to set up a committee and invite Solly to serve on it.

The Barlow Committee, so named after its Treasury Chairman, was charged 'to consider the policies that should govern both the use and the development of the country's scientific resources over the next ten years so as to facilitate forward planning in those fields which are dependent upon the use of scientific manpower'. The Committee, perhaps weighted down by such grandiose expectations, could only manage proposals which were safe, predictable and dull: the annual output of professional scientists should be doubled and there should be an Advisory Council on Scientific Policy (ACSP). For Solly, however, the Barlow Committee was important. Without the nudge to Morrison and his advisers, reminding them of his existence, and without their positive response in inviting him to serve, he might well have vanished from the Whitehall scene. Had he done so and devoted himself to science, focussing upon some major research project, it is at least possible that he would have put himself in the running for a Nobel Prize.

At that time peace was beginning to creep like a slow unwilling

1. Solly, aged 10

2. In Cape Province, South Africa, 1919

3. In liberated Tobruk, February 1943

4. Professor of Anatomy,
University of Birmingham, 1950

5. 'It is better to find out than to suppose': Norfolk beach, 1954

6. With Cony Jarvis and Alec Todd, President of the Royal Society, in Norfolk, *c.* 1958

7. With Nanou, Gaston Meyer's wife, in Bordeaux, 1957. Solly wears the hat of a member of the Commandeurie du Bontemps

8. A gathering at home in Norfolk, 1959: Solly standing (*right*) and Joan sitting (*left*)

'Sir Solly tells me that he's pretty sure that the Russian panda is "one of those"!!'

27.ix.64

'Ah well, I suppose we can't expect even the Americans to go on footing the bill for rockets and for Elizabeth Taylor'

11.xii.62

9. Cartoons given to Solly by Osbert Lancaster

10. Stella

11. Solly in Norfolk, *c.* 1963

12. November 1961, Washington: with Harold Brown (Director of Defense Research and Engineering) on the *Sequoia*

13. Aboard the aircraft-carrier USS *Enterprise, c.* 1964

14. With Khrushchev (*left foreground*) and Averell Harriman (*right foreground*) at the signing of the Test Ban Treaty, Moscow, July 1965

15. At the UN Chemical/Biological Warfare Conference, Geneva, January 1969

16. With George Bush, then Congressman for Texas, *c.* 1970

17. In the Galapagos, with Lord Mountbatten, Prince Philip and Princess Alexandra, 1971

18. Cutting his birthday cake, 1974

19. At the home of Aubrey Buxton, with Lord Brabourne, Prince Philip and Aubrey
Buxton, Sutherland, August 1976

20. Solly on his seventy-fourth birthday with Anita Mandl

21. At the opening of the new Lion Terraces in 1976, Charles Clore, Vivien Duffield (his daughter) and Vivien's daughter are presented to the Queen on her visit to mark the fiftieth anniversary of the Zoological Society of London

22. Solly leaves the Chapel Royal after the Order of Merit service. Harold Macmillan is on the left, Henry Moore on the right

23. With Edward Heath at a farewell dinner given for Solly at the Zoo, 15 May 1984

24. With Peter Krohn on Solly's eightieth birthday, 1984

25. With the Queen Mother, Robert Armstrong and Joan, 1987

26. At The Shooting Box, 1988

27. Solly with Denis Healey at the unveiling of his portrait by Derek Hill

28. Solly and Joan

dawn over the nation. While it pushed back – imperceptibly at first – the clouds and shadows of war, it revealed a changed world and a host of problems, new and baffling. The government of the day looked to committees to find answers to unanswerable questions, or, failing that, at least to give the impression that they were doing their best. Although Solly uncharacteristically had declared he was unnerved to find himself a member of the Barlow Committee, closeted with members of the scientific establishment, and taken aback by Morrison's invitation to join the new Council, he soon shed such cosiness and, with Patrick Blackett, won and enjoyed the reputation of being a Young Turk and a radical. Solly admired this good-looking, independent-minded nuclear physicist, a future Nobel Laureate, but thought him to be something of a one-man army fighting for reason. As with most such armies, Blackett, convinced that he was always right, tended to ignore both the status and the arguments of those opposed to him, and to lose more battles than he won. Learning perhaps from him, and more weather-wise, Solly was careful about whom he took on and why. He steered clear of pitched battles he could not win. He was, however, disturbed to find that Blackett had not been included among those invited to join the Council, and had some doubts about accepting himself; he nevertheless did so.

The Council affords an excellent example of how we in this country are accustomed to handle our affairs. First, there was a perceived need that in scientific matters, of which they had little knowledge, ministers should have available the best possible advice. Secondly, there was the proposal of a committee chaired by the Second Secretary to the Treasury that a Council should be set up for the purpose. Thirdly, eminent scientists were prepared to participate. Sir Henry Tizard was the first Chairman and, when he retired, Lord Todd succeeded him. For fifteen out of the seventeen years of its existence, Solly was Deputy Chairman. The processes of erosion, however, set in before the Council even met. In the interests of security, the Council was precluded from the whole area of defence. It should not interfere in matters which were the responsibility of individual Government departments; nor should it intrude into the territory of the quasi-independent and prestigious Research Councils. There was concern also that the Council should do nothing to interfere with the right of individual scientists to go their own way. As if to make sure that the Council would not be a nuisance, it would meet only monthly and so would not have time to look at anything in depth. Thus there was born an organisation so hobbled as to be incapable of fulfilling the purpose for which it was set up. Those who thought it up must have been pleased to have found a way of keeping scientists happy and quiet.

Those who had looked for a prestigious source of independent advice must have been disappointed. How, one can only wonder was it possible in the first instance to persuade men with knowledge, ability and integrity to join an organisation so clearly lacking in muscle? How were they enticed to remain, despite an almost total lack of achievements.

Invited early on in its life to study the national migraine of poor productivity, the Council embarked upon a series of intricate bureaucratic manoeuvres which had no very obvious point. It appointed a sub-committee. The sub-committee divided the subject into four panels, handing a part to each. The sub-committee, duly rewarded with a rise in status, became the Committee for National Productivity. Two years and two White Papers later, three of the four panels were abolished. The only panel to survive the slaughter was the one whose remit was Imports Substitution, which was chaired by Solly. As a further sign of the importance attaching to nomenclature and status, the panel then became the Natural Resources (Technical) Committee, its functions being unchanged. Solly, as its Chairman, cherished it for what it taught him rather than for anything more notable. Beyond what he himself learned from its proceedings, Solly regarded the Committee's achievements as minimal. Agriculture and forestry were, he thought, the only area in which it helped significantly.

The need to increase livestock production and yet avoid expensive imports of feed caused Solly and his Committee to look to improved grasslands as an alternative source of protein. By 1948, he had learned enough to write a paper on the subject, which Tizard submitted to the Chancellor and the Lord President, with the result that a major campaign to improve the country's grasslands was launched. Pleased to find Nye Bevan, with whom he had long been on friendly terms, enthusiastic in his support for the campaign, he mentioned it to Morrison and was surprised to be taken to task for having even spoken of it to Bevan: 'In future you leave the politics to me.' The incident taught him that the affection of ministers for their colleagues is subject to evaporation.

To complete the circle, the Council, having lived on for as long as seventeen years with nothing much to its credit, was replaced in 1964 by the Council for Scientific Policy, which after only a few months was itself replaced by The Central Advisory Council on Science and Technology. The last named, as Solly, its first Chairman, delicately put it, 'fell into disuse' following a change of government.

The Natural Resources Committee under Solly's Chairmanship, meanwhile, applied itself to the task of reducing the country's import bill by finding either home-produced alternatives or cheaper sources. He spent time studying and absorbing information concerning whatever was on the Committee's agenda: steel, copper, tin, zinc, carbon black, synthetic wood, tanning materials; he visited a sulphur mine in Sicily, tin mines in Cornwall, and in Birmingham he learned about the great mix of materials, some valuable, some toxic, which found their way into the city's drains and the country's rivers. Whatever they proposed and in whatever direction they looked, there was always an impact on the environment to be taken into account. Solly found it surprising that, in assessing the support needed for agriculture and forestry, no account was taken of environmental factors; nor was account taken of the possibility that, in a hungry world, food shortages might one day again be a problem. The farmer received for his product what his customer was ready to pay or what governments thought appropriate. The need to preserve farming land from being entombed in concrete had somehow been forgotten.

In the fifteen years from the end of the war to the time when he became a Chief Scientific Adviser and a top-ranking civil servant, Solly spent more than half his time in Whitehall, familiarising himself with the extraordinary ways of Government. As an outsider, he examined and advised on a great range of matters. In the course of it, he learned a great deal, not only about the problems themselves, but also about the processes and the atmosphere of

Government. He learned about the relationships between ministers and officials; he became familiar with the world of the Gentleman in Whitehall, who in Douglas Jay's immortal words knew better what was good for the people than the people knew themselves. The range of problems, larger by far than any ordinary educational curriculum, included scientific manpower, pollution, the cost of imports, improvement of grasslands, the use of toxic substances in industry and agriculture, productivity, and latterly the cost of government-financed research and development.

There is no precise record of how many government committees Solly sat on, or the number of meetings he attended over the years; nor, though this would be interesting, is there any analysis of the value of his labours. Beyond his own education, he himself judged it meagre. During the year preceding his move to higher things, there were two more committees which deserve mention. For a short time he chaired an Air Ministry Scientific Policy Committee, which considered deterrent policy. The Committee thought, for a start, that it was illogical to describe as the basis of national security a weapon which, if used, would provoke devastating retaliation. It went on to ask, without ever being answered, what the word credible meant when applied to the deterrent. It could mean that, if attacked, Britain would respond with nuclear weapons, or it could mean that the weapon system itself was both technically sound and invulnerable to attack.

Another assignment, and one which brought him back to Defence, was to chair a high-level committee set up at the behest of the Treasury, to consider the management and control of R&D carried out by government departments or research councils. Military R&D has long been a source of concern to those who pay the bills. It would be interesting to know whether or not those who purchased the English long-bow for use in battle at first attempted to resist the blandishments of its designers or were worried later by the cost. What is sure is that by the end of the century in which Agincourt was fought, Leonardo da Vinci, superb as artist, sculptor and military engineer, showed himself also to be a considerable arms salesman. He urged upon Count Sforza a whole catalogue of devices which might help to bring about the defeat of an enemy. Solly, as Chairman of the Defence Policy

Research Committee, with some sympathy for Count Sforza, was fond of quoting a letter which Leonardo wrote 1483:

> Having, most illustrious Sir, seen and considered the experiments of all those who profess to be masters in the art of invention of the apparatus of war, and having found that their instruments do not differ materially from those in general use I venture, without wishing injury to anyone, to make known to your Excellency certain secrets of my own.

There followed a list of items which Leonardo could provide: a process for the construction of light bridges; the means of tunnelling, draining moats, constructing scaling ladders, mining and destroying fortresses, producing cannon easy of transport and capable of ejecting inflammable matter or catapults. What Leonardo was saying to Count Sforza was that anyone buying his equipment would have an immediate advantage over his enemy. It was not, in essence, different from what mammoth engineering concerns were saying to armed forces and to their political masters five centuries later. It took that length of time to achieve the sophistication of a full-blown nuclear arms race and the participation of northern governments propelled by media pressures.

In the second half of the twentieth century, with, so it is said, more scientists at work than in all the preceding centuries put together, the amount of money required to equip the Armed Services and keep them up to date continued to spiral beyond anyone's power to control. The Treasury, more than a little restive at what it saw as a lack of effective financial management, insisted on a high-level, no-holds-barred inquiry. The ACSP, precluded from Defence and from intruding on government departments and research councils, would not suffice; so Solly was called on to chair a small and well-informed committee of five members. The problem was the way the eventual cost of defence projects regularly outstripped the original estimate by a large margin. Experience showed that a well-worded proposal for some new device with a keen potential user in tow, preceded by a barrage of scientific and technological data, was a hard combination to put down. Moreover, once money had been spent, the project developed a momentum that was irresistible. There would never be a right time to stop. Cancellation would damage industry, destroy jobs, involve writing off large sums and deprive the military of a key element in their plans, essential if they were to keep up with the enemy. Fear of losing face led people to talk of hopes as if they were facts. Common sense came to look like irresolution, if not treachery. The stories of two projects, one American, one British, are told in the next chapter, on their own, as a kind of cautionary tale. Skybolt and TSR2 both cost hundreds of millions of pounds; neither ever entered service.

The Committee heard a great deal of evidence; it lambasted Service Chiefs and pilloried the Defence Research Policy Committee for lack of co-ordination. It advised of the need for standardisation of weapons between Services and in NATO; it recommended that those responsible for framing operational requirements should have among them someone experienced in scientific and technical as well as operational matters. It advised the Government that cancellation, even when large sums had already been spent, was preferable to pouring good money after bad. 'However much money and effort may have been spent on a project, it is not worth spending more unless the development when finished will meet a real need in an effective way.' By one of those twists of fate which make everyone look foolish, Solly, by the time the report appeared, had himself become Chief Scientific Adviser to the Department it criticised and Chairman of the Defence Policy Research Committee which it castigated. He had little doubt, however, that despite the new Zuckerman procedures his committee had introduced, millions of pounds would continue to disappear down the development drain. What mattered was 'choosing the right projects and the right people to do the job', a precept which no combination of ministers, civil servants and scientists has yet been able to match.

During those early years in Whitehall, Solly seems to have been willing, in the pursuit of knowledge, to sit on almost any committee considering any subject. A summary of wartime researches into wound ballistics; a fuller report on the vulnerability of human targets to fragmentation and blast weapons; standardisation of weapons; smaller calibre rifles; dogs as mine detectors; all were additions to his huge workload. Much of it showed no useful result, but for Solly even the wild goose chases, the non-runners and the streets which led nowhere added something to his store of knowledge of Whitehall procedures, and his paramount need always to be doing something.

An invitation in 1959 to spend May and June in California offered a welcome respite from the insoluble problems of R&D and troubles at the Zoo. A chance to catch up with friends, the Gershwins, the Alfred Hitchcocks and the Charles Laughtons, was one not to be missed. Such people were always to him a source of interest and fascination, as indeed he was to them. What engaged and held his attention was the flame which gave them lift-off, and loosened a little the hold that earth's gravity has on ordinary men. The Gershwins had taken him up and made much of him on his first visit to New York in the early 1930s when he was penniless and unknown. Charles Laughton and his wife Elsa Lanchester had been frequent visitors to his small house in Oxford, which the actor enjoyed filling with his huge voice. Alfred Hitchcock had become a friend during the German Blitz on London, when Solly was studying bomb damage; they used to have supper together at the Savoy. Hitchcock's habit of sending him a case of claret from time to time was a welcome though not essential buttress to their friendship.

The California visit proved to be a good deal more than just an interlude, a holiday, after which he would continue as before. Soon after arriving, a letter reached him from Sir Richard Powell, Permanent Secretary to the Ministry of Defence, inviting him to become the Department's Chief Scientist. While he declared himself to be greatly disturbed, as he always did on such occasions, his doubts were more than equalled by the pleasure the invitation must have given him. The prospect of being in the inner circle of Government at that level cannot have been other than gratifying. There were, it is true, matters to be discussed such as his responsibilities in Birmingham and the Zoo, and he would not have wished to seem over-eager. Since, however, there was at the time no one within range with whom to talk things over, he left the question open till his return.

Meanwhile he applied himself to the role of visiting Professor to the California Institute of Technology at Pasadena and to the Commencement Address at the annual awarding of degrees. His subject, 'Liberty in an Age of Science', while of abiding interest to him, was less than enticing to a large audience of young men and women who had just been awarded their degrees, their proud parents or even the academic staff. Encased in heavy academic robes – he was never averse to dressing up – even Solly must have found that the plough did not move easily through the ground on that hot afternoon. Only in the last three lines of an address which ran to fifteen pages of typescript did he even mention the degrees handed out or those who had received them. Then he gently sprinkled them with cliches: being younger than most of those present, they would have longer to influence the shape of the future; the institution was famous as a fount of new knowledge; its reputation would be safe in their hands.

That day he was addressing questions about science, its meaning and worth to mankind, to which no one could be sure of the answers. He quoted George Gissing, who at the end of the nineteenth century was writing of how he hated science, which he saw as the remorseless enemy of mankind. 'What science is that', asked Solly, which is 'the enemy of mankind?' His concern was how and whether the cracked bottles of democracy could contain the new, virile wines trodden out in the unceasing process of scientific discovery. Science, he reminded them, had always revolutionised society; long ages ago it taught nomadic tribes animal husbandry and crop cultivation and caused them to settle. While the discoveries of recent years might, and probably did, transcend those of the rest of history, what was unprecedented was the speed with which they were disseminated and applied. 'The political and economic consequence of all this scientific activity will prove far more profound than those which resulted from past epochs of discovery.'

Science, he pointed out, was already determining choice. People were already enjoying the benefits of scientific discovery in many fields and wished to continue to do so. Neither rich nor poor would choose to arrest the process even if they could; it was irreversible and all but impossible to check. A popular yearning for some kind of control over scientific discovery, for time to reflect, discuss and debate, would involve a loss of time without adding to knowledge, and might even stifle the process of discovery. If that vital process was to continue, there could be no restraint upon the scientist to roam where he pleased. The nature and magnitude of potential discovery could not be defined in advance; nor could the scientist be held responsible for applications of which he knew nothing and over which he had no control. 'Faraday, Hertz, Curie – what could they have known of the ultimate uses to which their discoveries would be put in the field of electric power, wireless and nuclear energy; or of the social and political consequences of their uses?'

The scientific facts which transformed people's lives became more and more difficult to comprehend: 'The element of the unknown in Government increases with every step now being taken to apply the fruits of science.' The questions he asked were hard to answer and getting harder all the time. Did the Government or anyone else have either the power and the knowledge to decide which scientific development should be supported and encouraged, or were we simply obliged to live with and adapt to whatever came out of Pandora's scientific box? He ended his address with the plea that an understanding of social and political purposes was an aim of the liberal arts that could not be realised until their scope was widened. They had to find room for an understanding of the science which was rapidly transforming our intellectual and material environment. In a world where change was powered by scientific knowledge, it would be sensible to include a better understanding of science among the aims of the educational system.

Those who deliver such discourses, the fruit of long experience and earnest thought, are often mortified to find that the wisdom they are aiming at their audience is somehow not hitting the target. Although his speech on that hot afternoon may not have done so, it was an important statement of the conviction of a lifetime that, while all over the known world the influence of science is paramount, governments back away from it and are unwilling to make room in their ranks for scientists. Failure to come to terms with science could later take them in directions which they neither expected nor wished to follow.

By way of a postscript to a chapter dealing with committees and the use made of them by British governments, it is appropriate to find room for Solly's opinion. He did not know, he wrote in a letter in 1962, where the planners stood, but of one thing he was becoming quite sure: 'the human mind cannot operate lucidly and with genius in the atmosphere of a committee'.

10

Skybolt, TSR2 and the Harrier

'Man is the Reasoning Animal. Such is the claim. I think it is
open to dispute.'

Mark Twain

IN 1957, the year after the Suez fiasco, the Government understandably took a long hard look at Britain's defence commitments, at their effectiveness and their cost, and at what the
country could afford. They concluded that National Service,
costly, and, from a military point of view inefficient, should go.
Improved air defences meant that subsonic manned bombers
would find it increasingly difficult to penetrate Russian air space.
The costly V-bomber force would therefore be phased out. Their
key role in the deterrent would pass to Blue Streak, a liquid-
powered ballistic missile then being developed. The fears
expressed at the time that, installed in easily identifiable fixed sites
within the small space of the UK, it would be unduly vulnerable
to a first strike nuclear attack, continued to gain ground. Two
years and some millions of pounds later, the project was scrapped,
leaving Britain's cherished nuclear power status dependent on
American willingness to sell either Skybolt or Polaris. The two
Air Forces, American and British, fearing that the development of
long-range ballistic missiles would leave them without a strategic
role, were determined to retain the manned bomber. Skybolt and
TSR2 (Tactical Strike Reconnaissance) offered the means of
doing so. Although at the time Solly arrived at the MoD both

projects were only in development, such was the power of wishful thinking that, in the minds of their designers, makers and potential users, it was only a question of time before they became operational realities.

Skybolt was always a complex and highly sophisticated project. An air-to-ground ballistic missile would be carried to a precise and predetermined point outside Soviet air space. There it would be released and, with inbuilt knowledge of its own location and that of its target, at once lock on to the latter and proceed on course to attack it. The TSR2, in order to penetrate Soviet airspace, would have a capability of a 1,000 mile low-level all-weather supersonic dash; in other words, it would fly at supersonic speeds at a level below the enemy's radar screen in all weathers.

What must be a source of surprise is that the two Air Forces and the British Government should so completely have lost sight of the fact that Skybolt was never more than a project, attended by a number of unsolved technological problems. Moreover, they seemed not to hear the rumbles of doubt given out with notable candour by men highly placed in the American administration from the beginning. Herb York, head of the American Directorate of Defense Research and Engineering, and his Deputy, John Rubel, briefed Solly originally in Washington in March 1960, soon after he had become Chief Scientific Adviser. Rubel particularly emphasised how his own introduction to the project by the American Air Force had been 'almost insulting in its superficiality'. He had asked General Le May, then Deputy Chief of the Air Staff, 'Do you know how much has already been spent on Skybolt?' Le May: 'No'. Rubel: 'About $10 million. Do you know what you have got for that?' 'No.' 'You have reports about as thick as that pile of papers. Do you know what they're worth?' 'No.' 'About as much as the paper they're written on.' Rubel went on to warn that Skybolt was highly speculative and that the manufacturers, Douglas, were facing major technical difficulties. It would be some time, he said, before the US would be able to decide whether the project would survive and that it was as yet far too early for an inter-government contract.

A week or so later in Washington, Harold Macmillan obtained Eisenhower's agreement that as the British Government was cancelling Blue Streak, it should be allowed to buy either Skybolt or Polaris, the latter being a ballistic missile with a nuclear warhead carried in and launched from a submarine. Macmillan, understanding both to be in full development, preferred Skybolt, which, in prolonging the operational life of the V-bombers, would go some way to justifying the huge investment which they represented. At a meeting attended by Harold Watkinson, Solly and Richard Chilver in Washington, Rubel repeated the negative and gloomy briefing which he had given Solly two months before. Despite that, a Memorandum of Understanding, which can never have been more than a pious hope, was signed by the two Defence Ministers, Gates and Watkinson. The US would do its utmost to complete the R&D work; the UK would buy a hundred missiles, if they were completed. For the sake of appearances – it can hardly have been for any other reason – a form of financial and technical agreement followed.

Meanwhile, from the two Air Forces, the manufacturers and the RAF officer posted to the Pentagon there came a regular flow of reassuring messages. Although the British officer had access to Rubel and could easily have checked with him had he wished to do so, he was content instead to pass on the comfortable messages which he knew the Air Ministry would be happy to receive. By contrast, the information Solly received from his contacts in the higher reaches of the American Government, two Secretaries for Defense (Gates and McNamara), the Science Advisers to successive Presidents (Kistiakowsky and Wiesner), all conveyed the contrary view. While there is no reason to doubt Solly's assertion that he passed on what he heard, there is at least a lurking suspicion that, out of a desire not to upset the RAF, he spoke too quietly. He even began to wonder if he had lost all credibility, or if it was just another instance of there being none so deaf as those who do not wish to hear. Whether the Air Ministry view would have carried the weight it did, had there then existed a unified Ministry of Defence, is at least an open question.

Early in 1962, President Kennedy, over lunch in the White House, told Julian Amery, then UK Minister of Aviation, that there were doubts about the Skybolt system and that the British Government should not place too great a reliance upon it. By that time, however, so much had been made of its wonders and its key role in the deterrent that it was looked on in this country not as the project which it still was, but as an established fact. Amery, deeply shocked, responded with vigour: it must be made to work; without it Anglo-American relations would take a considerable jolt. Such words, however, availed nothing against the reality of rising costs and unsolved technical problems. A warning from McNamara led Solly to pay another visit to Douglas, the manufacturers; he had been there twelve months before and had come away reassured. Given a clear outline of all that needed to be done before a fully guided launch of a prototype took place in October, he again came away comforted. Brown and Rubel, whom he saw on his way home, soon let the air out of his revived hopes. Their information, from people they had working at the plant, was that there was no chance of any such trial being possible by that time. Wiesner's information was to the same effect.

In September 1962, Peter Thorneycroft paid a first visit to America since becoming Minister of Defence. He and Solly were invited by Kennedy to accompany him on a visit to NASA's space centres. 'You'll enjoy it,' the President said to Solly; 'you'll never see so many billions of dollars being spent in so short a space of time.' Harold Brown, watching Wernher von Braun as he introduced his team of German rocketeers to the President, remarked, 'They haven't had so grand a day since they were introduced to Hitler at Peenemunde.' On the crucial matter of Skybolt, Solly took the opportunity to call in on McNamara and to remind him of the storm which its cancellation would cause in the UK. Barely a month later (October 1962), he learned from Washington that the news of Skybolt was bleak. Another month passed before McNamara, with the agreement of the President and Secretary of State Dean Rusk, told the British Ambassador, David Ormsby-Gore, that cancellation was almost certain; and on the following day telephoned to Thorneycroft to confirm it. When McNamara and Thorneycroft met in London, their points of view could hardly have been further apart. As McNamara saw it, Skybolt had failed five tests and he was simply cancelling a project which had proved to be not only costly but unworkable. He offered to hand it over as it stood to the British. Wisely they did not accept. For

Thorneycroft, however, it remained a betrayal; the UK had relied absolutely on America. 'Did the US want to deprive the UK of its independent nuclear status?'

Less concerned with the politics and the loss of face, Solly understood very clearly the American position. They had, in his view, cancelled a development which should never have been started, to which the British had contributed nothing and for which the Americans had no military need, but which, in some marvellous way, 'the British had identified as their independent deterrent'. While the Americans fully understood the significance which in British eyes surrounded Skybolt, the British, in Solly's view, failed to give proper weight to the financial and inter-Service problems which McNamara faced: 'nor did we have experts to match John Rubel and Jerry Wiesner in assessing the technical feasibility of the Skybolt concept as a whole'. This inclination to sympathise with, if not to share, American opinions, upset a number of his British aviation engineering colleagues. A meeting in London in December, at which the argument moved on to whether the UK should be allowed to purchase Polaris missiles, made no progress, but somehow fell short of being a disaster. Unusually for him, Solly recorded nothing about the meeting beyond the fact that it had settled nothing.

Two teams, one American, one British, looked at what remained of Skybolt to see if there was anything worth salvaging. They found nothing; the total bill was five hundred million dollars. The verdict of a member of the White House Staff on the episode was 'a chapter of spoken and unspoken misunderstandings between the leaders of the two sides'. Others put it more bluntly, asking, 'Who was the crazy guy who had thought that an air launched "farting" ballistic missile could have its starting point fixed in space by means of stellar navigation accurately enough to hit a given target in the USSR?'

Following the demise of Skybolt, a summit meeting between Kennedy and Macmillan took place at the end of 1962 in Nassau. In order to avoid giving the affair too much of a military flavour, the Prime Minister left Mountbatten, the Chief of the Defence Staff, behind and took Solly with him. Solly's role in the proceedings turned out to be that of a fascinated spectator. The meeting was eloquently described by the US Under Secretary of State, George Ball, as 'probably one of the worst prepared in modern times'. For the British, and for Macmillan personally, the starting point could hardly have been worse. What was to have been the core of Britain's whole defence policy had disappeared; moreover, it followed immediately on that chill weekend in Rambouillet when de Gaulle delivered his magisterial rebuff to Britain's request to be allowed to join Europe. The two Ministers of Defence, McNamara and Thorneycroft, had reached a point at which further discussion between them was unlikely to be helpful.

Macmillan's performance was accounted a *tour de force*; he required that Skybolt should be replaced by Polaris, in such a way as not to suggest that Britain's status as a nuclear power was being downgraded. Kennedy agreed that the British could purchase Polaris on the basis that they would assign it to NATO with the proviso that it could be withdrawn, should the British government decide that 'supreme national interests' were at stake. After some hectic drafting, the agreement was enshrined in a document of which Arthur Schlesinger said, 'the drafters outdid themselves in masterly ambiguity'. Certainly no one has ever been able to say what in that context was meant by supreme national interests. Another unusual aspect of that extraordinary meeting was that no one so much as mentioned price. When this came up afterwards, McNamara proposed that the UK should contribute the same proportion of the development costs as the number of missiles bought bore to the total cost of the whole production run. Harold Macmillan was 'much concerned' and instructed the British Ambassador to offer instead 'to add 5 percent to the retail cost'; McNamara was indignant, but agreed. The repercussions were much what the Americans feared and Solly expected. In addition to his 'Non' to Britain, de Gaulle also took France out of NATO.

While no one spoke in quite such a vein about the Tactical Strike Reconnaissance system, the story was not dissimilar. In September 1960, the Prime Minister asked Harold Watkinson, then Minister of Defence, to take a look at both the Buccaneer and the TSR2. Both were fighter bombers, one for the Navy and the other for the RAF, the Buccaneer being at a more advanced stage of development. The similarity of their roles prompted the question, were both needed? Watkinson in turn looked to Solly for a personal review. Unwilling to become involved in an inter-Service dispute, Solly walked delicately, though not delicately enough to avoid the deep suspicions of Sir Thomas Pike, Chief of the Air Staff. The question, as Solly saw it, was, 'Were we being asked to pay too much . . . in order to satisfy needs that were possibly illusory'? He did not understand, nor was anyone able to tell him, how significant in relation to the aircraft's vulnerability were the greater speed of the TSR2 over that of the Buccaneer and the ability to fly supersonically at a lower level. The cost and weight of the aircraft and the difficulty of finding space for the increasingly complex avionics were matters of deep concern. Despite these grave worries, Solly's report concluded rather lamely that, if the operational requirement could not be relaxed, the technical specification should stand. The RAF, which throughout had refused even to consider an adaptation of the Buccaneer, insisted that it could not.

A meeting called by Watkinson with the Chiefs of Staff did not change anything; most of the talking was done by Sir Thomas Pike and by Solly himself. Mountbatten, who said little, explained afterwards in a personal note to Solly that, while he agreed with him, he could not appear publicly to challenge his RAF colleague. What he did not make clear to Solly was the extent to which, behind the scenes, he was supporting an inter-Service version of the Buccaneer. Following that meeting, Watkinson was able to persuade the Prime Minister that the TSR2 should go ahead; the contract for the engine having been placed towards the end of 1959, the one for the air frame was accordingly placed in October 1960. Watkinson later wrote of what a tough battle it had been; 'it was only achieved by my putting my total Ministerial and personal influence behind the project'.

While it is not difficult to understand the reluctance of all concerned to think in terms of cancellation, it is surprising that ministers who knew that the original specification had been breached, made no move in that direction. The cost and the weight had risen dramatically, and in particular the overall take-off weight had increased from a specification of 70,000lb to nearly 100,000lb. In 1960, Peter Thorneycroft, who had resigned two years earlier as Chancellor of the Exchequer, returned to the Government as

Minister of Aviation, in which position he must have learned all there was to be known about the problems of TSR2. Having replaced Watkinson in 1962 as Minister of Defence, he observed to Solly that the TSR2 was 'an albatross round our necks' which was seriously distorting the entire military procurement programme. Despite that, he continued to plead with the Treasury for support. That such an intelligent and courageous Minister should have continued to back the project while holding the views he did shows just how large the project loomed in the eyes of both the RAF and the aviation industry; scrapping it had become unthinkable.

Since the albatross would not of its own accord fall from around their necks, ministers saw no alternative but to continue to live with it. The problems, however, continued to multiply; increasing technical demands meant that the aircraft could not come into squadron service before the late 1960s. Ferranti warned of difficulty in fitting in all the avionics and that the aircraft was itself becoming so complex that supersonic flight would not be possible in all weathers at tree-top height. The cost, weight, size and engine-power required continued to chase each other upwards. There were other competitive designs – the F111 and the French Mirage – and apart from the RAF, still there were no buyers.

In October 1964, a new Government took office, with Denis Healey as Secretary of State for Defence. Asked again for his personal view of TSR2, Solly provided Healey with an update of what he had given to Watkinson three years earlier and he recalls him going over it line by line. Even for a new Government committed to reducing defence expenditure and scrapping the TSR2, cancellation of so longstanding and prestigious a project was not easy. The effects upon the industry, the RAF's capabilities, and jobs, and the loss of a huge investment, held the Government back until April 1965, when it finally took the plunge.

As Healey himself wrote later,

> My decision to cancel the TSR2 strike-reconnaissance aircraft was more difficult. The original estimate of its cost in 1960 had tripled to £750 million in the four years before I became Minister. Though its original target date for delivery was 1965, in 1964 there was still at least three years' development to go

before the RAF got its first operational plane. The programme over ten years was likely to cost at least £250 million more than the American alternative, the swing-wing FIII. However, the Prime Minister, Harold Wilson, was worried about announcing its cancellation with the other decisions, on 1 February, 1965; he preferred to smuggle it into the Chancellor's Budget speech in April. So I had to keep development going for purely political reasons at a cost of over £1 million a week until 6 April; I was deeply conscious of what could have been done with that money for more useful purposes.

Although Solly attracted the dire suspicions of the RAF, there are no grounds for believing that his undoubted misgivings were decisive. Indeed, the question can fairly be asked, why did he not make these clear to the Prime Minister directly when he had every opportunity to do so? Macmillan is on record as having expressed doubts in 1963, 'What will it cost? Will it ever fly?' There can be little doubt that the fate of the project was settled by three factors: cost, complexity and, to a lesser extent, competition. Frank Cooper who, from various positions in the Air Ministry and later the MoD was never far from the centre of the argument summed it up: 'An extraordinary and complex story. Cancellation was inevitable.'*

Healey then secured the agreement of the Cabinet to purchase the American FIII in the face of strong opposition from the Prime Minister (Harold Wilson) and the Minister of Aviation (Roy Jenkins). The subsequent cancellation of the order brought Healey to the brink of resignation; he had, after all, persuaded the RAF to accept cancellation of the TSR2 on the understanding that they would get the FIII instead. In the event, he held back, having heard from Antony Head the tale of his resignation as Minister of Defence after Suez. It seems that on his way out of Number 10, Head saw Duncan Sandys and realised to his horror (and too late) that Sandys was to be his successor. For Healey the moral – never resign without knowing your successor – came powerfully to mind and, fearing that if he went his successor would be Crossman, decided to stay.

---

* *TSR2 with Hindsight* (RAF Historical Society, 1988).

One reason given for cancelling the TSR2 was that it served no relevant strategic purpose. In Solly's view it therefore made no sense to purchase the American F111 as a replacement. He made use of his less formal position as scientific adviser to the Cabinet to lobby a number of Healey's colleagues against the proposal. In doing so he made things difficult for Healey, who in all the circumstances was both generous and understanding. The upshot was that Solly moved from the Ministry of Defence to the Cabinet Office with the title of Chief Scientific Adviser to the Government as a whole. Only a slight brush of face powder was needed to make the move look like a promotion. Whether it was or not, Solly had no option but to accept.

A third project, contemporary with both, was the P1125, which survived to become the Harrier. There were times when it seemed doomed to follow the other two on to the scrapheap, but it worked and it was lucky. To lift the aircraft vertically off the ground required an engine with a thrust of some 19,000lb. The Americans, always doubtful of TSR2, were interested and concerned that the Treasury might refuse proper backing. Interested also in the variable geometry or swing wing★ principle, they wanted to know if it could be incorporated. Solly inquired of Sir Arnold Hall, then Managing Director of Bristol Siddeley, who told him that he was already having sufficient difficulty in raising the performance of the engine to the level required without that further complication.

Events then took a turn of which Solly's account is scarcely credible. Returning from America, where he had been on an official visit, he learned that the RAF, never much interested in the P1127, had persuaded the new Minister of Defence, Peter Thorneycroft, that were a jump-jet aircraft ever to be developed for military service, it would have to be supersonic. Such an aircraft (dubbed the P1154) would require engines with a 30,000lb thrust, more than double the amount at that time attained from the engine for the P1127. According to all the best advice he could get, such a performance level was not then possible. Solly describes

---

★ After take-off the profile of the aircraft could be changed so that it took on that of a bullet, with lower wind resistance.

himself in his autobiography as staggered: 'I nearly went through the roof.' He could not, so he would have us believe, do anything about it because the Prime Minister, 'briefed very differently from the advice that I would have given', had given the project his blessing. While it is certainly possible that a new minister coming from Aviation would have known about and sympathised with the RAF's view, it is inconceivable that matters could have moved so quickly as to have caused Solly to have been confronted with a *fait accompli* of which he had no previous knowledge. Moreover, it would surely have been his duty, had it been so, to inform both his own Minister and the Prime Minister of his belief that a wrong decision had been made.

The project, however, was allowed to continue until 1964, when Healey cancelled it. Indeed, it was only with difficulty that he was persuaded, largely by Fred Mulley (then Minister for the Army) not to throw out the P1127 at the same time. The Americans continued to be interested, though McNamara, suspecting that the British wished to settle things at a high political level without too much detail, refused to release the funds required until detailed drawings were available. Eventually the Harrier emerged, having survived the changes and chances which stem from Government, and gave a good account of itself in action. It is still with us.

Crossman's question, asked afterwards in his memoirs rather than at the time, is one which many ministers concerned with such matters may have asked, but which few have answered, at least in public. 'How can Cabinet come to a sensible decision, when none of us know what these things really are?' Solly (in *Monkeys Men and Missiles*) echoed Crossman's question with one of his own. 'How indeed can Cabinets come to sensible judgements about the political consequences of technological ideas which they do not usually have the time even to try to understand?'

11

*The MoD and the
Zuckbatten Axis*

'He both fuelled the CDS with ideas . . and acted as a brake
on Mountbatten's impetuous extravagancies.'
Philip Ziegler, *Mountbatten*, 1985

B Y 1960, Solly constituted a morsel too large and indigestible to
be swallowed whole by Whitehall. As Chief Scientific Adviser
to the Ministry of Defence, he possessed unrivalled knowledge of
what he described as the macabre science of destruction. He
understood that terrible as conventional bombing was for those
who were in its path, its effects were local and possible to repair.
Moreover, it was seldom decisive. Area bombing of the towns and
cities of Germany did not of itself bring victory; the huge weight
of bombs dropped on Vietnam brought only death and destruction. As Chief Scientific Adviser, Solly needed to get a measure of
the destructive power or energy yield of the first two atomic
bombs which had destroyed Hiroshima and Nagasaki compared
with that attained with high explosives. He had to learn how later
versions of nuclear and thermo-nuclear weapons had developed
since, and consider their impact upon war.

Unusually he began his career in the Civil Service at the top
level, with the rank of Permanent Secretary; he also had access to
the Prime Minister, at that time Harold Macmillan. Had he
accepted Tedder's invitation to become his Scientific Adviser at the
Air Ministry after the war, he would either have lost his independence or found himself rejected as an intruder when Tedder

retired. He would certainly not have been in a position – nor was anyone else – to team up with Mountbatten and then assail, as he did, the whole strategic thinking of NATO on the role of nuclear weapons.

Offered the post of Chief Scientific Adviser in 1959, Solly was in the powerful position of being wanted. Moreover, having built up a substantial scientific department in Birmingham, he was recognised as an academic scientist of note; by his work at the London Zoo he had won a considerable reputation. He had also learned in a long apprenticeship the strengths and weaknesses of Whitehall; its ability to ride out almost any storm, its shyness of science, its taste for procrastination. He had renewed his wartime contacts in America and made others. Acceptance of the post on offer would make him a top-ranking civil servant in a Department concerned with matters of which he possessed exceptional, if not unique, knowledge. Sam Way, Maurice Dean and Eddie Playfair, Permanent Secretaries of three of the Departments most concerned, were his friends and admirers. When Solly's name did not appear on the first list of possibles, all three had protested and inquired why. In Mountbatten as Chief of the Defence Staff he had not only a friend and admirer, but someone whom he could feed with ideas and who would cause others to listen. So long as Mountbatten was there, it was said that Solly could walk on water.

He had, however, no wish to give up his work either at Birmingham University or at the Zoo. Not only would it mean putting aside laurels he had won, but he would forfeit that touch of reassurance which his visits to both gave him. Accordingly he made acceptance of the Government post conditional on his being allowed to remain in charge of his Department at Birmingham and as Secretary of the Zoo. As Vice-Chancellor, Sir Robert Aitken was prepared in the circumstances to agree that Solly should continue in his post as Professor of Anatomy, even though he would be spending the greater part of his time as a civil servant in Whitehall. The Zoological Society of London was hardly in a position to object; not only had he recently won a notable struggle against a tiresome rebel element, but he was the one who had pushed and shoved the Society into the twentieth century. Moreover, it paid him nothing. The Government, anxious to secure him, having fussed a little about allowing such flexibility to a civil servant, fell in with the arrangement; though Duncan Sandys, the Minister responsible, found it hard to understand why he should wish to continue to serve an institution which generated problems, but resisted solutions.

Once the Government and the University had agreed to Solly's terms, no barrier remained to his accepting the post. Moreover, Mountbatten's pleas were reinforced by his wife; Dickie's success as Chief of the Defence Staff would, she said, depend upon his having Solly to work with him. He, however, was not to be hurried into a decision; apart from anything else, she enjoyed being courted. A call from Bob Robertson, Chairman of the Pentagon's main scientific advisory board, urging him to accept and promising all possible help, finally decided him. So after much havering and hesitating he became in January 1960 Chief Scientific Adviser to the Ministry of Defence. His role was that of a one-man think tank and included the Chairmanship of the Defence Research Policy Committee. In rank, and this was a matter of great importance to him, he would be on the same level as the Permanent Secretary and the Chief of the Defence Staff. He was also, though this was to remain secret, to be the scientific adviser on defence policy and disarmament to the Prime Minister, Harold Macmillan. Such an outcome made him think that he had been right to wait and to decline such earlier opportunities as Whitehall had offered. He was now in on his own terms.

He had no problem in coming to terms with the top echelons of Whitehall. He particularly took to Richard Chilver, the Deputy Secretary, who became the most treasured of his Whitehall tutors. Chilver had had, like Solly himself, rigorous standards and, like Solly, had little time for those who failed to meet them. He accustomed himself quite quickly to files circulating like food to battery hens, to be pecked at and passed on, and to attending meetings at which nothing much happened, but which served to ventilate the system. Rows of empty bookshelves yawning at him caused him some unease; a threat, if they were not removed, to fill them with jars containing anatomical specimens was sufficient to make them disappear. He acquired a taste for intrigue, more because he enjoyed it than for anything he gained by it. Frank Cooper's illuminating comment, 'Solly was a rotten bad intriguer, he had that terrible streak of integrity', was plumb in the middle of the target.

Whitehall's processes have something in common with those of a concrete mixer. Though less drastic, they move people round and mix them together in such a way that those inside develop a community of outlook and approach. The system does not explain itself. To do so would not only be difficult, it might be a source of awkwardness, since explanations only prompt more questions. Above a certain level there is only room for men and women of exceptional ability who understand and cherish the system and who also have an eye for the future, looking for those with the ability to take over from themselves. They are members of an elite who would never use that word, and who even in these times do not relish self-advertisement. If they could arrange it without drawing attention to themselves, the windows of their offices would probably be made of glass through which only those inside can see. It was exactly the kind of club to which Solly relished belonging, even if he did sometimes feel obliged to break one or two of its rules.

As a newcomer, he needed first to look round and to get an idea of the country's defence commitments and the resources available to meet them. He took in the ruinous cost of the arms race and the terrible advances in destructive capability that a new generation of weaponry had brought with it. To update himself on nuclear matters, a visit to the United States was the first step. Recent relaxation of the McMahon Act at least made it possible for Americans to talk to their sometime allies and to show how things had moved since those first explosions of 1945. Solly had need too of people to guide him within the Department, and to explain him to the Civil Service staff, most of whom had never encountered his like before. One enquirer was assured that he would be like champagne after draught lager beer. Of his skill in pulling together a staff – he called them his équipe – there can be no doubt. Clifford Cornford came to Whitehall from the Royal Aeronautical Establishment at Farnborough after much coaxing, but having done so, he ended up as Chief of Defence Procurement, one of the few to break out from the scientific fold and into the top level of the Civil Service. His task was to look after Solly and keep him informed on the hardware requirements and their supply. Rather oddly, he once complained that Solly had such an effect upon him that he could neither think nor speak in his presence. He survived, however, with distinction. Robert Press had a role in nuclear matters similar to that played by Cornford in equipment. Having been involved since 1948 before the first British atom bomb was tested, he was well qualified. When in 1966 Solly went to the Cabinet Office, he took Press with him.

Within the Department, in addition to Cornford and Press he still required someone to keep an eye on technological developments and on policy generally. Believing government scientists in general to be vassals who saw it as their duty to provide a veneer of scientific respectability for their masters' policies, he sought help from Sir William Penney, Chairman of the Atomic Energy Authority. He suggested Terry Price who was then working for the Authority at Winfrith Heath and was looking at the time for a chance to work in London. Hearing of the post that was on offer, he enquired, 'Does Zuckerman carry much weight?' The answer 'None more so' was enough, and he agreed to allow his name to go forward. A meeting at Solly's home at Burnham Thorpe began with a brief statement of its purpose from Solly: 'I need help. The Scientific Civil Service doesn't seem to provide the kind of people I need. The Atomic Energy Authority has a better reputation; Bill Penney has given you good marks. Tell me something about yourself.' They then drove to Overy Staithe, where they went for a walk and discussed how the harbour could be saved from silting up. On their return to Burnham Thorpe, as he got out of the car Solly said, 'I'll tell the Permanent Secretary you can have the job,' adding some welcome details as to its grade.

Solly's judgement of Price, that he had 'a quick, brilliant and independent mind; it was a joy to work with him', marked him out as unusual; there were few of whom he spoke in such terms. In return, Price considered Solly dazzlingly quick to grasp a point; he avoided so far as possible the painstaking and time-consuming preparations for an important occasion that other men would make. He was interested only in what he personally judged to be important – a luxury not available to lesser folk. He read fast but made no attempt to read everything: 'Don't worry about the paper, the issues will make their own priorities.' Price quotes Richard Chilver with approval: 'You can say many things about Solly, but you cannot say he was made of common clay.'

The Ministry of Defence, when Solly first joined it, was a modest, inconspicuous affair, lacking in muscle and housed, as if apologising for itself, in offices which were no more than an annexe of the Treasury. It was a half-measure, admitting the need for a single Ministry in charge of Defence, but taking only a meagre step towards one. In the war, as Prime Minister and also Minister of Defence, Churchill had muscle of his own to ensure the co-ordination and compliance of the three Service departments. In 1951, he again assumed the role, but this time on a temporary basis, pending the return of Lord Alexander from Canada, where he was Governor-General. For more than a decade, an anaemic centre was left with the impossible task of co-ordinating the three Service departments, which were united in resisting any move which threatened their independence and in a grudging acceptance of Buggins's turn as a means of deciding priorities. Not until the spring of 1964 was Thorneycroft, as Minister of Defence, with the powerful backing of both Macmillan as Prime Minister and Mountbatten as Chief of the Defence Staff, able to bring the three departments together. Only then did the new ministry, by that time thirteen years old, gain effective control over the three Service departments. The change, long overdue, was one Solly particularly welcomed, since it brought with it the establishment of a single Operational Requirements committee reducing the potential for confusion and waste.

Having had time to explore, Solly's summing up of the situation was both clear and devastating. The Ministry of Supply was still supporting weapon development contracts which, having their origins in war, had somehow survived. As was made clear earlier there were as many as four new fighters – three were cancelled later – in various stages of development. The RAF was insisting on the TSR2 while the Navy was going for its own aircraft, the Buccaneer. For good measure there were the HS681, a military transport, and the P1127, which became the Harrier. In the early stages, Solly strongly favoured the cancellation of the last on the grounds that, having taken off vertically, it had only a limited range; only later did he become a supporter. On the civil side were the Concorde and the Viscount. Many of the procedures and attitudes of mind were little more than wartime relics, which had long outlived their purpose. Overall he was concerned to find Britain, with diminished resources, still shouldering many of the commitments of an empire which belonged to history.

One early cloud on the horizon, a sign of disagreement to come, was the requirement of the Permanent Secretary, Sir Henry Hardman, that all advice to the Secretary of State should come through him, having been co-ordinated by his office. Mountbatten demurred; he did not think the Chiefs of Staff would agree to their advice being thus filtered. Likewise, Solly did not relish the idea of scientific advice being put through the bureaucratic mixer by people who, not being scientists, would not understand its significance. With neither the make-up of a team player nor the inclination to become one, he was not prepared to give up his right to say what he wanted, whether or not it fitted in comfortably with the views of the Department or even with those of his own staff. Such a declaration of independence at an early stage in the life of the new Department doubtless caused Hardman some discomfort; he had started life as an economics don and was inclined to fussiness. It could well have been, as Solly thought, a contributory factor to his removal from the Department two years later.

Not long after Solly's arrival he found himself looking again at military R&D, this time as Chairman of the Defence Research Policy Committee, the same body that only a few months ago he had been roasting for its lack of effectiveness. Since the bulk of its substantial budget of some £10 billion was already committed under existing development contracts, the Committee was not much more than a gentlemanly forum for sharing out between the Services the relatively tiny amount of new money that was available. A useful reform which might remove some of the debris would be to require that every Government Committee, as the first item on its agenda at the beginning of each year, should review its achievements in the previous twelve months. If these were insufficient, the committee would be obliged to justify its continued existence or be wound up.

Haunted always by the memory of his beginnings and with no wish to return to them, Solly shared with the legendary Walter Mitty a lack of self-assurance. Searching constantly for something he did not have, he almost certainly envied Mountbatten and, given the choice as to who he would like to be, might well have opted to become the man who was now to be his partner and his champion at the Ministry of Defence. Admiral of the Fleet Earl Mountbatten of Burma, Destroyer Captain, Chief of Combined Operations, a Supreme Allied Commander, the last Viceroy of India and Chief of the Defence Staff, was a man who naturally drew attention to himself. Tall, good-looking, bred in the purple, he was a great-grandson of Queen Victoria.

His unique career is proof enough of his qualities; without them no amount of privilege or good fortune would have carried him so far. His faults, however, were so eye-catching as to divert attention from his merits and could even, at times, eclipse them. His appetite for the trappings of military life, uniforms, medals, swords and ceremonial was insatiable. His tendency, to which Solly drew attention, to tell of things as he would have liked them to be rather than as they were, and to hog the credit, caused him to be mistrusted by most of his fellow Chiefs of Staff, Gerald Templer, Thomas Pike, Sam Elworthy and Caspar John. Templer is credited with the comment – there are other claimants – 'Dickie, you're so crooked that if you swallowed a nail you'd shit a corkscrew'. Frank Cooper, an admirer of Solly, and a future Permanent Secretary of Defence, thought that Mountbatten's faults so grated on the nerves as to provoke opposition to whatever he proposed. His love of applause and curtain calls led him to claim credit which belonged at least in part to others. While a single Ministry of Defence might never have come about without the determined support of a prominent military figure such as Mountbatten, there were other players. Harold Macmillan as Prime Minister and Peter Thorneycroft as Minister of Defence both had a part in it. The two ministers readily acknowledged the importance of Mountbatten's role; sadly and mistakenly, he talked and behaved as if the whole idea had been his from the start.

As Chief of the Defence Staff, he tended to think that he was in charge of everything down to the smallest detail; one exasperated general observed that he seemed to think it his business to control every platoon battle anywhere in the world. Philip Ziegler, in a notable biography, saw Mountbatten's vanity as childish, but also monstrous. He admitted to being irritated at the way in which Mountbatten 'sought to rewrite history with cavalier indifference to the facts to magnify his own achievements'. In order to maintain his own balance, Ziegler placed on his desk a notice to himself, REMEMBER IN SPITE OF EVERYTHING HE WAS A GREAT MAN. Ziegler's acknowledgement of his own reaction and of his need for that simple reminder somehow helps the reader to look beyond the tangle of human weaknesses and to see the full stature of the man.

No one looking at Mountbatten and Zuckerman earlier in their lives would have recognised them as likely partners or would have foreseen what they achieved together. Occasionally they had their misunderstandings, as on one occasion when at a meeting Mountbatten was unwell and Solly, as a medical doctor, offered him advice: 'Good God, Solly, I'd no idea you were a doctor, I thought you were a vet.' Ziegler saw Solly as complementing Mountbatten admirably: 'sceptical, iconoclastic, analytical yet brilliantly perceptive, he both fuelled the CDS with the ideas that were to shape Britain's policies over the next five years and acted as a brake upon Mountbatten's impetuous extravagancies.' A book could be written about the relationship of these two out-of-the-ordinary men. If proof were needed of their mutual affection and admiration, it was provided by Solly's anguish at Mountbatten's murder and the steps he took to see that that sad and shattered family received the best medical treatment.

Mountbatten, the more generous of the two, readily acknowledged Solly's stature. He believed that, without Solly's insistence on bombing the French railway network, Overlord might have gone sour. He called him the cleverest man in the world. Solly, on the other hand, more inclined to seize on faults, did not hesitate to draw attention to them. 'Dickie was not a great reader' carried the message that, unlike himself, Mountbatten was no intellectual. 'In the latter part of Dickie's life, fancy about the past had a strong tendency to replace reality.' Both men were ambitious, both were arrogant, though in Solly's case the arrogance might have been a shield covering a lack of self-assurance. Both might have had difficulty in spelling the word humility or even saying what it meant. A shared taste for intrigue, often counter-productive, caused those who worked with them to be on their guard. Frank Cooper believed that their propensity for making enemies and the closeness of their alliance – the Zuckbatten Axis as it became known – caused the enemies of either to be the enemies of both.

Solly's need of Mountbatten and his regard for him 'despite everything' were constant reminders that, whereas he was free to think and speak as he wished, Mountbatten was not. Whereas Solly believed that the use of small or medium nuclear weapons on the battlefield would result in escalation, Mountbatten's advisers – the Joint Planners, his own creation – on the other hand, thought it would be unlikely to do so. Accepting, or even being seen to attend to, Solly's advice meant that the Chief of the Defence Staff was not only questioning the established wisdom of the time on which the whole of NATO strategy was based, but that he was turning a deaf ear to the advice and opinions of his own staff. An invitation to air his views on the subject at the 1961 SHAPEX gave Solly the chance he needed to express his doubts on an occasion when they would be noted. Mountbatten encouraged him to speak out plainly, but was not at that stage able to endorse all the Chief Scientific Adviser said; that came later. The speech Solly made on the occasion when General Norstad as Supreme Commander took the chair involved for NATO a wholly new look at the strategy on which all its thinking and planning had been based. During his first years at the Ministry of Defence, his alliance with Mountbatten, his friendship with key Americans and a substantial degree of ministerial support made Solly inviolable. The arrival in office of a Labour Government and the reliance placed upon him by the new Prime Minister further strengthened his position.

Such phases, however, cannot and do not last. Solly's disagreement with Healey, Mountbatten's retirement and his own removal to the Cabinet Office served to diminish rather than enhance his status. The time came for the old order, which must have found Solly to be something of a burr under its saddle, to recover lost ground. There was also the need to avoid another similar intrusion in the future. He sought in vain for a guarantee from Burke Trend, Secretary to the Cabinet, that when he, Solly, retired, he would be replaced and at his level. When eventually Solly retired, he was succeeded by Sir Alan Cottrell at a lower level. Three years later, when Cottrell in turn retired, the duties were taken on by Robert Press at a still lower level and the title was allowed to lapse. Cabinet Secretaries have this in common with elephants: they do not forget, nor do they lose the opportunity to correct error.

Mountbatten's conversion to Solly's view that nuclear weapons had no military use was the most important outcome of their partnership. Together they succeeded in dismantling the great network of scaffolding which propped up the established wisdom of the time, that nuclear weapons were just a step up in the already terrible weaponry of war. During the war, Solly persuaded Tedder that the bombing of enemy communications was crucial and Tedder carried that message to persons and places Solly's voice might not have reached. In the Ministry of Defence twenty years later, it was Mountbatten who, persuaded that it was right, carried Solly's message and thereby invested it with the authority of the Chief of the Defence Staff. It was a milestone not only for the two of them and for NATO, but for mankind. There was at least a chance that sanity might prevail.

12

The Nuclear Arms Race

'The men in the nuclear weapons laboratories . . . have
become the alchemists of our time . . . They may never have
been in battle, they may never have experienced the
devastation of war, but they know how to devise the means
of destruction.'

SZ (p. 106, *Nuclear Illusion and Reality*)

THE TWO explosions which in 1945 destroyed Hiroshima and
Nagasaki brought an abrupt and unexpected end to the
Second World War. They signalled too the beginning of an arms
race which at times looked as though it might lead to a third.
Possession of nuclear weapons was perceived to be the prerequisite
of safety, particularly by the Russians, who spared no effort first to
acquire the secret and make the bomb. Thereafter they were determined at least to match the Americans in the capacity to destroy.
Churchill's famous warning of an Iron Curtain dividing Europe
heralded the blockade of Berlin, the seizure of Czechoslovakia and
the successful testing of Russia's first atomic bomb. The West's
response was the establishment of NATO and the decision of
President Truman to set in train further development of all forms
of nuclear weapons including the so-called super or hydrogen
bomb. East and West, the Warsaw Pact and NATO, drew each
other into an arms race which, since it had no finishing post,
neither could be sure of winning. Although, as Solly wrote at the
time, a reopening of the shooting war would only add to 'our load
of misery', there were those on both sides of the Atlantic and both
sides of the East-West divide who began to see war as not only
possible but inevitable, even necessary.

As fear of Russia mounted in America, so the cancer of McCarthyism grew and flourished. It grew to a point where it could be said that there were many Americans who hated Russia more than they loved America. Robert Oppenheimer, the brilliant physicist who, as head of the Manhattan Project, directed the development of the first atomic bombs, thought the H-bomb unnecessary and said so with the full support of his committee. It would only add a new and horrifying level to the destructive power which already existed without contributing in any way to the security of the United States. Such an attitude was tantamount to treason in the eyes of men such as Edward Teller – a theoretical scientist, as Solly contemptuously called him – who believed that safety lay in numbers of bombs and in possessing the maximum of destructive power. Fearful lest Oppenheimer's opposition might discourage other scientists from working on the new project, Teller set out to unfrock him. The FBI was brought in, and on the say-so of the American Atomic Energy Commission, chaired by a friend of Teller, Oppenheimer's past was dredged for any shred of evidence that he was of the Left and therefore a security risk. That, in Solly's view, decided the matter and Oppenheimer, despite the massive support he received from the scientific community, was doomed. Teller's determination was such that he even told an official of the Commission that whatever the outcome of the hearings, he wanted Oppenheimer 'unfrocked'. The success he enjoyed in that grubby mission justified Rabi's dismissal of him as an enemy of humanity and cast a murky shadow on those who stood by and allowed it to happen.

Solly and Sir John Cockcroft (Director of the Atomic Energy Establishment at Harwell), hearing of Oppenheimer's disgrace, were deeply shocked. The incident showed how, in a climate of suspicion and hysteria, wisdom and integrity can be assailed and swept aside by the wicked or the mad. Looking back, it seems terrible that a man with Oppenheimer's record could have been thus trodden underfoot and that those in power did not see fit to intervene. Cockcroft commented that it would take America decades to get over it. In 1956, the ill-starred Suez venture and the Russian move into Hungary jangled nerve ends. Two years later, the launch of Sputniks I and II showed that the Russians could reach any target of their choice, and that America had some catching up to do. There never was a moment during those years when people were able to breathe easily or to think clearly. East and West continued to face each other like two heavyweight boxers, grunting rather than breathing or speaking, each aiming to be ahead of the other on points; each fearing the knockout blow, each ensuring that they possessed the capacity to deliver one. The money poured out as if there was no tomorrow, and there were times when it seemed there would not be one.

Such was the fevered temperature of the world when in 1960 Solly arrived at the Ministry of Defence. Until then, his role in Whitehall, tacked on to that of an academic scientist in Birmingham, had been to advise on how Britain could best tackle the problems and the changes that were the legacy of war. A new cause for concern was the impact upon the environment of the carelessness and dirty habits of a world interested first and last in producing and consuming. In those early years Solly had little involvement in Defence and none at all in nuclear matters. Although Deputy Chairman of the Advisory Committee on Scientific Policy, he had no part in – indeed he was not even aware of – the decision that Britain should develop its own atomic bomb. At a time when the McMahon Act forbade Americans even to discuss nuclear matters with foreigners, his contacts in military and scientific circles would hardly have been useful. Relaxations of the Act and his own arrival at the MoD at once enabled and required him to inform himself for the first time concerning the new dimension of destruction initiated in 1945 and developed since. He needed also to go back to the lessons he had learned first in the towns and cities of England, then in Tripoli and Tobruk, in Sicily and Italy and finally in France and Germany itself. Careful and detailed examination of countless explosions had taught him things which might otherwise have been missed. They concerned the bombs themselves, their weight, type and fusing, the casualties and damage they caused and the targets against which they were most effective. In 1960, he could lay claim to a wider experience in the planning of bombing operations than anyone at that time in high command on either side of the Atlantic.

To learn of what was new and to stitch it into his previous

knowledge, he went on a voyage of discovery. It took him to the major US plants concerned with the production of nuclear weapons at Albuquerque, Los Alamos and Livermore. At the first two, he met those responsible for the design of warheads who, he said, were very patient with someone who at the time knew next to nothing about a field in which they were themselves expert. At Livermore, developed in the first instance by the infamous Teller who was still influential there, the atmosphere was different. One of their products was the neutron bomb, a nuclear weapon which achieved its effects by radiation rather than blast. Intended for use by the military on the battlefield in local situations, it remained, despite some confused and confusing claims that it was somehow humane, a nuclear weapon. Its existence would lower the nuclear threshold, its use would trigger the use of larger and more devastating weapons. Another weapon developed at Livermore, the Davy Crockett, was a small bazooka which launched a nuclear warhead and could be carried by an infantryman.

What shocked Solly was the fascination that such devices had for those who were working on them and their keenness to produce weapons of ever more devastating power than those already available. None of them had ever been near a battlefield; none seemed to have had any thoughts as to the reaction of soldiers on either side to such weapons when used, nor any conception as to the consequences for humanity. Their eagerness to see a resumption of testing was just part of the picture.

Added to the huge growth in their destructive power since 1945, was the increased number of nations in possession of both the weapons and the knowhow. The speed and accuracy with which they could be delivered to their targets was a further dimension to the horror. Whereas in 1945 only the Americans knew the secret of the atom, at the time Solly was writing four or five other nations possessed the knowledge, and the number has more than doubled since. In 1945 delivery was by piloted and vulnerable subsonic aircraft. By the 1960s, the development of the Inter-Continental Ballistic Missile made it possible to hit any target on earth, with no defence being available or in prospect. Confusion within the one-time Soviet bloc, far from reducing the dangers, has added to them. The need of each nation achieving nuclear status to test its warheads has led to pollution and brought progress towards a comprehensive test ban treaty almost to a halt.

Reflecting on the developments of the fifteen years that had passed since their first use and what he saw as likely to follow, Solly reached certain clear conclusions, from which he never departed. First, atomic weapons were the most terrible anti-personnel weapons ever devised. Secondly, while their possession might deter an aggressor, once that barrier had been passed, there would be nothing to restrain or limit the devastation that would follow. Thirdly, their usefulness on the battlefield was a delusion. The distinction between strategic and tactical use was unreal, and in any event, escalation would be certain to follow, regardless of the size of the weapon. In essence and put in simple terms, nuclear weapons had no military use and NATO's strategy of relying on them was misconceived. At the time this thinking was heresy, but like other heresies, it became in due course respectable. When in 1966 he left the Ministry of Defence, Denis Healey was able to say, in a light-hearted speech after a farewell dinner, 'Sir Solly has no longer any right to lecture the Defence Council, because we have all accepted his views on nuclear weapons.' One needs to recall something of the background clamour, the doubts, tensions, suspicions and fears of the Cold War, to appreciate what a struggle it must have been to reach that point, dislodging on the way the views and opinions which had taken root over fifteen years and to which there had previously been no serious challenge either in military or political circles.

Some years after Solly's retirement, he remained so disturbed at the lack of understanding on the part of politicians, the military, the media and the general public that he wrote *Nuclear Illusion and Reality*. In it he brought the salient facts together. Shocking when he wrote them, they remain so today. The first two atomic bombs, exploded over Hiroshima and Nagasaki, killed 140,000 people. A further 100,000 died within months. Far from being the last word in destruction, they were just a beginning. Compared with a modern armour-piercing shell, they were the equivalent of a terrorist's home-made grenade. By 1982, when Solly wrote *Nuclear Illusion and Reality*, ten times, a hundred times the amount of explosive power could be packed in a single warhead, weighing less than a fifth of either of the first two nuclear devices. The largest weapon ever tested, according to an authoritative UN report, 'released an energy approximately four thousand times that of the atomic bomb that levelled Hiroshima', and there was, so the report went on, in principle, no upper limit to the explosive yield that may be attained.

Not until 1983, more than twenty years later, did he ever come across a clear account of what happened when a nuclear shell was fired. Bernard O'Keefe, a man experienced in the testing of warheads, published his account of a test which Solly believed to be unique in the West. A gun was fired by pulling a lanyard and those present at the exercise immediately jumped into a trench, from which, as O'Keefe wrote,

> I watched the fireball churning its way thousands of feet up into the sky, visible for fifty miles around, the familiar mushroom cloud identifying it to all the world as a nuclear explosion, then the shock wave, very powerful in the trench, rattling windows in Las Vegas, ninety miles away; I was aghast . . . My dark glasses protected my eyes against the first flash. What of the soldiers on a battlefield? The first flash would sear the eyeballs of anyone looking in that direction, friend or foe, for miles around. Its intensity cannot be described; it must be experienced to be appreciated. The electromagnetic pulse would knock out all communication systems, the life blood of a battle plan. In addition to its effect on troops in the vicinity, everyone for fifty miles in any direction who lived through it would realise that it was a nuclear explosion. It would seem like the end of the world, and it probably would be, for any man who had a similar weapon under his control who had a button to push or a lanyard to pull, would do so instinctively.

Having read that report, Solly wondered if all records had not been deliberately buried by those responsible for the test, for fear that it would show beyond all doubt that the weapons they were struggling to produce would be unusable in battle.

With the limited knowledge available at the time and barred in the nature of things from making experiments, Solly realised that if he was to have any chance himself of understanding the effects of nuclear weapons, let alone explaining them to others, it would be necessary to rely on 'war games'. Accordingly, in the autumn of 1960 he set up the Joint Inter Service Group for the Study of All-out Warfare (JIGSAW). The first exercises were to consider the consequences of a single one-megaton bomb exploded over Birmingham and of one of twenty kilotons over Carlisle. Birmingham, the studies showed, would have been devastated; one-third of its million inhabitants would have been killed at once by blast or fire or died from a lethal dose of radiation. 'Within a radius of a couple of miles from the point of burst there would have been total destruction and few survivors.' Carlisle, with seventy thousand inhabitants, would have suffered similarly, the proportion of people killed the same or a little less, 'but the survivors would have had just as terrifying a problem to contend with – fires, roads blocked, no water supply, no food, radioactive fall out, and so on'. Whereas in our time we tend to dismiss the uncomfortable from our minds, Solly deserves credit for having to the end of his life persisted in reminding people of the risks. We may all feel more comfortable for ignoring them, but the habit of doing so has not made us safer.

Increasing concern that the enthusiasm of designers and producers of weapons would cause them to lose sight of the horror of the whole picture led him to invite George Kistiakowsky (then Eisenhower's science adviser at the White House) to come to London, bringing with him some other members of the President's Science Advisory Committee (PSAC) for informal and off-the-record talks. Not the least of Solly's assets was his ability to get on terms with those in high places in the United States, win their confidence and persuade them he was himself worth listening to. That meeting was the first of a series carried on biannually, involving five different science advisers. They came to an end only when Nixon abolished the post and the PSAC as well. Despite his formal subordination to the ministers he was advising, Solly needed no permission from them, or from the Chiefs of Staff or from anyone else. He could invite whom he pleased; all he required were the funds to pay for his guests' entertainment. When it came to a return match in Washington, Kistiakowsky, more hemmed in by rules, needed the approval of at least three top people.

Solly's address, 'Judgement and Control in Modern Warfare' to SHAPEX 1961 (NATO's annual conference) was in response to a suggestion from General Norstad, then Supreme Allied Commander, and Bob Robertson, his part-time science adviser, that the question of battlefield nuclear weapons should be aired. Mountbatten advised him privately to 'prepare a real shock piece'. It comprised his thoughts of a year or so on nuclear strategy. He used the studies made of the results of theoretical nuclear strikes against Birmingham and Carlisle. He 'rubbed in' the fact that NATO's plans included nuclear strikes far behind the battle line and he reminded them of the vulnerability of the control apparatus, which would be the first casualty, leaving the commander of the operation without either information or any means of controlling the battle. No nuclear war game, so far as he was aware, had ever indicated the possibility of victory for the defenders, only death and disaster. It made no sense to rate nuclear weapons as tactical or strategic. Recent developments in weapons showed them to be the product not of the men who commanded operations, but of those in laboratories and factories who had never been involved in the heat and confusion of battle.

What Solly said was received in silence. General Earle Wheeler (Commander in Chief, US Forces NATO), talking with him afterwards, posed the question, 'We have painted ourselves into a corner. How are we to extricate ourselves?' One of those who had contributed to the painting was Edward Teller. At the same conference in the following year, claiming to speak for the whole of the scientific world, he went into raptures about a new and wonderful weapon called the neutron bomb, of which Solly had learned at Livermore two years earlier. It was, he said, a device the Russians would be unable to cope with. Solly, speaking next, said Teller spoke only for himself and his band of acolytes. Mountbatten weighed in, publicly for the first time, and trounced as 'military nonsense' what Teller had been saying about the neutron bomb, which was not new, but was a nuclear weapon. General Wheeler's question remains unanswered. So too does the one asked by Mountbatten after the Cuban missile crisis in the autumn of the same year (1962), 'What would we have done if the Russians had not turned back?' The question still awaits an answer. World leaders have brushed it aside.

Failure to answer or even to address these questions suggests that in that 'race between understanding and catastrophe', to which Professor Jerry Wiesner (sometime science adviser to President Kennedy) drew attention, understanding does not look a likely winner. It is so much easier and more comfortable for those with narrow horizons and small minds to stay within their range and win easy applause than to venture out among unknown hazards. To the question, 'how can the world be extricated from the nuclear corner into which it has been painted?' Solly's assertion that only widespread understanding of the realities of possible destruction can provide an answer, before it is too late, has met with little response. 'The brutal fact which our minds seem incapable of taking in is that were the explosion to take place over New York or Washington, London or Moscow, one megaton (the same force as one million tons of TNT) would be equivalent to a million instantaneous deaths.' It would be, as Solly put it, 'a catastrophe unparalleled in the history of warfare and one which would make even the worst natural disaster of which history tells us seem like a gust of wind'. In using such language he spoke, not as some latter-day Jeremiah savouring the gloom of his message, but as one who enjoyed life in all its aspects and whose knowledge was rare, if not unique.

That assessment, still valid today, is neither endorsed nor contradicted, but simply ignored. What could easily become the gravest problem ever to confront the human race has no place – or at least a low priority – on the agenda of politicians who preen themselves in front of the cameras and cultivate comforting images. It would make a welcome change if one or more of them would break their silence and suggest that it is time to intensify efforts to reduce the number of warheads which litter and threaten the world. There are other problems: the number of members of the nuclear club now and in ten years' time; the security of the arsenals and stockpiles; the danger of smaller but still devastating devices getting into wrong hands. Since, as Richard Garwin says in the note included at the end of Chapter 13, 'Nuclear weapons are likely to proliferate to additional states unless their possession is no longer seen to provide status and security'. In the minds of world leaders the subject seems to be relegated to the 'not in front of the children' category.

Learning about nuclear weapons, concluding that they have no military use and persuading others who held a contrary view, was a steep uphill climb. A request from Thorneycroft as Minister of Defence in 1962, for a statement of his personal views on the basic issues covering nuclear and conventional warfare and the use of tactical nuclear weapons, caused Solly to crystallise his thoughts. A first version in the form of an essay entitled *Twenty Propositions* included much of his previous thinking. On its way to and from the Department, it went through some nine or ten editions, growing in length if not in clarity as it did so. A summary is included here to show that minds were on the move and the façade of previously accepted dogma was beginning to crack.

A Government is responsible for the security and survival of the state it rules over; it has a duty to deter other governments from doing things it believes it would be contrary to the interests which it is obliged to defend. No power would deliberately undertake or permit action likely to result in unacceptable retaliation. Just as since 1946 East has been deterred from attacking West, so the West has, as a result of Russia's nuclear capability, been deterred from attacking the East. Since experiments in such a field are not possible, the only yardstick available is that provided by events – hindsight. To be deterred, an aggressor must be convinced of the real risk of retaliatory action and his own destruction. The invulnerability of a retaliatory nuclear force is more important than its size. It is not the number of megatons that tips the balance of nuclear deterrence, but opinions as to the enemy's capability and intentions.

A policy of mutual deterrence is valid until either a realistic defence against inter-continental ballistic missiles becomes available, or a delivery system becomes capable of a first strike so effective as to destroy all or most of the means of retaliation. The more nuclear powers there are, the more deterrent policies may be confused, less effective and therefore the greater the hazard. A NATO strategic force would be difficult to achieve. To be militarily effective, it would need to be under single control, and that might provoke counter-action. Sufficient conventional forces were required in order to contain minor military aggression; the size of the force is as much a matter for political as for military judgement. The notion of using tactical nuclear weapons in the field to redress an inferiority in numbers makes no military sense. It would be difficult to calculate the yield required and, in any event, escalation would almost certainly follow. The deployment, as distinguished from the use, of tactical weapons probably adds to the credibility of the deterrence. On the other hand, it carries with it the risk of accident or disobedience and adds to the difficulties of control. No known systems of command, communication or intelligence would survive the use of nuclear weapons on a battlefield.

The publication by the Government of Solly's SHAPEX address prompted questions as to whether there had been changes of policy. Solly's *Twenty Propositions* paper, having been first circulated within the Ministry was, on Mountbatten's insistence, put to the Chiefs of Staff. While Mountbatten declared himself to be in broad agreement with it, he put to Solly the question whether or not a small number of tactical weapons in the hands of NATO would act as a deterrent to limited aggression. The main burden of Solly's answer was that putting more weapons into NATO's nuclear stockpile would be expensive without bringing any benefit; indeed, it would heighten tension and obscure the real problems. By that time, as the next Chapter makes clear, Mountbatten had moved sufficiently far in Solly's direction to insist that they should be considered by the Chiefs of Staff and the author given a chance to explain them. As matters stood, Mountbatten declared himself as being 'in agreement with Sir Solly Zuckerman's paper'. Sir Richard Hull, Chief of the Imperial General Staff, made clear his total disagreement, putting on two presentations to challenge Solly's view. In the second of them, as many as 200 nuclear weapons, with average yields of 15 kilotons, were assumed to have been exploded in an area stretching from Whitehall to Reading. It was a scenario which Solly said made absolutely no sense to him. Particularly he wondered at the assumptions that the Russians would either not use nuclear weapons at all or that they would use fewer than NATO, and that one of their nuclear strikes would do less damage than NATO's. The argument continued, with Solly stating with increasing conviction that nuclear warfare made no sense militarily and that it would be wrong to pretend otherwise simply to maintain a façade of NATO solidarity.

Whether they are aware of it or not, the most widely shared interest of human beings, old or young, rich or poor, the world over, must be that no nation should attack another with nuclear weapons. There can be no one with any claim to be considered sane, who would not opt to be rid of weapons capable of destroying all civilised life. Yet in a world ruled by suspicion and fear and steered, if at all, by showmen rather than statesmen, no one seems willing to mention the existence of 40,000 warheads. The number is absurdly in excess of what would be necessary to destroy the planet. It is an odd and wrong-headed doctrine that teaches us to pass over a problem which is a source of danger because its solution is difficult. Persistence in doing so has come near to making the possession of nuclear weapons seem like the shirt of Nessus the Centaur: whoever put it on could not take it off again. Dying at the hand of Hercules, he passed it, stained with his blood and bearing his curse, to Hercules' wife, telling her to give it to her husband, it would keep him faithful to her. Hercules put it on and the Centaur's curse proved fatal to him.

13

'A Race Between Understanding and Catastrophe'

'We have found that the men who know the most are the most gloomy.'

Russell-Einstein Manifesto

SCIENTISTS ARE frequently and unfairly loaded with the guilt of having developed nuclear weapons and other attendant horrors. The power of the new weapons to devastate, their proliferation, and the monstrous stockpiles which East and West had accumulated, together constituted an unprecedented threat to the planet and to the human race. The fact that they had only once been used in more than half a century afforded no comfort. If a major conflict were to break out, determination to settle things quickly, fear that the other side would use them first and desperation to avoid defeat would all be powerful spurs to their being used again. If they were, the consequences were likely to be terminal. In 1956, Bertrand Russell and Albert Einstein issued a manifesto – signing it was almost the last act of Einstein's life – calling upon scientists to 'appraise the perils that have arisen as a result of the development of weapons of mass destruction'. They spoke 'not as members of this or that nation, continent or creed, but as human beings, members of the species Man, whose continued existence was in doubt . . . All equally are in peril, and, if the peril is understood, there is the hope that they may collectively avert it.' Halfway through the manifesto, there occurred this laconic but chilling assertion: 'We have found that the men who know the most are the most gloomy'.

A year later a group of scientists from East and West assembled in Pugwash, Nova Scotia. The choice of this little-known village followed an offer from Cyrus Eaton, a wealthy Canadian industrialist, to pay all the expenses of the first meeting, on the one condition that it should take place in the village where he was born, Pugwash. The name was adopted by the movement which that first meeting inaugurated. Such an international get-together of eminent scientists taking place without even the possibility of official chaperonage or political guidance caused the American and British Governments considerable concern. Believing scientists generally to be as politically naive as they, the two Governments, were scientifically ignorant, they saw the event as simply providing the Russians with a unique opportunity to gather information and bewitch the innocent scientists with propaganda. Events showed them to be wrong and that the scientists probably understood the situation and each other better than did the politicians.

At much the same time tripartite talks began in Geneva between Russia, America and Britain to explore the possibility of a treaty in clear and enforceable terms which would put a stop to testing and so halt the arms race. Although a Russian proposal of a moratorium pending the signature of such a treaty was accepted, the subsequent talks meandered on in an atmosphere of suspicion and mistrust until American insistence on on-site inspection for verification of reports of underground tests, and Russian refusal to allow adequate access, proved a breaking point. The Americans then proposed that underground testing should be excluded from the talks and that only tests in the atmosphere, which could not be concealed, should be banned. They would not accept the Russian suggestion that the moratorium on testing in the atmosphere should continue indefinitely pending a treaty. Solly and Jerry Wiesner, President Kennedy's science adviser, exchanging ideas in July 1961, were of one mind in thinking that further advances in nuclear weapons would contribute nothing to national security. Solly raised two questions, the answers to which supported that view. First, if testing were resumed, what weapon could the West develop which would add anything to the deterrent they already had? Secondly, what advantages would the Russians gain if they, but not the West, were able to carry on clandestine tests? The answers to both questions being none suggested that the weeks of argument had been futile.

The atmosphere of mutual distrust permeated every exchange and made certain that whatever one side proposed, the other would reject. Delays, disappointments and recriminations gave hawks on both sides the opportunity to urge a resumption of testing; and at the end of August, the Russians declared that they were about to do so. Some fifty warheads were exploded, mostly above ground, and including one with an estimated yield of 58 megatons. At that point Solly was invited by Bertrand Russell and others to attend a later meeting of Pugwash, which was to take place in Maine. Knowing that Wiesner intended to be present, the Foreign Office, by that time less apprehensive than previously, urged acceptance. Both Kennedy and Khrushchev sent messages of support and one of the Americans present told Solly, 'Before, we would have lost our security clearances if we had attended a Pugwash meeting; this time we have had to get special clearances to show that we can be trusted to be here.' The calibre of the scientists attending was, Solly observed, very high, four being Nobel Laureates. Since at the time of that meeting in 1961 Solly was a civil servant, he went as an observer.

Pressure on Kennedy to follow the Russians and resume testing soon became irresistible and led first to a series of underground tests, and six months later to a series of tests in the atmosphere. To that the Russians replied in August with further tests, including one 30-megaton shot. Further tests by the Americans planned for the following year were, however, cancelled in the face of massive international protest. In their place, negotiations for a partial test ban were resumed, and with them the reiteration of the familiar arguments about how many inspections should be allowed and how large an area they should cover. British belief that recent developments in seismic science made it possible to monitor the observance of a test ban, without the need for on-site inspection, cut no ice with the Americans. Wiesner reported cryptically to Solly that his man (Kennedy) was getting cold on the need to secure such a ban, would Solly get his (Macmillan) to give him a shove. Solly, who throughout was impressed by and wholly shared Macmillan's determination to go for a comprehensive ban on all tests (CTB), thought the West gained nothing by turning down what was on offer. His friendship with Wiesner led to him seeing Kennedy quite regularly, and on occasion alone. At Glen Ora, the President's retreat in Virginia, after dinner one evening, the President repeatedly asked the question, 'Why do you think the Russians are now prepared to agree a partial test ban?' To which Solly replied, 'For the same reason as you should be, because they must be scared stiff about the possibilities of proliferation and the prospect of an unending nuclear arms race.'

In Paris for a NATO meeting in June 1963, Solly, with the prospect in mind of a weekend of superb wine in Bordeaux and food to match, was disturbed to receive a message from the Embassy. President Kennedy was expected to spend Saturday as the Prime Minister's guest at Birch Grove, his country house in Sussex, where Solly would also be needed. Accordingly, he met Joan at Le Bourget, took her into Paris and put her and his suitcase on the train for Bordeaux. He would, he assured her, not fail to be there himself in time for the special Sunday lunch given for him every year by Raymond Dupin. In Bordeaux in 1956, to lecture on the interaction of the nervous and hormonal systems of the body, Solly had taken the opportunity to familiarise himself with 'the magnificent cuisine of the region'. While so engaged he had had the great good fortune to meet M. Raymond Dupin, the owner of Grand Puy Lacoste, one of the great wine growers of the Medoc, and also a shipper. Solly, as was his way, had made the most of the chance to learn and enjoy, and to lay the foundation of a future relationship. He had named M. Dupin his 'godfather in wine' and quickly became both a customer and a friend. Without claiming to be a wine connoisseur in such company, he found 'there was something gratifying in being regarded as a bit of an expert and in always having good wine on our table'.

On this later occasion, time and the need to be at Birch Grove for the duration of Kennedy's visit were against him and the last vestige of a chance to get to Bordeaux in time for that lunch slid away. With no sign either of when he would be needed, if at all, he waited at Pooks, a small house near Birch Grove, the home of the Prime Minister's son Maurice and his wife Katie Macmillan. Looking for something to do and someone to talk to, he found his way to the kitchen where Katie was preparing a mountain of pasta to feed those of the President's high powered escort who were to be her unexpected guests for the night. They included the Secretary of State, Dean Rusk, the American Ambassador, David Bruce, and McGeorge Bundy, Special Adviser to the President on National Security. The sight of anyone with a problem – and Katie certainly had one – as usual triggered Solly into offering a stream of advice. He instructed her on how pasta should be handled, cooked and presented. Katie, anxious to make progress, told him with some sharpness to go away and attend to his sums or whatever it was he was supposed to be doing. He was, he said, too tired and needed a rest, but he still found energy enough to bombard her with unwanted advice.

Later in the evening, he was summoned to the big house and told by Lady Dorothy that he would have to spend the night; he could use a pair of Harold's pyjamas. He continued to wait until eventually the President emerged, looking tired and saying he was going to bed. The Prime Minister, older but indefatigable, took Solly into his study, saying he wished him to help find a book. Fumbling with one on a top shelf, he said to Solly, 'Stand closer, closer still. I am slipping into your pocket the paper which the President gave me stating the objections of the Joint Chiefs of Staff to a continued moratorium on tests. I want you to look at it tonight and give me an answer which I can pass on to the President in the morning.' Solly, back at Pooks, where he was to spend the night on a sofa, read it over but found nothing new, just the old arguments that you couldn't trust the Russians. In the morning, sitting on his sofa, scratching his head and wondering what he could say to Macmillan which had not been said many times before, he was surprised to see Frank Long, a member of the President's Science Advisory Committee and Assistant Director of the State Department's Arms Control and Disarmament Agency. He had with him John McNaughton from the Pentagon. They knew that Solly had seen the Chiefs of Staff note to the President; what was now urgently required was an agreed statement on detection and other matters, signed by both of them, to go to the President and the Prime Minister; here was a draft. After some discussion and a few changes they signed it.

As an event, the sole importance of that gathering at Birch Grove lay in the fact that it happened. It altered nothing, it decided nothing. It required the attendance for a very short space of time of quite a number of prominent persons in a small and not particularly convenient part of Sussex. It must have involved a legion of unknown planners in preparing for every possible need and contingency. The one thing that was sadly missing was an irreverent person with a sharp pen who, without departing from the truth, could have written a hilarious play. For Solly, the bottom line was probably a modest plus; the enjoyment of being in the middle of it all at Birch Grove against the loss of a spectacularly good lunch at Grand Puy Lacoste.

As soon as the farewells were over, Solly dashed off to Bordeaux. Joan recalled that on his arrival, the excitement of the preceding twenty-four hours caused him to take quite philosophically the loss of a lunch which, dish by dish and glass by glass, she described to him. M. Dupin, understanding Solly's anguish, arranged a compensation lunch on the following day at a small inn in the Medoc woods. Twenty-five years later, Solly could still remember every course they ate and every one of the freshly bottled 1961 vintages they had drunk. Not without satisfaction he reflected how improbable it was that any of the other participants in that quite extraordinary event at Birch Grove 'had enjoyed as pleasurable a sequel'.

A fortnight later Solly was in Moscow, as a member of the British team taking part in the negotiations for a treaty banning all nuclear tests in the atmosphere. Sadly, underground testing had by agreement been left off the agenda. While the formal version of the agreed treaty was being prepared for signature, Solly attempted to get the Americans and the Russians to look again at the question of a total ban on all tests. Neither were willing. Although he remained anxious to keep the question firmly on the agenda, he had little opportunity to move things forward until a conference in Toronto three years later, by which time a Labour Government was in office in Britain. Informal talks with those Russians present led to his being invited to Moscow, bringing with him a British seismological expert. Delay in replying to their invitation, and his late arrival in Moscow caused by the cancellation of an Aeroflot flight, were sufficient to awaken Russian suspicions that, for the British, the visit had a political edge to it in addition to its ostensible technical purpose. After a slow start, however, the Russians agreed that Solly could sound out the Americans as to whether they would be willing to resume the technical discussions which had been broken off in 1962. Millionchikov, who had chaired the talks, commented that agreement involving the three nations always proved to be unattainable and it looked as if on this occasion things would go the same way. Harold Wilson and George Brown, then Foreign Secretary, laid it down that the matter was so sensitive that it was not even to be mentioned to any Americans until George Brown had an opportunity to tell Secretary of State Dean Rusk face to face. Solly's view that such an embargo would be unhelpful was confirmed by events. The Americans, aware that something was going on, suspected that the British were trying to take the lead which was properly theirs. The Russians, always suspicious of Western duplicity, saw in the delay the likelihood of a trap.

That failure in 1963 to achieve a comprehensive test ban was to Solly and many of his American friends, including Glenn Seaborg, Chairman of the American Atomic Energy Commission, 'a world tragedy of the first magnitude'. Whereas Solly was advising Prime Ministers whose views he and most of his fellow countrymen shared, Kistiakowsky and Wiesner and others were advising Presidents who lived and worked in the fiercer Cold War climate engendered by those whose aim was to stay ahead in the absurd competition of who could accumulate the most destructive power. It was an aim which Solly considered to be unattainable and, having regard to the huge existing arsenals, meaningless. In the prevailing climate of fear and suspicion, people tended to concentrate on destroying the enemy rather than on surviving themselves. The senseless clamour to increase those arsenals proved, however, irresistible. Political leaders, East and West, were carried along at a pace they could not control to a point from which, though neither has gained anything, withdrawal proved to be all but impossible. The impasse remains. Those who see nuclear disarmament as an essential step back from the precipice, are thought by the politicians to be naive and to ignore the political realities. The politicians, on the other hand, seeing those political realities, and not much else, become hemmed in by them, unable or unwilling to move. Solly's lifelong concern that on scientific matters it was important that a scientific view should be brought to bear, becomes increasingly compelling with time.

Although the original purposes of prevention of nuclear war and disarmament remain central, Pugwash's concerns have widened to embrace chemical and biological weapons, conventional forces, arms transfers and regional security. 'The destruction of the environment on a global scale' was the subject of a special declaration in 1988. Those who attended the first conference were for the most part natural scientists: recently many other disciplines have been included; indeed, as many as 40 percent of the participants have had backgrounds in economics, history, law, political science, psychology and social science. Participants are invited personally; they are scientists and scholars and professional people, speaking for themselves, representing neither governments nor political parties.

The Pugwash movement is unusual in that it confers opportunities upon well-informed people to meet together informally, exchange views and 'contribute to the resolution of the many profound and pressing problems facing human societies all over the world'. Representing no one but themselves, they are not hobbled by the views of governments or their parties; they do not need to look for popular favour. Among the signatories of the Russell-Einstein manifesto was Professor Joseph Rotblat (now Sir Joseph Rotblat); he presided over the meeting which issued it, and is now President of the movement. Asked, at the age of ninety-one, why he did not write the story of his own life, he replied, 'I am still too young, there is too much to look forward to.'

In 1995, Rotblat was awarded the Nobel Peace Prize. In his Nobel lecture he appealed to the nuclear powers, to his fellow scientists and to his fellow citizens throughout the world. He spoke as a scientist, but also as a human being; he saw science as being in harmony with humanity; it was linked always in his mind with the benefits it conferred on people. Never in his earlier years had it occurred to him that he would spend the second half of his life in efforts to avert a mortal danger which science itself had created. He quoted from Solly's address in 1979 to the American

Philosophy Society, 'When it comes to nuclear weapons . . . it is the man in the laboratory who at the start proposes that for this or that arcane reason it would be useful to improve an old or devise a new nuclear warhead. It is he the technician, not the commander in the field, who is at the heart of the arms race.'

Rotblat made three appeals. First, he besought the nuclear powers 'to have in mind the threat to humanity', and to begin to move in the direction of its elimination. Those who signed the non-proliferation treaty were already committed to nuclear disarmament, but they had done nothing. Secondly, he turned to his fellow scientists, begging them to think in terms of the impact of their work upon society and not to excuse themselves with false precepts such as that science has nothing to do with politics. He quoted Professor Hans Bethe, a Nobel Laureate and the most senior member of the Manhattan team at Los Alamos: 'I feel the most intense relief that these weapons have not been used since World War II, mixed with horror that tens of thousands have been built since that time – one hundred times more than any of us at Los Alamos can ever have imagined.'

Rotblat's third appeal was to his fellow citizens everywhere:

Man has acquired for the first time in history the technical means to destroy the whole of civilisation in a single act. The whole human species is endangered by nuclear weapons . . . With the global threats resulting from science and technology, the whole of mankind needs protection. We have to extend our loyalty to the whole human race.

He reminded them of the formidable obstacle that lies in the way, that the abolition of war will demand limitations of national sovereignty. Such limitations, however, should be measured against an alternative as hard to contemplate as its effects would be unendurable. There is nothing in that notable address which is out of tune or does not echo the things that Solly thought and said in his lifetime. It is rare for the experts to be of one mind on such important and large questions; yet on this profound hazard to the human race, the scientists agree but the politicians hang back, hardly daring to frame, let alone express, an opinion.

Three reviews have been made on behalf of the United Nations of the status and function of nuclear weaponry, the first by Solly in 1970; a second by a Swedish friend followed ten years later, with a third by Richard Garwin, eminent American physicist and long time friend and collaborator with Solly. In 1993, shortly before he died, Solly was reviewing *A Nuclear Weapon Free World* edited by Joseph Rotblat and others in The New York Review of Books, to which he was a frequent contributor. It contained the results of an authoritative study of the nuclear arms situation organised by the Council of Pugwash and carried out by men whose combined knowledge could not, in Solly's view, be bettered. Since he died before he could complete the review, it was left to Richard Garwin, who knew his mind, and shared his opinions, to prepare it for publication. Solly once said of him that he was the cleverest man he had ever met.

That review, which appeared under the heading 'The New Nuclear Menace', is Solly's last word on the subject. It shows how in his ninetieth year, when he might have been ready to put such matters aside, he was determined to lose no opportunity to remind those who would have to live with it in the future, for longer than he, of the massive peril which they faced. He began with a reminder of the failure of early efforts to prevent the build-up of national arsenals of nuclear weapons. He went on to point out how the Test Ban Treaty of 1963, in forbidding tests in the atmosphere, had checked pollution but had done nothing to curb production or prevent proliferation. He dwelt on the absurdity of the arms race which had continued far beyond the numbers required to devastate the planet and destroy the human race with it. Nothing and no one had been able to stop the Gadarene rush. It was sustained, so the book's authors suggested, by a number of factors. The temperature was kept at fever pitch by profound ideological antipathy and demonisation of each side by the other, the time-lag between ordering new weapons and their deployment, undue reliance on worst case analyses, pressures from industry and concern for jobs.

The Russians' obsession with secrecy, and the success of their bluffs concerning the size and capability of their forces, had been a further spur to the arms race. The American belief that it would always be possible to sustain technological superiority had been a further push in the same direction. In agreeing with the conclusion of the authors that 'the UK's reason for becoming a nuclear power was overwhelmingly political', Solly added that much the same could be said of the United States. The pressure exerted by the military, by scientists and by industry, each grinding its own axe, played a huge part in fashioning the nuclear ethos of the US with the USSR inevitably following suit. The mass media readily joined in. So powerful was the tide generated that no one, not even heads of state nor any of those who understood how useless it all was, could either stand against it or prevent the monstrous waste that it involved. Solly, like the authors, was impressed by the huge expenditure of energy and ingenuity devoted to showing that nuclear weapons have a practical value, something which he believed to be profoundly untrue. He agreed with the author's conclusion that 'the only plausible scenario for the use of nuclear weapons is a situation where there is no possibility of retaliation'.

In the course of his review, he was dealing with matters about which he had as wide a knowledge of the facts and as sharp an awareness of the perils as anyone anywhere in the world. He sought to remind others of the sources of the anxieties so familiar to him: that 60 grams of matter when fissioned produced the same energy as 1,000 tons of high explosive; that only a few kilograms of plutonium – in plentiful supply – were required to manufacture a nuclear warhead. The advent of Multi Independently Targeted Re-entry Vehicles (MIRVs), Davy Crocketts and neutron bombs have contributed to an atmosphere of nightmare in which facts have tended to get lost. If the world is to succeed in finding its way back from the precipice, that rather strange collection of people whose fingers are in the neighbourhood of a nuclear trigger will need to understand that were one of these devices to be used, they themselves would be unlikely to escape the ensuing chaos. An arrogant and impatient age may find it hard to be humble and to go carefully, but the way to safety will not be easily found by people who are not even looking for it.

A world authority with the will, muscle and resources required is of the stuff of dreams. To be effective, it would need wisdom, which it would be unlikely to possess, and powers, which it would be equally unlikely to be given. The conundrum, to which there is no easy answer, is how stocks of existing weapons, plutonium and enriched uranium can be controlled and the development and testing of new weapons stopped. There would be the usual arguments about the surrender of sovereignty, a nightmare to those who are unable to haul their minds out of the past and focus them on what already is and what is likely to come in the future. Such people might reflect that the countless millions who won't be much consulted would see it as preferable to incineration. There might be something to be said for attempting to make a dream real as against accepting a nightmare.

There have been statesmen, presidents, prime ministers, scientists and military men who have seen the dangers and have made efforts to turn the tide; the fact that there are no nuclear tests in contemplation, and many thousands of warheads have been dismantled, stands to their credit, the more so since their successors have lacked the understanding or having understood, have not had the courage to move. Pugwash has been a move in a more hopeful direction contrary to the general flow of events since 1945. It is at least hopeful that scientists from all nations are more aware of the terrible possibilities than others and able to talk to one another. It must be the prayer of all that they will take steps to educate their Governments.

Richard Garwin presently Fellow for Science and Technology at the Council for Foreign Relations, New York, kindly produced the note that follows to update the situation.

NUCLEAR WEAPONRY AT THE BEGINNING OF THE TWENTY-FIRST CENTURY

At the beginning of the twenty-first century two nations possess enormous nuclear weapon stockpiles, neither with any apparent aggressive intent. The United States has some 12,000 nuclear warheads of which some 8,000 are operational – mounted on launchers or ready for use. Russia has perhaps 18,000 nuclear warheads, with some 10,000 operational. Britain, France and China have 400–500 warheads each, with about 80 per cent of them operational. These are the five 'nuclear weapon states' as defined by the 1970 Nonproliferation Treaty. In addition, Israel is thought to have some 200 nuclear weapons, never tested, while India and Pakistan may have some scores of warheads; each had several nuclear tests in May 1998. Despite these enormous numbers, the only two nuclear weapons used in warfare were those at Hiroshima and Nagasaki in August 1945. Those were less than 20 kilotons of high explosive equivalent, compared with the typical modern thermonuclear weapon of 100 to 500 kilotons yield, although some are much more powerful and many are less. The world's stocks are down from the peak of 70,000 nuclear weapons, and there have been no recent nuclear tests in the atmosphere and no tests at all since the signing of the Comprehensive Test Ban Treaty in September 1996, except those of India and Pakistan.

But the program to reduce nuclear weapon numbers has stalled, in part because of the critical economic situation of Russia. Added to this is the lack of understanding of the enormous destruction that a few or even one of these nuclear weapons could wreak and the reluctance of the world at large to mobilise its resources and efforts to reduce world stockpiles.

It would require no great change in strategic view for Russia and the United States to reduce their strategic holdings to 1,000 deployed warheads and their tactical (primarily aircraft-delivered) to a similar number. This would be a modest extension of the strategic arms reduction treaties, but there would remain 10,000 or more reserve warheads on each side. The next step would be to reduce to 1,000 warheads on each side, total – including any reserves or fissile material available to make warheads. Twenty warheads could still kill 25 million people in the target country.

A major concern at present is the reliability of command and control over the Russian nuclear force, and especially the prevention of theft or diversion of warheads or warhead materials at a time when corruption and poverty are both rampant in that country – an explosive combination when teamed with the nuclear threat. In 1998, the British government announced that henceforth its nuclear weapons would be limited to the Trident warheads on the strategic submarines, and that in the normal course of operations, these would be ready to fire in a matter of days rather than minutes or hours. France is limiting its nuclear weapons to its strategic submarines, plus some on the aircraft-launched cruise missiles, and the United States in recent years has eliminated the airborne alert – the carrying of nuclear weapons aloft in peacetime. It has also stopped flying its airborne command post.

In 1997 the Committee on International Security and Arms Control of the US National Academy of Sciences published a monograph, *The Future of US Nuclear Weapons Policy*, recommending a reduction in the nearest term to 1,000 nuclear weapons each for the US and Russia, with the reductions after that to include the other three nuclear weapon states. It recommended also that nuclear weapons serve only the function of deterring nuclear attack or responding to it, and should not be used in response to or to deter chemical or biological weapons. These latter are banned by international agreement, and the violation of those agreements should be met with a universal response by the community of nations. The 1997 report urged that the United States adopt a posture of No-First Use of nuclear weapons.

At the year 2000 review conference of the nonproliferation treaty (NPT), the 155 nations meeting in New York reaffirmed the importance of the NPT and urged Cuba, India, Israel and Pakistan to join. They emphasised the importance of entry-into-force of the Comprehensive Test Ban Treaty (CTBT), which needs to be ratified by forty-four nuclear-capable nations. Britain, France and Russia have done so, but China and the United States have not. In October 1999, a vote in the US Senate to ratify the CTBT failed, and its future is uncertain, although no important public figure in the United States advocates the early resumption of nuclear tests.

It is likely that nuclear weapons will proliferate to additional states unless their possession is no longer seen uniquely to provide status and security. To this end, negative and positive security guarantees issued to the international community by the nuclear weapon states would reduce the nuclear threat to non-nuclear weapon states. The statement by the five nuclear weapon states at the 2000 NPT Review Conference, that they are 'unequivocally' committed to the elimination of their nuclear weapon stockpiles, is helpful, but not enough to prevent the spread of nuclear weapons and the continued threat to survival.

14

Living with Labour

'You are to be my Minister of Disarmament.'
Harold Wilson to SZ, 18 October 1964

GOVERNMENTS IN this country employ an odd mix of ways of telling the public of their thoughts, intentions and plans. First they put into the mouth of the Monarch a speech of monumental dullness, setting out a list of the measures they intend to bring before Parliament in the new session. Secondly, they make statements to Parliament, either indicating some change or attempting to show they are in control of events. Thirdly, they hold press conferences and seek to persuade the sceptical and the unbelieving that they are about to take some bold, new, imaginative step into the future. An alternative to all three is to leak it, in the hope that it may thereby acquire some news value. A fourth way is to publish a White Paper. At one time these used to be printed in black type on cheap paper, with a brief indication of its presentation to Parliament by such and such a minister; no name, certainly no picture. Their contents, often obscured in clouds of verbiage, tended to be dull. While that dullness remains, the paper itself has become glossy, coloured print gives it an eye-catching quality and, to round things off, the publication bears not only a signature, but often nowadays a picture of the minister himself. The finished document, suitably contemporary, dispenses with taste and vision.

The publication of a White Paper ordinarily and rather oddly redounds to the credit of the minister responsible. That cannot, however, be counted on when it takes the form of a Defence Review. The Defence White Paper of 1960, smarter looking than its predecessors, made its appearance soon after Solly joined the Department. It showed the massive commitments Britain still shouldered and how we still looked back longingly at the trappings and ceremonial of imperial days. It also contrived to convey the comforting impression that the post-Suez pattern was both viable and valid. It was not long, however, before the facts of Britain's post-war situation reasserted themselves. The cost of meeting commitments which were the legacy of a vanished empire, and of keeping up with technological advance, called in 1963 for periodic reassessments which never seemed to catch up with reality. It is, however, in the nature of things that events get in the way of tired governments. They are denied the breathing space to look again at old problems or get to grips with new ones. President Kennedy had been murdered. The Government in its determination to remain a nuclear power had just signed up for Polaris. A partial Test Ban Treaty was in the course of negotiation. British troops were in action in Borneo. On top of that, the Prime Minister, Harold Macmillan, had departed, leaving behind him a Government battered and in no shape to embark on anything so immediately unrewarding as a defence review. As the general election approached, the appetite for one and even the opportunity vanished.

A general election in the autumn of 1964 brought in a Labour Government, pledged, as new governments tend to be, to wiping out original sin and conferring other similar benefits. Prominent among them was the reduction of annual defence spending to a level the country could afford, £2,000 million at 1964 prices. Blocking the way to such an achievement were obstacles as familiar as they were formidable. There were, first, the commitments which, though they had roots in a vanished imperial past, still bound the present; and secondly, the spiralling cost of the vast defence paraphernalia required to meet them. The speed of technological advance called for and fuelled by the arms race hardly left time for breathing, let alone second thoughts.

Still, after only four years in the Ministry of Defence, a new-comer, and — as a scientist in non-scientific Whitehall — an outsider, Solly can hardly have expected to be much involved in the political aftermath of the election. Yet only two days into the new Government, he found himself immersed in its affairs. Not only was he invited by the new Prime Minister to accept a ministerial post in the new Government, but when he turned it down found himself drawn in to advise on a range of issues stretching well beyond the merely scientific. Maybe it was the sheer unlikelihood of the unknown immigrant and budding anatomist of twenty years before finding himself in such an exciting situation, that propelled him into keeping a diary. Whatever the cause, he began it on the day after the election, Friday 16 October 1964. He continued it for over three years, the last entry being for Wednesday 21 February 1968, at which point his secretary, Pam Warwick, to whom he dictated every word, retired.

Rather strangely, and as if he thought it unimportant, he seems not to have looked again at the several hundred pages of typescript that emerged from hurried dictation and speculative typing. Had he done so, his concern to get things right would have prompted him to clear up at least some of the more obvious errors and uncertainties. What emerged has the quality of a spotlight offering vivid glimpses of those who had a place in the chain of events. It shows too how this unusual, non-conforming man contrived not only to fit himself into the system and survive, but as the joker in the pack, significantly to influence it. His autobiography, written twenty years later, is, by contrast, a large and somewhat unappealing pantechnicon. Loaded with information, it leaves the reader cramped for space and unable to sort things out from the mass.

On the Sunday morning following the election, Solly had a preliminary talk with Denis Healey, the new Secretary of State for Defence, at his house in Highgate. They touched on the problems of the Department, particularly the perennial pain involved in keeping commitments within the bounds set by financial resources. They agreed to meet for supper that evening at Solly's small house in Hasker Street, where Mountbatten would join them. Having parted from Healey, he returned there in time to keep an appointment with Frank Cousins, who, at the Prime

Minister's request, sought advice on his new role as Minister of Technology. Solly suggested that he should use the short period of freedom normally enjoyed by a minister following his appointment, to get clear in his mind the agenda he wished to follow. He should set it out in a note which he would present to whoever became his Permanent Secretary; Sir Maurice Dean would be the one to go for. He then went on to the Zoo, where he gave lunch to George Brown, the new Secretary of State for Economic Affairs. He found him 'beaming with happiness', delighted with his new job and thrilled at the numbers of people who recognised and greeted him as they walked round after lunch.

Back at Hasker Street to prepare for supper that evening, he had a call from Number Ten bidding him to be there at seven o'clock to see the Prime Minister. What then occurred is best told in Solly's own words, taken from the third day of the new diary.

While I was waiting outside the Cabinet Room door, about two minutes before the hour, the Prime Minister came along the corridor and took me into the Room with him. No one else was present. He was in terrific form, and after I had congratulated him he said, 'Look, I don't want to waste a word. You can guess what I have always thought I wanted you to do. You are to be my Minister of Disarmament and go to the Lords'. I gulped and immediately replied, 'This seems a crazy idea, I can help you and the country much better in my present job, and, in any event, I had assumed that if there were to be any change in my function I was to be given a wider remit and operate openly as your Scientific Adviser and as Adviser to the Government'. He immediately replied that that was all very well, but I didn't realise the importance he attached to the business of disarmament. I was internationally known for the work I had done, and his fear had been that Sir Alec Douglas-Home would have beaten him to the post and appointed me as a Minister himself. I reiterated my objection and he then rang for a drink and went on pressing his proposal. I assured him that I was unlikely to change my mind, and he asked me not to give a flat refusal, but to think about it and ring him later that night. He told me he wanted a Government of professionals, hence me. I told him that I had Healey and Mountbatten to dinner and asked his permission to discuss the matter with them, and also with Joan. This he agreed, but the whole time went on insisting that he knew best what was good for the country and for me. I then left him, having been with him about half an hour, and returned a much shaken man to Hasker Street.

Healey and Mountbatten arrived more or less simultaneously and we sat down over a drink before moving to the dining-room. After about ten minutes an opening was provided for telling them that I had just returned from Number 10, and that I had been asked to take on the Ministry of Disarmament, but I had in fact refused. I had, however, been asked to consider the matter further and been given permission to discuss it with them. Both took the view that I was completely right to remain in my existing job and not to do as the Prime Minister asked. We quickly dismissed this matter and went on to other issues.

During the course of dinner, however, the telephone rang and the Prime Minister came on the line wishing to speak to Healey. Their conversation lasted about ten minutes, and when Healey returned he said that he had told the Prime Minister that he had advised me not to accept and that the Prime Minister had argued pretty firmly with him. I was to ring the Prime Minister either late that night or first thing next morning.

Since his guests both stayed till nearly midnight, Solly made the easiest decision of the day, to leave it until the morning.

In his autobiography, he gives a rather tidier version of his answer to Wilson without in any way altering the sense: 'Either I serve this Government as I have its predecessor, or I leave Whitehall.' He added that he was not a politician and had no intention of becoming one. On the following morning, Wilson still declined to accept Solly's refusal until he had called on the new Foreign Secretary, Patrick Gordon Walker, and discussed the matter with him. The latter, at first surprised, in the end accepted that finding someone to replace him as an official might be harder than to find an alternative for the ministerial post. Joan, in recalling a telephone call from Solly telling her of Wilson's offer, gained the clear impression that at the time he had no thought of becoming a Minister. She did not for a moment see herself as the wife of one.

The Prime Minister, while accepting Solly's refusal to join the Government, was convinced of Solly's worth and anxious not to lose him. His thoughts of using him on a broader front than defence caused some difficulties, however, with Sir Laurence Helsby. As Head of the Civil Service, Sir Laurence was much concerned that a civil servant should not stray from his own department, least of all in the direction of Number Ten. He sought to ensure that the broader front should be as narrow as possible and that Solly should either have no direct dealings with the Prime Minister or, if he did, should immediately report back everything he said or did. Solly, more and more irritated by what he saw as Helsby's failure to understand what 'science in government meant', felt that he would not be of much use if his wings were to be thus clipped.

The upshot, given Wilson's determination, was that Solly was to have free access to him, but would keep Helsby informed. Burke Trend, Secretary to the Cabinet, also had worries about Solly's new and, as he saw it, intrusive role of advising the Cabinet. There would, Trend suggested, be no need for him to do much; he came close to saying that the less he did the better it would be for everyone. Maurice Dean, by that time Permanent Secretary to the Department of Technology, struck a similarly negative note, asking why he allowed himself to be so put upon, he had a lovely house in Birmingham, another in Norfolk, he collected silver and he had other interests. Why did he bother? Solly's answer – 'curiosity' – had the merit of being true, even if it was not the whole truth.

It is not difficult to understand what a deep and constant irritant Solly must have been to Trend and Helsby. They must have been mortified that a civil servant below them in the pecking order should have such easy access to the Prime Minister which was denied to them, his proper and pre-ordained advisers. They would be left – and this was what hurt – with no sure means of knowing what was said and agreed. Both had ample experience of the muddles which ministers contrived to make when left to themselves. To a lesser extent, Henry Hardman, Permanent Secretary to the Ministry of Defence, was similarly put out. In the interests of tidy administration, he required that advice to the Secretary of State from all sections of the Department should come to his office for assimilation and digestion. He would then, like some mother bird, regurgitate it to the Secretary of State. For Solly, this was anathema; science was his province and he was not going to have those who might not (almost certainly would not) understand the science, poring over, amending and confusing his advice. Added to that, he was himself always exceedingly sensitive to possible infringements of the rights and privileges of his own position. Only occasionally did he allow that others might have similar concerns. He did not, as Michael Cary, Permanent Secretary to the Admiralty, once remarked, like people coming too near the throne.

Soon after the change of Government, a proposal surfaced to establish some kind of multi-national nuclear force (MLF). This had already been aired in Kennedy's time; President Johnson accepted, as his predecessor never had, that there was no other way of satisfying German aspirations. The general feeling was that Britain would have to support it, albeit reluctantly. The idea was that America would provide a missile launching submarine and that the crew would come from its allies. Everyone would have a finger if not on, at least somewhere near, the nuclear button. The Germans, conscious as they were of their nearness to the Soviets and their own lack of nuclear capability, were enthusiastic. Rather like the proclamation issued by the pigs in George Orwell's *Animal Farm* that all animals were equal, the idea sounded good. The trouble lay, as ever, in the small print, or in this instance the lack of it. The question of control was one difficulty. While some thought it should be by majority decision, the Americans, though ready to consider giving a right of veto to each of the participants, were never going to agree to share the decision to fire. The amount of sensitive information involved and the considerable number of people to whom it would inevitably be divulged was another worry. In Solly's view, the proposal was certain to increase East-West tension, accelerate the arms race and delay détente. The total hostility of the Russians, who regarded it as a stepping up of NATO's strike power, which would in itself be a bar to any reconciliation, was considered normal.

The Americans saw themselves as offering a measure of comfort and reassurance to their allies, sharing the deterrent and threatening only an aggressor. Their allies, however, particularly those lacking a nuclear capability, thought that what was on offer gave them nothing of substance. Neither the Foreign Office nor the Ministry of Defence favoured the idea, but thought it unwise to go against the wishes of an American President who was so fully committed. In the coming months, however, the Ministry of Defence did have a measure of success in pointing out to all concerned the obvious defects of the plan. Mountbatten felt that it was the most serious problem that the Alliance faced. Professor Neustadt, a member of the White House staff, came to London to voice American concern. His message was that President Johnson had the Germans on his back. The British must help get them off, and setting up a Multi-Lateral Force (MLF) was the only way of doing so. The President could not stand a rebuff. Wilson, for whom the Multi-Lateral Force had little appeal, proposed a compromise in the form of an Atlantic Nuclear Force (ANF), which would take in the British Polaris. At that stage, it seemed that any arrangement emerging out of all the talk would be expensive, hard to handle, probably unworkable and satisfactory to no one. The change of Government in the autumn of 1964 did not, at the beginning, alter matters and the question continued to rumble on until it looked as if a generally unwelcome development would have to be swallowed by everyone.

By early November, however, the feeling of commitment in Washington to MLF was beginning to fade. A diary entry of 2 November states that Walter Lippman encouraged Solly to believe that 'a firm stand by the UK could get the USA off the hook'. Two weeks later his message was much the same. Washington was far less insistent on the MLF than it had been. Changes in duties at the State Department had made American attitudes less rigid. At about the same time, Terry Price, accompanying Solly on a visit to Washington, called on Mark Raskin, who had been a member of the White House staff in the early days of the Kennedy Presidency; they had met on previous visits and had become friends.

Raskin, having set out what he regarded as unanswerable arguments against the MLF, expressed surprise at the failure of the

British to understand that there were two governments in Washington: one in the White House, the other on Capitol Hill. Congress, he reported, was unhappy with the MLF, but would go along with it if the British signed up, as they were expected to do when Harold Wilson was in Washington a week or so later. If he did not, and Raskin thought he should not, the plan would be dead. To Price's question, how he could be so sure, came the blunt answer, 'I've just written the speech for the Senate Majority Leader.' At supper that evening in the house of General Sir Michael West, Chairman of the NATO Standing Committee, Price opposed the MLF, deploying the arguments used by Raskin. Walter Rostow, a senior State Department official, is said to have supported it 'with all the zeal of a missionary'.

On the following evening, Solly and Price were guests of Harold Brown, the Director of Defense and Engineering, who was a good friend of Solly's. Price took the opportunity to inform Solly of what Raskin had said. 'He's very controversial,' was Solly's immediate and cautious response. In the end, however, he came round, admitting that the information Price had given him was 'immensely valuable'. While it is not possible to say either what advice Solly gave or what its impact was, Wilson did not sign and the plan faded away. The Russians eventually accepted that the planned force was not going to happen and agreed that there should be private talks between President Johnson and Mr Gromyko, the Russian Foreign Minister, on arms reduction. Rather strangely, Solly makes no mention of Raskin or of this seemingly important development in either his autobiography or his diary. The only entry for the relevant day, 5 November, was to the effect that he had dined on *Sequoia*, the presidential yacht originally commissioned by Roosevelt and used for entertaining.

When early in December the President and Prime Minister met in Washington, the British tabled a paper on the MLF, which the Americans studied with interest. In discussion, the British somehow managed to avoid giving a direct answer to the key question, would they contribute to a multi-manned surface fleet? While there had been expectations that the Americans would press the British to join, they did not. There was, it would seem, no moment when the Prime Minister either declined to sign or was pressed to do so. The plan that only a short time before looked certain to be adopted, vanished, its demise barely noticed.

Meanwhile there occurred in the House of Commons one of those incidents in which a mixture of frivolity, opportunism and earnestness combine to produce total absurdity. Ted Heath, in winding up the debate on the Queen's Speech for the Opposition, drew attention to Solly's various roles. He added, 'I think that it is appropriate that an expert on tadpoles should be an adviser to the present administration.' That light-hearted comment proved explosive. George Brown accused Heath of referring to Sir Solly Zuckerman 'in a contemptuous phrase as a Professor of Tadpoles.' The incident, having generated some heat, was finally closed by Heath sending Solly a five-page, handwritten letter of explanation, in which he made it clear that the last thing he intended was 'to give offence to you personally or in any way to reflect upon your position or the work you carry out.'

It is clear from Solly's diary that his relations with the new Government were all that he could have wished. He enjoyed Wilson's confidence and gained access to him almost as he pleased. One entry, for 14th December, showed just how easy and informal was the relationship between them. They were alone and without any formal agenda:

When I got to the office I decided to have a word with the Prime Minister, whom I saw at about 5.00pm, and with whom I stayed for about an hour. I had intended discussing with him joint Research and Development, but instead he focussed practically the entire discussion on the question of the independence of our strategic nuclear weapons. We were alone throughout, presumably by some instruction he must have given his private office. He was well rested and very clear about the kind of information he wanted to elicit. Occasionally, in response to something I said, his mind would flash off speedily and pick up another theme which he would then develop before returning to the main drift of his questions. I explained to him as well as I could the nature of our relations with the Americans in the field of nuclear weapons and nuclear propulsion, and told him about the Treaty arrangements on which they were based. Only towards the end of our talk did he put in a word about co-operative research and development with the Americans. Here he appeared to have accepted the point I wished to make, and to which I had referred earlier on. When I got up to go he asked that if I thought of anything else which I felt he ought to know, and which might come up in the forthcoming debate on Wednesday and Thursday would I let him know.

In the evening when I returned from the Prime Minister I asked Dr Press, a member of my staff in charge of nuclear weapons [there was in that an element of exaggeration], to set out on paper for me the essence of our arrangements with the Americans in the nuclear field, my object being to check whether I had slipped up in any of the information I had given the Prime Minister, and also to prepare a note regarding the conversation.

It is one of the recurring phenomena of politics that new governments seem like rockets propelled upward into the sky, not so much by great new ideas as by the rather older and simpler one, that it is Buggins's Turn. Reaching their peak, they spread both light and sound to the chagrin of their opponents who, crushed, disappointed and at odds with each other, make premature and ill-conceived attacks which hurt only themselves. They even come to see themselves as a defeated remnant with no place in which to hide from events. In their first phase of upward climb, governments seem to carry all before them. Although not every minister loves his neighbour, the sounds of friction are muffled.

The new Government had committed itself to bringing defence expenditure within a budget of £2,000 million at 1964 prices and to do so by the year 1969/70. The new Defence Review laid out how it should be done. A so-called island strategy was proposed as a means of obviating costly seaborne communications and the need for aircraft carriers. A chain of conveniently placed islands round the world would serve as bases for a force of F111s (the American alternative to the TSR2 – a supersonic strike aircraft) which would be able to move from island to island and operate from the one nearest to a trouble spot. The fact that the islands were not always in the places the strategy required was conveniently overlooked. The fallout resulting from the Review took with it the Minister for the Navy, Christopher Mayhew, and the First Sea Lord, Admiral of the Fleet Sir David Luce. Solly's known unease meant that it was only a question of time before he left the Department.

At the beginning, Healey, as Secretary of State for Defence, and Solly, as his Chief Scientific Adviser, had worked easily together. Solly noted in his diary how brilliant Healey had been at one meeting of the Defence Council, how he had again demonstrated his virtuosity at another or been absolutely superb at a meeting of Ministers. With time, however, and the stresses of office, their relationship began to fray at the edges. Some shared characteristics served also to separate rather than to unite them. Both were clever, quick to see a point and unwilling to suffer fools gladly. Neither found it easy to conceive the possibility that they might be wrong. In addition, Solly's unpublished role of adviser to the Government as a whole became a source of irritation between them. For his part, Healey was determined, as was his right, to rule the roost. The Department and everyone in it were there to promote policies which he, as Secretary of State, had accepted on advice and then put formally to his colleagues in the Cabinet. It was intolerable that Solly, as one of his principal advisers, should take it upon himself to approach other ministers, including the Prime Minister, and seek to persuade them (as he did over the F111) that his own Minister's policies were mistaken. Solly, no team player, saw things differently; he was there to advise on the facts as they appeared to be at the time in question. If the facts changed, then so should his advice, regardless of what anyone else thought, be they the Secretary of State or even his own staff.

Solly found quite early on that Healey, like himself, did not accept advice without questioning it first. Nor did he consider himself tied to previously expressed opinions. In Solly's autobiography, written twenty years later, some of the rough edges were smoothed over, and in any event, as Solly himself admitted, Healey's personal attitude to him had been more generous than he could have expected. The diary, written soon after the event, reflects the mutual irritation which each felt with the other. A note, for example, on current nuclear problems was not in the form in which Healey thought it could go to his colleagues; it would have to be rewritten. Healey, by Solly's account, was in his 'usual bullish frame of mind, knowing most of the answers'. Solly told him that his attitude to scientists and the Scientific Civil Service was almost as old-fashioned as that of saying that people ought to be on tap and not on top. He told him plainly that he would continue to fight the case of scientists. Denis, according to another entry, was working the Ministry to death, someone was bound to get hurt.

In a friendly discussion after dinner one evening, Healey opened up on the Cuban crisis. Kennedy's achievement had been trivial, and he himself a pretty poor politician. Cuba resolved itself because the Russians realised they had gone too far. Solly thought Healey failed to take account of the tension at the time; it was wrong to treat a test of will of the scale of Cuba as just an everyday affair. Healey replied with some 'pretty blunt language'. Though there were times when all was calm and, as Solly saw things, Healey seemed 'less rejecting of things I said than usual', questions such as the purchase of F111s and the need for carriers were always there as seeds of discord.

From 1965 until 1968, when it was finally cancelled, the F111 became an increasingly sensitive issue. 'A cross Minute from Denis Healey about my having briefed the PM. Replied formally.' Healey challenged him about his contrary views on the F111 and the carriers, asked him why he had changed his mind, and was not persuaded when Solly said that he had doubts about the F111 on military, economic and technical grounds Healey was incensed by Solly's lobbying of other ministers, including the Prime Minister and George Brown. Solly's explanation, that he had seen the Prime Minister as of right, and it was at his request that he had talked to George Brown, whom he was going to see again, did nothing to assuage Healey's annoyance.

In order to clarify his own position, Solly went on to see Burke Trend, and outlined his serious doubts about the conclusion of the Review 'in the hopes that he would relay them correctly to the Prime Minister', whom he wished to see personally. A couple of months later things had cooled down between them: 'Denis was in an amiable frame of mind and thought I should be very pleased because the paper (on tactical nuclear weapons) was, as he put it, pure Zuckerman doctrine'. By that time, however, doubts as to Solly's future were beginning to firm up into a certainty that he could not stay in the MoD. The Prime Minister, when he saw Solly on 7 April, was of a mind that he should move not into the Cabinet Office, but direct to Number Ten.

To return to the autumn of 1964 and those early days of the Labour Government: Solly was at that time about as close to the centre of the Government web as it is possible for a non-politician to get. Roy Jenkins was a friend to whom he could always resort for advice. Interestingly, he became friendly with Frank Cousins, possibly because they were both outsiders, possibly also because he listened to and acted on Solly's advice. 'He may not be everybody's cup of tea,' Solly wrote on 13 May, 'but I find him very interesting and friendly.' Moreover, he listened to and acted on Solly's advice. Solly thought him a strong character and was amused by the abruptness with which he put down a suggestion of Mountbatten's; it had left 'Dickie very downtrodden'.

Solly's opinions of people, as opposed to his final judgements, tended to vary with his mood and with how they themselves were faring. He was in regular touch with Alun Chalfont, whom Wilson had chosen in Solly's place to be Minister for Disarmament. At first he tended to dismiss him as brash and sanguine. He became more sympathetic later, as Chalfont became depressed by the difficulties and the lack of progress. On one occasion, on leaving with Solly after a dinner, he was in a great fury following an encounter with Enoch Powell. Having suggested that they might get together for a talk, he was shocked by the reply that they were opponents in politics and that Powell didn't want to meet him. Solly's comment in his diary was 'I like Alun.' He and his wife Mona became friends and indeed regular visitors at Christmas to The Shooting Box, Solly's home in Burnham Thorpe. Friendship with Solly could, however, be an up-and-down affair. Stella recorded shock at the rude and rough way in which her father treated his guests from time to time, and surprise at Chalfont's restraint.

George Brown must have been the man for whom the phrase 'his own worst enemy' was coined; he looked for situations he could put his foot into. So skilled was he in finding them, that it needed all his considerable array of talents and, when he used it, his real charm, to get him to, and keep him in high office. Solly liked him, was on good terms and understood his variations of mood. On one occasion he had arranged to see him somewhat after hours at 11pm. The diary entry for 8 November 1965 relates how, when Solly arrived at 2 Carlton Gardens,

He was not in, but a very miserable Mrs Brown greeted me, saying that she did not know when he was going to come in; that he had left the house in a temper earlier, to go to a political meeting at Hampstead; and that life with a politician was terrible! Looking around her vast drawing room she said 'This is no home'. She then insisted on getting me a sandwich, I said I had already eaten, but realised that it would give her pleasure to provide me with something. I followed her into the kitchen and she cut me a ham sandwich. There was no drink around. She told me that a politician's wife had to be there for their husbands to take things out on. She seemed to be getting comfort out of a new small dog – in a big apartment where there was nothing personal lying around.

George arrived at 11.30pm in an ebullient frame of mind, and refused soup and food, and Mrs Brown was affronted about this.

He took me next door where we started talking about the Defence Review. He broke off after a few moments and said there was no point in our going on. He then rang up his office to find out what had happened to some letter which he had left for the PM, and got in a frightful temper because he could not get through to his own switchboard. He kept saying that here he was, the First Secretary, and he could not even get a telephone connection. He then settled down and we spent three-quarters of an hour discussing what he called 'the impossibility of working in Presidential Government' and indicating, what everybody knows, that he had had a big row with Frank Cousins, and that it was a case for the PM to choose. I had better not report any more.

George Wigg cannot have been a congenial colleague. He gave the impression of unsleeping watchfulness and suspicion. As

Paymaster General he had a roving brief which made him free to take a look into anything that attracted his attention. It is said that Wigg did not altogether welcome Solly's presence so near the Government; the protective zeal which he applied to realms of Defence led him to keep a close careful eye on Solly. 'George Wigg asked me to drop in on him. This took an hour, in which we discussed a number of matters which were worrying him.' Four days later, 'George Wigg had called for me and we discussed the thin edge of the psydon (sic) wedge etc'. A week later, 'Again saw George Wigg about the aircraft business, nuclear policy and defence'. 'My talk to the Paymaster General was about the usual business, he goes on being very suspicious of the coherence of Denis Healey's policy.' Solly's diary is littered with entries indicating the carefully nursed unease with which Wigg regarded his colleagues. 'More than an hour with George Wigg – his private war with Dick Crossman.' A long heart to heart with George Wigg, at his request, on what is wrong with defence policy.' 'Usual hour's talk with George Wigg discussing the sins of various colleagues.' 'An hour with the Paymaster General on where are we going in our defence policy.' 'Off to see George Wigg about a number of matters.' It is not surprising that Solly called him 'a very persistent man'.

For some of the minor figures in the chorus line he had scant regard; he was particularly scathing about C.P. Snow, who though he had corridors of power in his novels, had little understanding of them in Whitehall. He was also pompous in the way he talked about the universities and how he had handled them in the war. For Lord Bowden, Minister of State for Education, Solly had a special disregard, recounting with some relish their first meeting in the waiting room at Number Ten. Bowden extended a wet hand and expressed surprise that they had not previously met. He then proceeded to cut his nails, leaving a small heap of debris on the carpet. Roy Jenkins, who had joined them, made no verbal comment, but when they got up to leave, delicately pushed the parings aside with his foot.

From time to time, Solly caught a glimpse of Mary Wilson, who seemed like someone who had strayed from what is sometimes called the real world into the weird, esoteric one of Number Ten. She was, she told Solly, finding it very difficult to get accustomed to being pinned down, unable to move without being watched or followed. She came with a bottle of sherry, which she had bought round the corner, thinking that Solly might care for a drink. With no corkscrew in sight, however, neither of them were able to open it, nor was Harold Wilson when he came in. She departed, leaving them to discuss the old problem of cost of defence, which, powered by the arms race and technological development, defied all efforts to contain it.

When eventually in April 1966 the time came for him to move from the Ministry of Defence on one side of Whitehall to the Cabinet Office on the other, the distance was so short as to make the customary farewells at the Ministry of Defence seem superfluous. He wrote much later of how the transition could not have been smoother, and he at least seemed to find it painless. Solly had ruffled too many feathers to remain *persona grata* – if he had ever been – in the Department. Mountbatten's retirement left him on his own, and in Healey's eyes his conduct in lobbying other ministers against the purchase of the F111 had made it impossible for him to continue as his adviser. The Prime Minister, liking and admiring Solly as he did and wishing to continue to have his advice available, had no wish to see him lose face. He therefore invited him to become Scientific Adviser to the Government and accompanied his invitation with the suggestion that he should be named as Head of the Scientific Civil Service. Solly cannot have failed to be aware that since the Scientific Civil Service did not exist, to be made head of it was simply a pleasant bouquet which meant not much. The Cabinet Office, however, provided him with what he always valued, a position. Moreover, it was one which was near enough to the centre of the web to be informed of what was going on and from time to time to contribute.

On the other hand, that move across the road, short as it seemed, meant for Solly quitting a Department in which he had both staff and muscle; it meant leaving an area in which he had some ascendancy, and finding himself in the position of a consultant. While he could be called on by ministers to advise in circumstances of difficulty or embarrassment, no one would be obliged to follow his precepts. The move brought him into calmer waters, gave him more leisure – and less influence. Appointments with the

Prime Minister began to be cancelled, not for reasons of regard, but because of other more urgent calls on his time. Solly came to depend on Burke Trend, and became more friendly with him. There were from time to time no new papers on his desk; he said it was a relief. He found time to search the War Office Library and track down Mountbatten's claims that he had been informed about the atomic bomb and its intended use before McArthur. Solly, thinking such claims improbable, showed them to be impossible, and did so in time to get Mountbatten to alter a film about his life in which he had said 'some pretty incorrect things' about McArthur. He was able to leave it all behind him and enjoy two and a half delightful weeks in Majorca.

15

The University of East Anglia

'If one had it in mind to do something absolutely new and
fresh in science . . .'

SZ, Letter to Sir Christopher Ingold

RATHER AS children in the age of steam trains would decide to
become engine drivers, without much likelihood of doing
so, Solly nursed thoughts of becoming a Norfolk country gentleman. To achieve it, he would need roots. Accordingly, in 1949, he
bought a holiday home, The Forge House, in Burnham Thorpe,
the birthplace of Nelson. Later he exchanged this for The
Shooting Box in the same village. It had a garden and a cellar,
which he enjoyed filling, and it became his permanent home. He
fell, however, a long way short of his aim, for he lacked that essential aura of lazy detachment which the archetypal country gentleman wraps round himself. Even in old age, there remained a
tension, a concern as to what he should do next. He was still at
heart a nomad and nomads are not made of the same stuff as
country gentlemen. What he thought might become a way of life
was more a base from which he organised affairs, his study being
the engine room. He had roots, but they were in science and they
were long ones, which permitted movement not only between
disciplines, but to places far removed from the laboratory and
lecture room of earlier years. By the mid 1950s, his involvement in
either was slight. Instead he faced in non-scientific Whitehall a
range of problems very different from those encountered in the

laboratory; he was working with men who, though ready to use what it provided, misunderstood science and were mistrustful of scientists. There was the deep, ill-founded yearning to control the processes of scientific discovery. As he had pointed out years before in that speech in Pasadena, it is not possible to control what is still unknown.

To understand the place the University of East Anglia had in Solly's life, one needs to go back in time and recall how the feats of scientists in war brought to the British Governments a dawning awareness of their importance. In the closing months of the war, the Minister of Works set up a committee to advise his department on scientific matters generally and in particular on the revival of cities shattered by bombs. Though kept in being by the incoming Labour Government, it made little impact. Solly, a member from the outset, wrote not to Tomlinson, the sponsoring Minister, but to Herbert Morrison, the Deputy Prime Minister, suggesting that it should be wound up and replaced by a Science Secretariat. The outcome was, as has already been related, an Advisory Council on Scientific Policy. Like most efforts to please everybody, it failed. Despite the efforts of Sir Henry Tizard, its first Chairman – and indeed of Solly himself, his deputy for many years – the Council was used by governments as not much more than a cosmetic which gave them the appearance of scientific respectability. Its advice was either cherry-picked or ignored. The Council, in short, took up the time of conscientious and able men, but in its recommendations seldom strayed outside the safe, the respectable and the dull: to be fair, it was denied the opportunity.

The supply of scientists was a matter which the Council rightly regarded as crucial. The absurdity of attempting to monitor the expansion of the universities and the output of scientists by informal, irregular swapping of off-the-cuff opinions soon became obvious. He suggested that a specialist sub-committee, able to give time, would be better fitted to handle the problem. Tizard agreed, and, as Solly must have anticipated, made it a condition that he should be its Chairman. He learned, as he always did, from the high powered and experienced civil servants who sat on the sub-committee. Men like Eddie Playfair (War Office), Otto Clarke

(Treasury) and Gilbert Flemming (Education) had something to teach anyone who was willing to learn. They none of them had much regard for C.P. Snow, who joined them. 'More of a novelist than a scientist', was Solly's judgement; 'If he tells us to move in one direction, turn smartly round and go in the other,' was Clarke's verdict. Long experience of working in committees had made Solly doubtful of their usefulness, and particularly of their statistical and sampling techniques. He also had considerable reservations as to the wisdom of the Robbins Committee in decreeing that the doors of the universities should be open to all who wished to enter.

Living in Norfolk, he joined a committee, chaired by Lord Mackintosh of toffee fame, to press the claims of East Anglia to be the home of one of the new universities which were to come in the wake of Robbins. Later, as a member of the Academic Planning Board of what became the University of East Anglia, he had in mind the need 'to do something absolutely new and fresh in science'. He wondered whether Norwich could not embark, in its Faculty of Science, on a Division of Environmental Sciences – meteorology, oceanography, geology, conservation etc. If it did, he was certain that 'nobody would ever be able to say that scientists were trained in a narrow way'. The breadth of his own science, covering anatomy, anthropology, biology, reproductive physiology and zoology, led him to favour a university education free from those unnecessary and pettifogging barriers which inhabitants of ivory castles use as fortifications. He believed that students would benefit from knowing what was going on next door and that they should be encouraged to find out. He deplored the British tendency to treat scientists as mere technicians who had no claim to a voice in policy matters; it was different in other countries. One of his particular talents, as many of his students and his erstwhile colleagues can testify, lay in his ability to aim people at a target, wind them up and launch them on their way. The blueprint for a school of environmental sciences, which was his particular contribution to the new University, reflected both his aversion to narrow, imprisoning partitions and his readiness, having sown the seed to let others grow the plant.

As early as 1961, he outlined the main directions he thought the new School should follow; meteorology, oceanography, conservation, land use and population studies. He saw no need for divergence until the student's third year; he had thoughts of a possible bridge with social studies and economics in the second and third years. The numbers envisaged at that stage were 150 to 300 undergraduates, fifty to a hundred graduates and thirty to sixty members of staff. In nearly forty years there has been amazing growth, even surpassing Solly's hopes. There are now 60 teaching staff, 94 research staff, 148 postgraduates and 320 undergraduates.

The appointment of Frank Thistlethwaite as the first Vice-Chancellor was a stroke of good luck for the new University. He and Solly were natural allies, in that they both disliked the man-made barriers which people fearful of innovation devise for their own protection. Just as the new Vice-Chancellor wished to bring the humanities and the social sciences together, so Solly was concerned to see an end to the divorce between the natural and the physical sciences. Frank saw in an alliance with Solly a heaven-sent opportunity to bring about the innovations which they both sought. He came to admire 'the wonderful sweep of his mind' as being 'uniquely precious'. Solly's suggestion that the University should 'embark on a division of environmental sciences,' and his thought that 'in a sub-faculty something could be produced . . . a bridge between science and the humanities,' were so completely in tune with Thistlethwaite's own thinking that a School of Environmental Sciences became an important priority. His next step was to look for a Dean to run it.

Keith Clayton, who first arrived at UEA in 1967 as Dean of the new School of Environmental Sciences, is one of those men it is easy to underrate at first meeting. He is slow to claim the credit for his achievements and bases his opinions on accumulated knowledge, experience and thought. He would never kowtow to those he believes do not deserve respect and is the last to hide or back away from his own considered judgments. 'You could do something with the universities of this country if it were not for the Committee of Vice Chancellors and Principals' is a thought on which those responsible for higher education in this country would do well to reflect. Meeting Solly for the first time, his impression was of a charming rogue, a skilled operator, ambitious, good at handling important people. 'When Solly wanted you to do something for him, he could be a real bully, but if you stood up to him, he would listen.' Keith was the one who, with the aid of his colleagues, developed the school, as he thought, 'incredibly close to what Solly Zuckerman had intended, but it was quite by chance in the sense that, faced with the same problem, he and I came to the same conclusion about the sort of courses we could have'. While UEA was not the first in the field of environmental studies, others faltered, and it grew the fastest and quickly became dominant.

Conscious of the merits of the University and doubtless with his own contribution to it in mind, Solly came to think that those on the outside should be told of its existence and purpose. A series of seminars on the environment, using the University as a forum, greatly appealed to him. 'The aim', he told the Prime Minister in a minute of February 1970, 'is to have an informed review of several aspects of the unfolding scene, including population changes, prospects for economic growth (general and regional), the provision of food and water, the treatment of waste, the possible impact of long-term climatic changes on development programmes, environmental amenities etc.' He added that while he first had in mind a seminar in which he could be educated, it was now 'obvious that the professionals, whom I have invited, and the academics who are being invited by the University, are equally stimulated by the idea of being educated about each others' problems.'

A question arose concerning the participation of civil servants. Sir Matthew Stevenson, then Permanent Secretary to the Ministry of Housing and Local Government, who was himself a particularly frank and fearless adviser of ministers on their policies behind the scenes, was distinctly coy when it came to civil servants explaining or defending those policies in public, and replied to a letter from Solly in a letter, which is something of a gem:

I find your request rather embarrassing. Quite apart from the difficulties which would arise from the shortness of notice, I am not enthusiastic about Civil Servants forecasting, explaining or defending Government policy at gatherings of people outside the Civil service. I think that this is a function of Ministers which should not be usurped.

Another even more familiar problem was money; the University had no funds for such a programme and the Government would not even have thought of providing them. The Ford Foundation, from whom Solly sought help, generously came up with the lion's share of what was required to finance 'the Ford Seminars'. The first, which took place over a weekend in March 1970, was attended by a mix of academics, civil servants, directors of research establishments, business people and one or two politicians. Delegates were well cared for, especially when it came to food and drink. Busy men were, Solly believed, more likely to be persuaded by such means to give up a weekend and would benefit, as he did, from the magical powers of claret. Interestingly, it was the University's practice to base its wine prices on the original cost; in practice, this often meant that the oldest and the best were also the cheapest.

A 1977 report to the Ford Foundation, drafted by Keith Clayton but signed by Solly, emphasised the value of privacy and informality of the proceedings and how rare the opportunities were for such open discussions between those who, though they saw the same problems, did so from very different angles. 'The best testimony to the value of these seminars are the repeated requests and suggestions for the resumption of the meetings. They clearly represented a unique forum, and the case for continuing them is strong.' Keith, upon whose shoulders fell much of the labour, commented, 'It was new ground to me; they were very able people, but there were a lot of things they didn't know and they certainly didn't know much about the environment'. It is easy to forget how quickly opinions shift and facts seem to change when seen in a different light. At the first of the seminars, on the subject of climate change, the speaker was concerned not with the consequences of global warming, which is now the cause of real anxiety, but the prospect of another ice age. Keith, having been Dean at the beginning, had a second spell in the same role twenty years later in 1987. Reflecting then on the success achieved by the School, and looking forward to what might be done, he wrote to Solly suggesting that a Scientific Advisory Panel be set up; it should cover the whole range of the School and should consist of distinguished people. He invited Solly to be the first Chairman. The Panel met for the first time in June 1988 with Solly in the chair and thereafter twice a year until 1993; that last meeting, after Solly's death, was chaired appropriately by Lord Dainton, who testified in his obituary to the major hand he had had in shaping the University and as a prime mover in creating a School of Environmental Sciences.

Solly's involvement with the University continued from the time of its foundation until he died. For a few years as Professor at large he had a Chair, but no executive responsibilities. Later he was given the title of Professor Emeritus. During those years, the University provided him with office space and shared with him the services of Gillian Booth and Deirdre Sharp. Those two remarkable and devoted women came to know and understand him well. They learned, and they were not the first to do so, how adept he was at getting his own way, and that excuses, no matter how valid, did not appease. Icebound roads or the likelihood of snow or an injured knee were not grounds for either leaving early or not coming to work at all. The need for a holiday was not only an unwelcome interruption, but a sign of thoughtlessness. The fact that he had work for them to do hid from him that other fact like blindness, that they had their own lives to live. Nevertheless they stayed, and they remember him, not as slaves would, but with fascination and affection. He was also in his way thoughtful, appreciative and generous. When he died he left the lion's share of his estate to the University, and also an overflowing archive; to Gill a case of his best claret, and to Deirdre a valuable piece of glass and some nineteenth-century books on the history of science.

While in Birmingham University, sadly, there is little left of the Department of Anatomy which Solly spent more than twenty years of his life building up, nor much trace of him, in the UEA he is remembered and honoured. Professor Trevor Davies and Professor Peter Liss, who barely knew Solly but who, at the birth of the millennium, were intimately acquainted with the School, have written warmly of his vision and of how it has become a reality.

Although I met him a few times, I did not know him well. However, the legacy of this visionary is at the forefront of my mind, every day, as Dean of the School of Environmental

Sciences. His prescription for the School, propounded almost forty years ago, was then regarded by many as a step too far in his quest to lead scientists away from the 'narrow way'. I like to think that we have made a very decent contribution to his vision of 'something absolutely new and fresh in science'. His vision was so long and robust that this prescription in 1960 is a very good description of what today's successful school does. As methods and understanding improve we are seeking ways of increasing the connections between, and extending the web of, the separate disciplines concerned with the environment and society, in anticipation of the science of the new Millennium being more holistic and inclusionary. The vehicle may get a little sleeker and more efficient, but the objectives are still rooted firmly in Zuckerman's ideals.

Trevor Davies

Solly Zuckerman was a man of great independence of thought and action. There is no need for me to elaborate on the former, but an example of the latter was the sight of him well into his eighties pushing a baggage trolley at Norwich Station to get himself on to the London train in order to attend the House of Lords or some other august body. Another prized quality was his foresight and vision. There are many examples but one close to home is the School of Environmental Sciences at the University of East Anglia. Thirty-five years ago he thought up the, then, radical, concept of studying the environment from a holistic standpoint. With its 5 star research grading and demonstrated ability to tackle the large multi- and inter-disciplinary environmental problems, the School has amply fulfilled Solly's visionary idea.

Peter Liss

The School has achieved some notable successes. It is to be the home of a new Institute for Connective Environmental Research (ICER), a prime aim of which will be to give an interdisciplinary base to environmental research and win for it a new and higher profile. Business partners will participate directly in its programmes and in decisions concerning the management of the environment. The hope is that the Institute will bring about a new degree of co-operation between organisations which, despite a common interest, have in the past gone their separate ways. An important part of it will be the Tyndall Centre, named after the Victorian scientist who first recognised 'greenhouse gases'. Based within the School, the Centre will, in the words of the Dean, 'involve a partnership with nine other UK institutions, which contains unparalleled expertise in the field of climate change and ensures the participation of many leading scientists, social scientists and engineers.' The aim of the Centre will be to learn more of the causes and consequences of climate change. In that work it will be reinforced by the new Laboratory for Global Marine and Atmospheric Chemistry. With equipment unique in the world, it will be able to learn how far and how fast the global climate is likely to change. Other component parts of the ICER will be two Centres, one concerned with environmental risk, the other with environmental decision making. In the view of those who now steer the School, public understanding of the risks is one of the important pieces that are missing from the jigsaw.

It is a basic aim of the School as a whole to encourage by all means available to it a broad interdisciplinary approach and the elimination of barriers and the allaying of something near to enmity which separated disciplines and inhibited communication between them. Solly would have approved without reservation. He would also have applauded the growth of the School from nothing forty years ago to a total complement of nearly 700 today. It can be said of the School that it has learned from Newton's famous words, 'If I have seen further, it is by standing on the shoulders of giants'. In recognising Solly's status and the quality of his vision, it has gained a position for itself, and a potential which few can have foreseen or even hoped for when, forty years ago, Solly suggested doing 'something absolutely new and fresh in science'.

16

The Environment

'The most precious thing we have is the tiny, damp, curved
space which is our living room. The pleasantly warm
moment we now enjoy in it will not last forever.'

Crispin Tickell

MORE THAN half the twentieth century had passed before
some traces of real anxiety as to the state of 'our living room'
began to permeate the non-scientific mind of the human race.
Until about 1970 the great complex of land, water and air that surrounds us, and all the problems arising from it, had no officially
approved name. Since it is difficult to grapple with things
unnamed, someone searched through the words available and hit
upon environment as the one least open to objection. Whereupon
it was ordained, after the manner of Humpty Dumpty – 'when I
use a word, it means just what I choose it to mean, neither more
nor less' – that that word, which until then had meant no more
than surroundings or locality, should bear the weight and dignity
of a new and enhanced meaning. It was given a capital 'E' and, in
this country, a government department to take care of it. Since
then, the world has been coming slowly and patchily to accept that
what it had named as the environment is not simply a vast unlimited emptiness into which waste can be freely tipped. Continuing
to do so might have consequences as dire as they would be unexpected.

Human numbers and needs have spiralled upwards together.
While advances in science and technology have gone a long way to

meeting those needs, they have also created new problems. They have brought industrial development on an unprecedented scale to much of the world. New levels of food, health, housing, comfort, movement, information and energy have been achieved. The accompanying shadow has been a vast and ever-increasing quantity of waste, much of it toxic. Easily created, it is hard to dispose of. The pollution caused to land, water and air has not been limited in terms of either time or space. It is cumulative, enduring and global. It is reversible, if at all, only with patience, not yet a conspicuous feature of modern times, and with an acceptance of restraint which sheer weight of numbers may rule out. Time, always in short supply, is needed for facts to be established and to gain a foothold in the human mind. Meanwhile, standing in the way of something being done is the headlong race led by the rich and the powerful to get and spend – and forget the rest. Those still young may take comfort in dismissing the predictions of disaster as the scare-mongering of crackpot scientists; those who are older, in the thought that they may not be around when the chickens head for home.

As in war Solly's knowledge of destruction began and grew, not from any conscious decision of his own, but from a chain of circumstance and chance; so too in peace did his concern for the environment. In his youth, much of it spent in the open in the veldt of Cape Province, his fascination with the host of creatures he encountered must have made him aware of the importance of climate and habitat and food and water. Attending two conferences on environmental matters in 1949 marked the beginning of his public involvement in the subject. The first, sponsored by the United Nations in 1949 at Lake Success, was concerned with the protection of nature. As a member of the UK delegation, he chaired one of its plenary sessions. The purpose of the second, under the auspices of UNESCO, was declared by Julian Huxley, its Secretary General, to be the promotion of 'a better understanding of man's relationship with his environment and the maintenance of nature's equilibrium'. Huxley had been a friend and an important influence in Solly's life ever since that first meeting at the Zoo soon after Solly's arrival in London. They shared a lively and well-justified concern at the increasing human population. Sadly, the British, lukewarm and superior, sent only observers to the UNESCO conference, of whom Solly was one. Chairmanship of the Natural Resources Committee (already mentioned in Chapter 9 as seeking ways of saving on expensive imports) caused him to look at a great range of materials and made him aware of the frequency with which their production and their use impacted upon the environment. He was surprised to find that the close relationship between agriculture and environment was neglected or ignored when the level of support for the former was being considered.

A chapter in his autobiography entitled 'Poisons, Pollution and Population' reflected his growing interest and concern with the subject. At the request of ministers, he chaired committees which considered the hazards for both workers and consumers which the use of toxic materials involved. In an attempt to handle questions which reached him daily from a multitude of sources, he developed a practice of passing them on with short covering letters to those he thought should be able to provide the answers. The meagreness of the replies led him to see the worth of inter-disciplinary education and to lament the lack of it. Living near the Norfolk coast, he was from time to time reminded of the way the elements exert pressure on the environment. In the early 1950s unnaturally high tides smashed through coastal defences, flooded thousands of acres of agricultural land and drowned more than three hundred people. In the same year (1953), intense and prolonged smog in London caused the death of some thousands of old people and others with breathing difficulties. The resulting outcry pushed the authorities into something resembling action. In 1958 they gave their blessing to the Clean Air Act, which started life as a Private Member's Bill introduced by Gerald Nabarro. An earlier invitation from the Ministry of Fuel and Power to chair a committee on the subject was one too many, even for one with Solly's insatiable appetite for committee work. He turned it down with a brusque 'Tell the minister that what ought to be done is obvious, it doesn't need a committee.'

Solly's interest in population growth dated back to his prewar studies of reproductive physiology. At the time of the first United Nations conference in 1954, he was engaged in doing a report on the subject. He was therefore invited to join the British delegation.

He told later in graphic terms how Pope Pius XII, 'a very elegant figure in white borne in on a palanquin by his Swiss Guards', addressed the delegates. He had, he told them, instructed the Vatican to seek ways in which population growth could be curbed 'within the framework of the Christian faith'. Having with those last words brought his audience sharply back to earth, the Pope made a graceful exit, waving farewell to his visitors, as well as to their hopes that the problem posed by the sheer numbers of the human race might at last be faced. Twice when Solly raised the subject of birth control in relation to over-population, neither the Advisory Committee on Scientific Policy nor the Medical Research Council showed any eagerness to pursue it. The subject is one which politicians and their advisers the world over pass by, in the certain knowledge that the pitfalls are numerous, and the rewards for facing it so thin as to be non-existent.

In 1964, Harold Wilson set up the Department of Land and Natural Resources. He intended that it should take over the functions of the Natural Resources Committee, which under Solly's chairmanship had become more and more involved in environmental matters, but which, without his leadership, had wallowed in the doldrums. The hostility of Crossman at the Ministry of Housing and Local Government, who saw the new Department as a threat to his own, was one nail in its coffin. Another was its failure to answer the unanswerable question, still very much with us, of how the social and economic aspects of land use can be reconciled with the requirements of amenity and conservation. Its demise showed how a hopeful and sensible initiative, disturbing to settled patterns and influential persons, can be squeezed out.

In 1967 there occurred one of those incidents in which natural forces combine with what is rather coyly known as human error to show how man's efforts to keep abreast with current problems fall short of what is required. It was a further reminder of the part the elements can play, and of just how vulnerable the environment has become in the scramble to supply modern needs. The air of unreality and farce gave opportunity to the cartoonists, embarrassment to everyone else. The *Torrey Canyon*, fully loaded with crude oil, hit a reef sixteen miles west of Land's End on Saturday 18 March 1967. A Dutch salvage team got on board in the hope of floating her off the rock and winning a rich prize, but only succeeded in getting in the way. Solly was put in charge of the scientists from all the departments concerned and told to make a plan. Convinced that nothing could shift her and that it was too dangerous to attempt to pump out the remaining 90,000 tons of oil, he concluded that the only course was to open up the compartments holding the oil and hope to fire it as it gushed out. This, however, was not possible so long as the Dutch salvage team remained on board. Solly, with a slipped disc and sciatica and feeling sorry for himself, retired hurt to Burnham Thorpe.

There was to be a meeting at the Naval Air Station at Culdrose in Cornwall on the Sunday morning which the Prime Minister wished Solly to attend. He at first said he could not, but gave in when an ancient Pembroke aircraft arrived to collect him. The tasks by then were how to deal with the remaining oil, how to remove the slick already on the Cornish beaches, how to prevent more from drifting ashore, and somehow to find a way to persuade the brave but greedy salvage team to leave the ship. At the end of the meeting, with nothing much decided, Solly embarked on the Pembroke to return to Norfolk; before doing so, they flew over the ship. It so happened that, at that moment, her back was breaking and more oil was gushing out; the stern was attached by tie-lines to a tug and a man was still on board. Attempts to fire the huge oil slick failed, and more oil washed on to the Cornish beaches; no one could say whether bombing the ship would succeed in firing the oil that remained in her, or what incendiaries would do to the oil slick. The whole affair was a dramatic warning – not lost on Solly – of the power of the elements and the unwisdom of leaving them out of the reckoning.

In 1969/70, the environment at last achieved official recognition in the scheme of things. Tony Crosland, then President of the Board of Trade, was summoned to return from Tokyo, where he was taking part in talks on Anglo-Japanese trade, to be told of his new appointment as Secretary of State for Local Government and Regional Planning. Bewildered and alarmed, he asked Solly, 'What is Harold up to, am I being sold down the river?' Reassured that the Prime Minister had no such intentions, he learned that he would have within his own office a Central Scientific Unit to provide him with expert advice and support and to co-ordinate action on pollution. The idea of co-ordination is often given an airing in official programmes, where it has a certain decorative effect, but not much else. Solly, as Chief Scientific Adviser to the Government, had a hand in what was a notable step forward. Indeed, the Prime Minister, in appointing Crosland, told him of the considerable amount of preparatory work Solly had done. A further move was to appoint a Royal Commission on the Environment. Like others of its kind, it was both an indication of the importance which the Government attached to the problem, and an admission that it had no clear ideas as to what it should do. In the event, the Commission produced its quota of reports, papers and letters, but nothing of any great consequence. Solly himself, having served on it for three years, was then re-appointed, but with his enthusiasm at a low ebb, resigned after one further year. He did not care to give his time to processes which achieved nothing and taught him nothing.

Martin Holdgate, invited to become the first Director of the Unit, had not encountered Solly before. His first and clear impression of him was of 'an extraordinary man, an increasingly powerful scientific influence in Government; he made certain that the voice of science and the voice of Solly (he sometimes had difficulty in separating them) were heard everywhere . . . Charming, brilliant, vain, persuasive, tyrannical and a past master of Whitehall intrigue. I found him rather overpowering.' Those who move in high circles, whether they admit to it or not, nearly always take a lively interest in protocol and pecking order; Solly was no exception, as Martin Holdgate quickly discovered. When word reached the new Government that the Americans handled environmental matters differently and better, Solly was invited to lead a team to Washington to see whether it was so. Holdgate, who accompanied it, was told by Crosland, his Secretary of State, to report, and on his return did so direct, with a copy to Solly, who was far from pleased and quick to say so. 'The meeting in America was my meeting. You came as one of my delegation. If anyone is to brief the Cabinet it is me.'

The new Department of the Environment, set up in 1970 and housed most unsuitably in a graceless building, constituted another hesitant step in the right direction which did not quite come off. Having swallowed three existing Departments, Housing and Local Government, Transport and Works, the new creature lacked the stomach to digest so vast and disparate a meal. Missing also was the single-mindedness to develop the fresh attitudes that were needed. Moreover, the concentration upon those three Departments and the omission of others left the whole venture looking distinctly lop-sided. Hindsight suggests that it would have been better had the new Department been given a period of intensive care in the Cabinet Office. It might then have been able to develop a persona of its own, and sufficient clout to extend its influence over all departments whose activities affected the environment.

While there were constant reminders from such phenomena as nuclear waste and acid rain of the pressures on the environment, Solly tended to think of them as more easily manageable than the social and political problems that existed in a world in which nuclear weapons could not only slaughter people on an unprecedented scale, but devastate the physical environment as well. He saw the disparity between rich and poor as an endless source of tension. He recognised that, while it would be relatively easy to get the environmental science right, hopeful and positive, a far more difficult task would be to have its implications accepted by the Government and society. The imperatives were clear enough, but insufficiently to remove the entrenched resistance to them. Conferences, speeches and resolutions do nothing to dissuade people from doing what they have become accustomed to do. Burning fossil fuels for warmth or for travel anywhere and everywhere in cars and aeroplanes, even keeping cows which generate large quantities of methane, are so integrated in people's lives, that restraint of them will be resisted.

People are not going to relish being told by officialdom that *vis-à-vis* the environment, such day-to-day activities are dirty habits which should be curtailed. Moreover, governments the world over, bossy rather than persuasive, are seen to be prone to error. Ready enough to bully individuals, they flinch when it comes to curbing powerful and articulate lobbies. 'The sense of hopelessness that we shall never be able to solve our social, political and environmental problems', which Solly perceived, has not gone away.

He pointed to a 'growing volume of protest that in our greed we have allowed science and technology to run away with us, that our material civilisation is leading us inevitably and rapidly to our doom'. In a notable address to the American Philosophical Society in 1979, he returned to the theme, calling attention to ever-rising material expectation and to the spectre of overpopulation which resulted from biomedical advances. It would seem that a deal of persuasion, reinforced by events, will be needed before *Homo sapiens* (man still accepts the nomenclature without a blush) is ready to accept a degree of self-discipline and regulation which he would find inconvenient.

The events and developments of half a century, Solly suggested, called for new attitudes and a new look at institutions which were beginning to look inadequate. What had sufficed in the days of bows and arrows, and even gunpowder, would suffice no longer. A shared determination to understand, to explain and to act before time ran out or someone did something wicked or foolish, was, in his view, urgently necessary. The demonstrated inability of mature and sophisticated nations to meet and decide, without much messy lobbying and accusations of cheating and bribery, which of them should host a football tournament, suggested that more serious problems might be beyond them. Although the perceived likelihood of some worldwide catastrophe might induce some fresh thinking, the nearness of the threat would not give much time for it to bear fruit. The habit of jostling for position is too ingrained to be quickly shed. Modern technology has not left much unchanged over the latter half of the twentieth century; it has made the world smaller and led to a huge increase in human numbers. Separation is a thing of the past; yet the United Nations, the single global institution of government, lacks the clout even to oblige its members to pay their dues, let alone live up to the hopes its founders cherished half a century ago. Meanwhile, national governments, quick to forget the lessons of the past, jealous of encroachment and more fearful of the loss of sovereignty than concerned with the safety of the planet, talk far beyond the limits of their powers to perform.

In the speech which he delivered to the young graduates at Caltech in 1959, quoted earlier in Chapter 9, Solly argued that the scope of the liberal arts should be widened to make room for an understanding of 'the scientific knowledge whose application is now so rapidly transforming intellectual and material environment'. Although it has continued to do so, science and the scientist are still somehow subordinate, relegated to a below-stairs status. The notion of a Nobel Prizewinner even thinking of standing for Parliament or of a political party inviting him to do so is unreal. Yet it seems almost as absurd that, in a world and at a time influenced by science as ours is, the voice of science should be so little heard, and its message so little understood. Even in Whitehall, scientists serving in government departments are there to advise their ministers and to marshal the scientific arguments which support their policies. Scientists with Solly's breadth of knowledge and experience are seldom seen or heard there. Professor Keith Clayton, the first Head of the School of Environmental Sciences in the University of East Anglia, gives Solly the credit for having understood, long before most scientists, that population increase, economic growth and the means used to tackled them interact with each other in ways and with effects which no one even began to foresee.

> Chemicals can limit damage to crops or eliminate the insects which carry disease, but many can pass more widely into the environment and threaten the survival of animals further up the food chain. Fossil fuels, accumulated over a few hundred million years, have been burnt in a few hundred years, hanging the heat balance of the Earth in space to produce global warming that will take decades to stabilise and centuries to reverse. Clever new chemicals such as the CFCs, unknown before 1950, have carved an ozone hole in the stratosphere that will persist for another hundred years even if we achieve world-wide regulation through the Montreal Protocol.

Clayton's concern is directed not only to the specific problem of global warming or climate change, call it what you will, but also to the small numbers who know and understand sufficient about it. Scientists in modern times tend to specialise; few have the interdisciplinary base which would give them a view of the whole scene. Similarly, there are not many social scientists or politicians who are

qualified even to begin to think how change, unwelcome but necessary, might be handled. Further difficulties in the way of understanding include the way in which attention is diverted from the
whole problem to minor but popular aspects of it. There is also that
Luddite army ready 'to flout', as Clayton has put it, 'their ignorance
of difficult ideas by doubting whether the idea of global warming is
real, or, if it is easier to accept the concept, to propose that we shall
all enjoy a warmer world, indeed the warmer it gets the better!'
Clayton, like Solly before him, speaks to the few who understand,
or at least have some wish to do so; they have little to say to those
who neither know nor greatly care. There are many who, in our
world, are not much worried either by the waste they cause or the
destruction they leave behind them. If the destruction of other
forms of life, the extinction of a diversity of creatures and the tread-
ing underfoot of the variety of creation are matters of importance,
mankind is either unaware of it or thinks it a price worth paying.
We forget how useful were other forms of potato or cocoa bean,
when something went wrong with the 'popular brands'.

In April 1992, two months before the international conference
in Rio on the global environment, Solly wrote to Prince Philip,
'The very fact that we still don't know what part, if any, the US is
going to play . . . would seem to indicate that the world is in worse
array about the environment than we were twenty years ago.' Not
only were the old problems of population, poverty, illiteracy still
with us, but their consequences were in danger of being
intensified by the resurgence of nationalism and the growth of fun-
damentalism. There was 'a danger' – and no one can suggest that it
has disappeared since – 'of environmental problems escaping from
human control through the ineffectiveness of our international
institutions'. An article in the journal *New Scientist* echoed
his gloom. The two great issues that were not tackled in all the
documents accompanying the Summit were 'the role of the
multinational companies – the agents of rainforest destruction,
the generators of greenhouse gases, the plunderers – and the
corruption that they and their clients, the unelected leaders of
many of the world's nations, conspire to perpetuate.'

In an article in *Nature* (July 1992), written when he was eighty-
eight, less than a year before he died, Solly summed up his

thoughts. There never were grounds for the hope, built up prior to the Rio conference, that governments were ready to reach a mandatory international agreement on stabilising, or even reducing, the levels of carbon dioxide emissions by a given date. Members of the European Community having failed to agree to a tax on such emissions, the Commissioner, Carlo Ripa di Meana, had declined even to attend. What he sought was 'a policy based on facts, obligations, constraints and precise commitments, not pretty words'. The President of the United States, the country alleged to be responsible for a quarter of the world's carbon dioxide emissions, had said in the run-up to the conference that he could not accept a fixed date for limitation. As at Stockholm twenty years before – and here Solly endorsed Barbara Ward's warning of potential conflict between man's two worlds, the one he had inherited and the one he was creating – so at Rio the lessons were the same. The problems were more complex than the trumpeting in advance allowed for. Not only did the long-term problems differ from the short-term and the global from the national, but those of the advanced nations were far from being the same as those of the less forward. Complexity, however, was only one roadblock on the way to progress. Others lay in expectations so large that subsequent disappointment was certain, and in the number of the nations involved – 150 – and the variations in size and strength of their delegations. Another major lesson was that, in practice, the solutions to most environmental problems lay almost entirely in the political and economic domains. The blame for the sense of letdown that Rio had left behind could be shared between 'those who for political reasons had made the world expect too much from it, and the over-enthusiastic environmentalists who had proclaimed that the meeting would be the most important ever to be convened'.

Towards the end of the article, he returned to Barbara Ward and her thought that 'we should not linger too long on the . . . fact that our total natural system . . . in the biosphere of air and water could be irretrievably upset by man's activities'. At that point Solly rather surprisingly put off the mantle of Jeremiah and concluded that because what Barbara Ward had said was now understood by all literate people, he continued to believe that 'in the end man will not destroy the only planet, which to our knowledge is the habitat of what we call the living world'. He ended another letter to Prince Philip, written a week or so after that article, on a similar note: 'I continue to hope that *Homo sapiens* has the wit to save the planet and itself from extinction. I cannot believe that it won't.' He seemed to be making more of a frantic plunge in the direction of a happy ending than expressing a conviction that there would be one. More cautiously, he admitted that he would hate to have to provide a blueprint for the kind of political system he thought could be relied on to safeguard the environment as we know it.

Crispin Tickell, at the end of a recent lecture, asked two peremptory questions, as easily understood as they are hard to answer.

'Do we know where we are going?'

'Can we cope with the problems raised by the unstable and unsustainable society we have created for ourselves?'

If one more question were permitted, it might be, by how much have we overloaded the planet?

Just as Solly was ready, as Head of a Department in Birmingham, to encourage students who could show the necessary stamina and intellect, so, later, when new recruits of the same quality took up the environmental theme, he gave them unstinted encouragement and support. In 1975, he wrote in a Foreword to Crispin Tickell's book, *Climatic Change and World Affairs*, 'Man's present political problems are miniscule in relation to what could result from major changes in climate, and someone from outer space, viewing our globe in the units of geological time, could well suppose that nations of today behave like people who quarrel violently and murderously over immediate trivialities on the fifth floor of some huge, modern Tower of Babel, oblivious of the fact that it is blazing away merrily below them.'

17

An American Dimension

'The helmsman is playing it by ear, but he is stone deaf.'
Isidor Rabi, letter, 7 September 1981

T HERE WAS a large and important American dimension to
Solly's life. It began in the 1930s with an eighteen-month spell
at Yale, which allowed for lively intervals in New York. There was
no obvious reason why anyone in that pulsating hive of a city
should even notice an unknown immigrant who knew and cared
about monkeys. Yet celebrities such as the Gershwins welcomed
him as if he were one of their own. Maybe as a rootless immigrant
he was at home in a country built by and belonging to people
who, like himself, had something to prove. In the years during
which he was advising successive British governments, his friendships with many of those with key roles in the American administration and in NATO were of great value. No other scientist from
another country was allowed to sit in on meetings of the
President's Science Advisory Committee (PSAC).

The four men with whom this chapter is particularly concerned, all of them American, were Solly's friends. In their variety
and in what they did they represented what he loved and admired
in America: General Carl (Tooey) Spaatz, Air Force Commander;
Admiral Hyman Rickover, 'the father of the US Nuclear Navy';
Isidor Rabi, physicist and sometime Chairman of the President's
Science Advisory Committee; and lastly the poet e e cummings (as

he wrote his name). Solly included the first three in his book *Six Men out of the Ordinary*, published in the year before he died. He chose them, he said, because he wished to show what they were like and what it was like to work with them. He also wished to show the link between the men who conceived and developed the implements of war and those who fought with them. The claims of the fourth, a poet, are based on thirty years of friendship and the fact that he was at least as out of the ordinary as the other three.

Spaatz was the grandson of German immigrants who arrived in Pennsylvania halfway through the nineteenth century. An airman all his life, he was, when Solly first met him in Algiers in 1943, the Commanding General of the North West African Air Forces. David Metz, his biographer, credited him with 'one of the rarest of all gifts, an uncanny sense of what would work'. In Sicily and in Italy, Solly was a member of his mess and continued to advise him, together with Tedder, on the choice of targets. He had, he said, rarely met a man who was 'so forthcoming in his friendship'. It was from Spaatz that he received the instruction to judge whether the island fortress of Pantelleria could be taken out by bombing. If this were possible, it would avoid the need for a costly seaborne invasion; one was planned to take place in two weeks' time. He was, if he thought it could be done, to draw up a plan showing how and what forces would be required in terms of aeroplanes and bombs. Spaatz would see to it that they were available. It was, to say the least, an unusual partnership between an American General and a non-military academic scientist from South Africa. Its success, and Solly's role in it, was generously acknowledged by Eisenhower as well as by Spaatz, who presented Solly with a special citation.

One minor incident, in which Solly was not involved, shows a side of Spaatz's character not always found in high-level commanders. Frank Cooper, thirty years later Permanent Secretary to the Ministry of Defence, relates how, as a Flight Lieutenant serving with the Spitfire Wing of the Desert Air Force, he was sitting in the mess in Corsica when two Air Force Generals walked in, told him they had never flown Spitfires and asked him to arrange for them to do so. He and a friend then walked them out on to the airfield, where they commandeered four planes and, after brief explanations, took off. After a short flight, all four returned safely. Spaatz was one of the Generals.

The muddle and confusion which are endemic in human affairs become the more intense in war. No matter how detailed the evidence available or how carefully it is analysed, it is unlikely that the full truth of what happened will ever emerge. Early in 1944, there were three views as to how the Allies should use their growing superiority in the air. Harris was determined to sustain what was by then the established strategy of Bomber Command, namely, to strike by night at German towns and cities with the aim of breaking the economy and cracking the morale of the people. Spaatz, on the other hand, disapproved of the bombing of purely civilian targets. His daughter, Mrs Walter Bell, tells of how, on a visit to London in 1941, he went on to the roof of his hotel and shook his fist at the waves of German bombers flying over, declaring that they were setting back the use of air power by many years. He was a firm believer in a strategy of daytime precision bombing, its first aim being the destruction of the Luftwaffe; particular targets were selected on the strength of what they could contribute to that aim. Both Harris and Spaatz believed the war could be won from the air, and both saw Overlord as hazardous in itself and prejudicial to that possibility. Eisenhower and Tedder, on the other hand, committed to and responsible for the invasion, both believed, on Solly's advice, that the paralysis of that part of the French rail network which served the Channel area was crucial. It was essential to deny to the Germans the means of reinforcing quickly their defences against an Allied landing. This would require the diversion of a part of the strategic air forces. The powerful support accorded to all three views generated considerable heat and recrimination at the time, and subsequently.

While Solly felt that the Air Barons, who of course included Spaatz, arrogated to themselves a degree of sovereign independence allowed to no one else, Spaatz considered that Solly had a fixation about the transportation targets. While their staffs may have argued, between the two of them there was no serious friction. In the early months of 1944 Spaatz was Solly's guest at a dinner in Christ

Church Oxford, where by Solly's account he was a great success. He would have been more so had he brought his guitar with him, for then he would have been able to lend weight to his assertion that Bach sounded better on the guitar than on the organ. Solly claims that while he was helping him to bed following a somewhat festive dinner, Spaatz brought their talk back to military matters, insisting that he was not opposed to the Allied Expeditionary Air Forces (AEAF) plan in principle. What disturbed him was the thought that while he would be diverted to supporting an invasion that might never take place, Harris would be free to continue his attacks on Germany and so might win the war on his own.

In the last phase of the war in Europe, Spaatz commanded what was, and is likely to remain, the largest air armada ever assembled. His aim, in which he succeeded, was to win the right of way in the skies. When, later, he was ordered to the Far East to command the operation which was to launch the first atomic bombs on Japan, he first consulted his wife as to whether he should take part in such a mission. He received the clear answer, he was a West Pointer and must, as such, obey orders. He demanded that he be given those orders in writing and kept them always with him. A minor panic ensued when one day a zealous orderly sent his trousers to the laundry without realising what was in the pockets.

Never a man of many words, on his return home he could hardly bring himself to speak of the business in which he had had a part. When a neighbour congratulated him on his part in bringing the war to an end, he could find no words and turned away in silence. He was, in any event, not one who talked much. Whereas some people never used two words when one would do, Spaatz would never use one when none would suffice. Clare Boothe Luce once complained to Spaatz's wife, 'I got nothing out of your husband; maybe I should sleep with him.' 'You still wouldn't,' was the immediate answer. The man who commanded that huge American air assault on Germany, and was then entrusted with the awful mission against Japan, needed to be and was out of the ordinary. Solly regretted that the disputes inevitable between Allies in the heat of conflict were given new life in memoirs and biographies when it was over. Spaatz, who refrained from such exercises in hindsight, in reviewing books by Alanbrooke and Montgomery, allowed himself the dry comment, 'How the Allies managed to win the Second World War, handicapped as they were by American Generals, is a mystery.'

Hyman Rickover the next of Solly's collection, possessed like him unlimited energy and absolute determination. Unlike Solly, there was little room in his make-up for charm, and he used what he had sparingly. He was the son of poor Jewish parents who, at the turn of the nineteenth century, came from Poland, first to New York, and finally settled in Chicago. Not much is known of his youth, though he was said to have been bullied at school and at the Naval Academy. Certainly he emerged with and kept a man-sized chip on his shoulder. His only seagoing command, of an ancient minesweeper, was not a success. He was seen to have no future as a line officer and was relegated to the engineering side of the service, generally regarded as inferior and far from being a breeding ground for Admirals. Promotion to Rear Admiral did not come until he was over fifty; he was over seventy when he was made a full Admiral. His appointment then owed more to his standing with Congress and with the public than to the regard in which he was held by the naval authorities. Solly described him as 'one of the most outstanding military technologists of his age, and at the same time one of the most disliked officers who had ever graced the US Navy'. He seemed to relish lambasting authority and, unsurprisingly, was not much loved by it as a result.

In the years immediately following the war, the US Navy set about adjusting to the arrival of nuclear weapons, and began to have thoughts of using nuclear energy for the propulsion of ships. Rickover saw this as his opportunity. He devoted his energies to learning about nuclear propulsion, ensuring that he and no one else controlled the development of the reactor that was required. Admiral Hills, the head of the Bureau of Ships, who knew that Rickover would out-work, out-manoeuvre and out-fight everyone, set up a nuclear power branch in the research division of the Bureau and put him in charge of it. A decision was made six months later to give the branch the corresponding role within the newly-formed Atomic Energy Commission's naval reactor branch.

Rickover thus wore two hats. Wearing one, as an official of the Bureau of Ships, he could request the Atomic Energy Commission to do something and then, wearing the other as an officer of the AEC, put it in hand. He set about creating the nuclear navy. With a finger in every aspect of the project, selection and training of officers and men, with his own men in the construction yards, and working with his contractors, he knew an exceptional amount about what was going on. He developed considerable expertise in bypassing individuals who might be a source of delay or resistance and was skilled in his handling of Congress and obtaining the development funds required.

In 1962, Solly was lunching in the house of General Sir Michael West when someone came in to tell him that Admiral Rickover was sitting outside in his car; he would not come in, would Solly go outside to meet him. Referring to a recent article of Solly's, the Admiral said, 'That was a fine piece of yours; keep it up. We military are not made to think. Keep in touch.' It was, as Solly said, an odd beginning to a strange friendship that lasted for more than twenty years.

Solly was convinced that Rickover had played a part in securing the amendments to the McMahon Act, and that without his active support, the American Government might never have agreed to sell Britain the complete nuclear propulsion plant without which the Polaris venture might have gone lame. Unhappily, all Solly's efforts, supported by Mountbatten and the British Ambassador in Washington, to get him a knighthood failed; Rickover was as much detested in the Royal Navy as he was in the US Navy. He had his own way of doing things; having established relations with Solly, he insisted on conducting business with the British Government through him. If he wished to visit Holy Loch, he would notify Solly when he expected to arrive, leave it to him to fix an aeroplane and then perhaps spend a weekend in Norfolk. He did not bother with the Navy Department in Washington or the American Embassy in London. So far as the British Government was concerned, if they wished to say anything to Rickover, as they frequently did, they must do so through Solly; it gave Solly an added importance which more than survived his retirement.

It was extraordinary that a man so unconventional, so little

given to the ordinary politenesses of life and at times so devastat-
ingly rude, should, despite a host of enemies gathered on the way,
have gone so far and achieved so much. Eventually, after reaching
his eighties, he was retired. A special ceremony was set up at the
White House to honour him and take the pain out of the occasion, which proved to be as unusual as the rest. Rick, as he was
known, took trouble to let Solly have a blow-by-blow account of
what occurred. Lehmann, the Secretary of the Navy, approached
to shake his hand: 'What the hell are you doing here?' was followed
by a stream of abuse. In the Oval Office, when the President began
to speak of his great achievements, Rickover interrupted, 'Why
are you firing me?' and pointing at the Secretary for Defence,
Weinberger, accused him, 'They told me you ordered me fired.'
He then called Lehmann 'a piss ant'. Turning on the President,
who had tried to calm things down, he shouted, 'Are you a man?
Can't you make decisions for yourself? What do you know about
this problem? They say that you are too old and that you're not up
to the job either.' 'Are you a man or not?' he demanded of the
President. 'I thought this was going to be a meeting between you
and me.' He then asked for and was given some time with the
President alone. Solly saw him as a man who did not belong, one
who, bruised by the anti-Semitism he met in earlier days, was
fuelled by resentment.

'So you're the redoubtable Solly Zuckerman,' was Isidor Rabi's
greeting when they met in 1958 at the first meeting of NATO's
newly constituted scientific committee. Solly, who must have been
delighted, declared himself amused. It marked the beginning of a
friendship that grew in warmth and understanding till Rabi's death
thirty years later. 'He was', Solly wrote, 'to reveal himself as a
statesman who as much as anyone I knew had a realistic view of
what scientists could do in the promotion of understanding and
world peace.' Intended as a tribute to Rabi, the words encapsulate
the vision that lit his own path. Such men ought to be remembered, yet they tend to slip out of life and memory. What they said
is too often submerged in a torrent of the glib, the superficial and
the unhelpful.

He was the son of poor, strictly orthodox Jewish parents who emigrated in 1899 from Poland to New York when he was a year old. The anti-Semitic feeling of the time and area he grew up left him unscarred, but streetwise. The school he attended left him free to learn or not as he pleased. He won a scholarship at Cornell, where he studied first chemistry then physics. Physics to him had a deep emotional quality, which he described as 'a higher truth': 'You're trying to find out how God made the world, just like Jacob wrestling with the angel.' A two-year tour of Europe and finally a lectureship at Columbia University completed the foundations of a brilliant career. Working on radar at the Massachusetts Institute of Technology at the outbreak of war, he declined Robert Oppenheimer's invitation in 1943 to become his deputy in the Manhattan Project at Los Alamos. He did, however, agree to become his chief adviser and consultant, and remained so until the war was over. Fear that Hitler might be the first in the race to unlock the secrets of the atom and his revulsion at the Nazi treatment of the Jews were the factors that moved him and many others to take part in that most grim of competitions

With the return of peace, Rabi went back to Columbia as head of the Physics Department. He was one of the first members of the President's Science Advisory Committee, set up by Eisenhower, and its Chairman for a year. He played a key role in 1955 in the International Conference on the Peaceful Uses of Atomic Energy; he was a Nobel Laureate. He regarded the hydrogen bomb as intrinsically evil and focussed upon Edward Teller, one of its protagonists, his especial contempt: 'He is an enemy of humanity.' Another of Solly's *Six Men out of the Ordinary*, Rabi is the only one in that slim volume whose words are quoted at length. They are memorable, incisive, clear; we do not hear the like today. In 1965, he lamented that whereas the mature scientist could listen with pleasure to the philosopher, the historian or the literary man, 'this channel of communication is a one way street . . . science seems to be no longer communicable to the great majority of educated laymen'.

If we survive into the future we can hope that men will realise deeply that their most noble goal is to understand themselves within the universe and that this goal will override all the petty and parochial aims that so disturb the peace and endanger mankind's future existence.

His life, he said on the day of his retirement as Head of the Physics Department of Columbia in 1967, had been separated into two parts.

The first was the prewar, where we devoted ourselves whole-heartedly and continually to scientific efforts' . . . [second was the war in which we] 'devoted ourselves completely to the war effort because it was then that we were fighting a beast which was inimical to all nationalities, to all humanity.

The years that followed drew from him this warning, 'While I feel quite confident that we have a great Department of Physics, I do not feel so confident that we have even begun to tame the atom so that it doesn't kill us ultimately . . . I far underestimated the problem; I far overestimated the rationality . . . of human beings. I far underestimated the capacity of people to put the obvious, the fearful, out of their minds, to refuse to look at the longer distance for the sake of immediate advantage.' If people were to move their minds away from that immediate advantage for long enough to read those words again, they might find in them cause for reflection. Rabi, as Solly said, achieved that synthesis of knowledge and experience which leads to wisdom. It would be reassuring to know that men such as Rabi had a voice in government. What he said would come as a welcome change from the endless cascade of bromide and triviality which pours out over us.

That the human race has been able for so long to co-exist with nuclear weaponry without disaster being injected by either wickedness or accident, was, Solly thought, to be taken as ground not for thankfulness and profound relief; certainly not for concluding that alarm signals of peril were exaggerated, even groundless. Facts are awkward, uncomfortable things to live with, and the truth is often far from what we hope, pretence being a more cosy, comfortable companion. The media provide us with what we are willing to pay for, a diet of football, sex, scandal and crime, which will keep the viewer, the listener, the reader content and coming back for more. Politicians, even those who are not swept along with the herd, who have had glimpses of truth, are reluctant to share them for fear they might frighten, bore or otherwise disturb. World leaders are for the most part silent on issues of survival which used to concern their predecessors. Their chosen way of handling the unthinkable is, it would seem, to avoid thinking about it. They are ready enough to take advantage of the fact that mankind has grown used to living with perils, of which it has never taken the measure. The world needs the Rabis and the Zuckermans to remind it of facts, which otherwise slip its mind.

What such men have said has not been denied, contradicted or challenged; it has been ignored, not by accident but on purpose. It is as if one were to walk round Trafalgar Square and decide not to notice Nelson's Column. Solly's belief that *Homo sapiens* would not be so mad as to risk self-destruction remains unproven; he could yet dispense with the *sapiens* and prove himself an idiot, even though a clever one. *Nature* ended its admirable obituary of Solly with these words, 'His most fitting memorial would be that his friends would now press for an answer to the awkward questions on nuclear policy the British Government has not yet answered.' This book is intended to remind people of questions, which despite our efforts to bury them, are likely to re-emerge. Politicians from time to time express their concern as to where scientists and the greater knowledge they have brought are taking us. They turn a deaf ear to the anxieties of scientists. Rabi, wise as any, expressed his fears in a letter in September 1981: 'The USA is now governed by an energetic and devoted group equally divided between madmen and fools. The helmsman is playing it by ear but, he is tone deaf.'

e e cummings, painter and poet, wrote in a letter to Solly that all his heart was 'on a New Hampshire hill, gifted with blue mountains'. His wife Marion, enchanting as she was beautiful, left the Ziegfeld Follies to marry him, loved him, cherished him, enjoyed him as a poet and was amused by his opinions, without always sharing them. They entered Solly's life in 1934 during his first visit to America, and thereafter had a compartment of their own; they welcomed Joan when she married Solly. The friendship was a feature in the lives of all of them. For Solly, enthralled by the wonders science revealed in the world, excited and shocked by the cleverness and follies of those who ran it, a poet who preferred to stay away from it in the woods was something new. 'I was fascinated by cummings' wry conversation about the madness of the world.' He attempted to comfort cummings with the thought that it was the same everywhere, the peasants were on the move. The letters they exchanged over a span of thirty years, almost coded and written with no thought that an outsider might one day read them, gave a flavour of themselves. They said little of what they were doing or where they were, unless it held some prospect of their meeting. They told of England, bleak, cheerless, hungry and poor, and of food parcels that flowed eastwards, 'the cupboard love' they generated and the hams they contained. One ham meant that Solly would now be able to face the new economic blizzard with confidence. Another made it possible for him to 'face the future with greater courage than that of any other inhabitant of this fighting back tough glorious little island'. cummings was inspired to reply with a limerick,

> give our sadists *carte blanche* in atomics
> let our masochists flaunt economics
> . . . if I understand Freud
> no-one need be annoyed
> while our narcissists stick to their comics.

Solly passed the limerick off as his own, but could not answer the question 'What difference would it make if the masochists handled atomics and the sadists comics?' Meanwhile, he was helping 'to find staffing that doesn't cost dollars to fill the gap in our shining balance of payments'. Joan still had not seen the wonderful ham (another one); she was not yet back from the wet and rainy seaside, to which she had taken the children and their whooping cough. He sent his 'warmest salivatory thanks', and would invite her to attack it (the ham) on her return without further delay.

In answer to Solly's protesting that he was himself a scientist, cummings wrote, 'It hadn't occurred to ignorant me that you might be a scientist; I'd have sworn that my favourite rogue was a human being.' A.J. Ayer, the philosopher whom Solly introduced to cummings, said of him that of the men he had met, cummings was one of three whom he most admired; the other two were Einstein and Russell. cummings wrote a poem to mark Ayer's birthday with two memorable lines which explained their friendship,

You walk on tightropes as if they lay on the ground
And always, bird eyed, notice more than we notice you notice.

18

A Man out of the Ordinary

'It is wiser to find out than to suppose.'

Mark Twain

SOLLY WAS an enigma to rival the Sphinx: a loner who looked for support; gregarious, provided people did not come too close or stay too long; a nomad who feared encumbrances yet sought to put down roots; a self-centred man who yet looked far beyond the carapace of his own self. It was as a scientist that Solly, aged twenty-one, first explored the development of a baboon's skull. It was as a scientist that throughout his life he looked at man's growing power to create and to destroy; to heal and to wound; to conserve and to consume. It was as a scientist also that he reflected upon the impact of man's activities on the land, water and air on which all life depends. What made him different was that, though he applied himself to the detail, he did not get caught up in it. He was aware that the fragment he was looking at could not be properly understood on its own; it belonged to a structure of which no one knew the beginning or could see the end.

While those early years in South Africa left their clear and indelible imprint upon him, they left him unchained and free, as soon as his education was finished, to go to England where he knew great things were waiting to be savoured. In telling his own story, he made much of the overpowering taskmaster his mother had been, perhaps to excuse himself for the way in which he had left home and family and thereafter cut himself off from them. He saw his family as being a hindrance and had no wish to risk an entanglement from which escape might be difficult.

South Africa came near to making an anthropologist of him. 'You had the whole gamut of evolution around you near Cape Town from almost naked bushmen to Government House,' he wrote. Tribes of baboons were his neighbours. He spent time looking for signs of early human habitations. When, however, Elliot Smith, who had first launched him in England, encouraged him in 1935 to accept the Chair of Anthropology at Peking University, he declined. Respect for facts and an unwillingness to involve himself in unfounded speculation about man's origins kept him away from a field of study he felt to be still in shadow. The exposure of the Piltdown Man hoax went some way to justifying his caution. He returned only twice to South Africa, in 1931 for reasons zoological rather than family, and again in 1975; by then he was famous. The hero's welcome accorded to him at his old school seemed to stir in him an awareness of what it had done for him, and even a touch of gratitude. He had not been crammed with knowledge, he had been given an appetite for it, and had been allowed to leave with an inquiring mind. An invitation to deliver the Cecil Rhodes Memorial lecture took him to the University in Grahamstown. He asked his audience, without getting much of a response, what they thought a modern Rhodes would make of his forebear's vision that an international scholarship scheme would help to bring peace and understanding in the world. Something of a shadow was cast over the remainder of the visit when, unwarned, in a speech in Cape Town he cast a slur on an Afrikaner hero. A hostile press surprised and upset him and he pulled down the blinds on his native land and never returned.

That ability to pull the blinds down on what was of no interest and to turn back from roads that led nowhere was important. It left him free to unravel, explore and challenge. Boundaries and partitions which hampered access to knowledge were anathema to him. He saw them as devices erected for their own protection by those who could not stand exposure. Without being a great scientist in the sense of driving a salient into the unknown, he was an influential one. The breadth of his science – biology, anatomy, physiology, endocrinology, zoology – made him so and lent weight to his belief that in both government and education, science should have a voice on the same level as the humanities.

Solly was ambitious in that he wanted to go a long way. Though content to wait for opportunity, he was ready always to seize it. He saw no need to hobble himself with a plan. He had his own star to follow and it took him on a long and varied journey, from the wild places of Cape Province to the calm of the Norfolk countryside; from the lecture room to the battlefield; from the dissecting room to the Cabinet Office. It took him away from the precision of scientific experiment in Birmingham to the ordered confusion of Government. It showed him how inexact and unscientific are the processes of handling the affairs of a nation. The backcloth to his journey is so crowded with people jostling one another for space and massive events running into each other, that perspective is lost. What belongs in the background of the picture seems at times to surge forward, swamping, confusing and almost blotting out what was once easy to see. It becomes hard in the tumult to get the measure of either people or things or events, or their importance to us.

To help him on his way, he had a rich endowment of intellect, energy and stamina. At turning points, he was accustomed to leave the decision to circumstance, chance and other people. When, in the early days of the war, he put together the Oxford Extra-Mural Unit, he could not have foreseen that it would lead him to advising Eisenhower and Tedder on a vital aspect of one of the most significant military operations in history. Nor, in accepting Morrison's invitation to join the Advisory Council on Scientific Policy in 1946, can he have realised that he was taking a step on a path which would take him to the top flights of the Civil Service. What he called a stimulating tutorial was not part of any considered plan, yet it turned out to be essential training for what followed.

His practice of collecting people, successful, interesting, promising or just useful, and the fact that some had titles and were famous, earned him a reputation for being a name dropper and a snob, and to an extent he was. What set him apart from the generality of the breed was not only the size and variety of his collection, but the fact that he knew them all, and they knew him, and were pleased to do so. The Government's Chief Scientific Adviser had in mind the memory of the young Jewish immigrant who knew about monkeys and loved them. The people Solly cherished were those who helped him to believe that the world he now lived in was real and not a dream. A roll call of them seems appropriate, even at the cost of repeating what has been said elsewhere. Jackie Whitworth, the friend who took him rock climbing; Ruth Bisbee, the visiting lecturer from Liverpool who showed him what a fine field of study zoology was; Elliot Smith, a leader in medical science, his sponsor in England; Julian Huxley, who gave him his first job at the Zoo; J.D. Bernal, crystallographer, who collected him from Oxford and took him into war; Tedder, whom he advised – and honoured – and who believed in him; Peter Krohn and Anita Mandl who sustained him in Birmingham; Terence Morrison-Scott, who helped him through the troubles at the Zoo; Richard Chilver, his guide in Whitehall; Mountbatten, who looked for ideas in others and took Solly to people and places Solly on his own might not have been able to reach; Rabi, the American physicist who was his friend and from whom he learned.

There were of course others, extra-mural so to speak, who saw him against different backgrounds. Two perceptive and dazzling women, who loved and admired him, came as close as anyone to unravelling the enigma of Solly. Martha Gellhorn, a friend for sixty years, wrote to Joan when Solly died,

> No doubt he was a strain as a husband, even as a father, but what a wonder he was in himself. The tirelessly inquiring mind, the energy for work, the variety of his thinking. As he grew old, his vanity was touching, as if he didn't really know his own unique value and he had to reassure himself with the names of all the important people he was seeing, when he was far more unusual and far brainier than any of them.

Peggy Willis, also a friend for many years, noticed the value he placed on social success and his envy of Isaiah Berlin that he should find it so easy. She summed him up, 'Probably he would always about everything, have wanted what was beyond his reach. He achieved so much, but I don't believe it was ever enough; nor could it ever have been.' They were both aware of the inquiring mind, the stretching for something that was out of reach and the lack of contentment. They saw too how his admiration of others caused him to lose sight of his own worth and stature.

Most people face problems; Solly fed on them. They were grist to his mill, they kept his wheels turning. They ranged from the immense and almost insoluble, from how to restrain the human race from destroying itself or poisoning its habitat, to the mesh on the Snowdon Aviary at the Zoo or how Cadbury Schweppes should keep the bubbles in soft drinks. Although he contrived to dovetail together his roles in Whitehall, Birmingham and the Zoo so that he could more easily handle them, they had little in common. Like an actor playing by turns Hamlet, Lear and Othello, he was a different person in each. In Whitehall he was an adviser, part of a huge, diverse machine which hardly knew one end of itself from the other. He was a part of it without belonging to it. As elsewhere in his life, those who worked with him seldom saw the same man. One saw him as interested only in impressing his equals and, even more, his superiors, having little time for those who worked for him. Another remembered him as warm, distinguished, larger than life, the model of an *éminence grise*. A third had him as charming socially, reserved professionally and slow to show his hand. In Whitehall, Solly learned lessons about the political realities which beset governments and how hog-tied, they limp along behind events, half-aware of dangers ahead, trumpeting that they know what to do, but still afraid, even if they know what might be done, to disturb people with the unpalatable. They fear that those whom they have encouraged to be frivolous may not welcome invitations to be serious.

The Department of Anatomy in Birmingham University was a world away from Whitehall. Solly was himself in charge. Those who worked in it were a team which he assembled and held together. In Peter Krohn he had a man who was not only a considerable scientist, a Fellow of the Royal Society, dedicated to his work and loyal, but one who sought nothing for himself. Anita Mandl, also a scientist of distinction herself, not only kept in touch with Solly for thirty years after her own retirement, but was at pains to keep together and informed about each other 'the Old

Gang from the Department . . . part of his family – or at least we felt we were'. Solly's faults were obvious, plain for all to see. Those who make much of them ought not to dodge the question, what was there about him that gave rise to that feeling of family, that caused them at the time to be aware of his physical presence in the Department and many years later to remember him with gratitude, admiration and affection? Rather strangely, he seems to have been unaware of the extraordinary impact he had on all their lives. There is a lingering regret that he did not give more credit to others for the scientific work they had done together; it would have cost him nothing.

The Zoo again was different. Whereas in Whitehall he was an adviser and in Birmingham something between chairman and managing director, in the London Zoo he seemed more like a proprietor, but one who was paid nothing for running both the Society and the Zoo. For many years a treasured part of his life, it kept him close to the creatures which were always to him a source of wonder, and gave him a position in London which he enjoyed. His papers are sprinkled with mentions of its problems, the need for money, the improvements he had in mind. He was proud of what he had achieved there; he had saved the Society which owned it as a scientific institution. He had also put down a rebellious and selfish clique and given the Zoo new life following the staleness and decay to which war had reduced it. Thirty years are a long time for one man to dominate an institution, and the time came when even his energy was insufficient, and complacency took the place of vision. When he retired, he left not much in the way of organisation and certainly no one of his stature. Some at least of the new buildings seemed designed more to impress the onlooker than for the comfort of the occupants or the convenience of those who cared for them. He thought the animals were themselves sufficiently wonderful to draw people in. He did not trouble to explain what was there to those who did not know, or to provide adequate amenities for visitors. The conviction that he was right may have annoyed people in Whitehall, but as often as not it gave him the power and the push to get things through. It was, however, more the way of a politician than of a scientist, and it led him into error at the Zoo.

Such was the frame of Solly's public life: university, menagerie and government. A combination of intellect, energy and determination enabled him to handle the huge range of problems they threw up. But even in that public area of life where he enjoyed prodigious success, he was not an open book, easy to read. He was a man of variable moods. While he would be listening to and receiving what was said to him, he would at the same time have in mind other problems which interested him, needed his attention. He would be getting ready for the next major encounter and quite often wondering how to persuade, convince or impress. Those who came close to Solly tended to find, as they did so, that his defences increased rather than diminished. His almost paranoid concern with privacy, originating perhaps in early youth, led him to fence himself in and to make it difficult for others to reach him; impossible for him to explain himself.

In 1968 the award of the OM delighted him and might have marked the end of his career; it did not. Retirement for Solly was like the end of the rainbow, a point which, though close at times, never seemed to come nearer. In 1969 he told Harold Wilson that since he was in his sixty-fifth year the time had come for him to retire. Wilson replied that he saw no reason why he should, nor did he want him to do so. Since neither Wilson nor Trend would give any assurance that there would be a successor, Solly decided to stay. Two years later (1971), by which time there had been a change of government, he tried again. Ted Heath replied in much the same vein, but added that if he insisted on going, he hoped he would stay on as a consultant on a day-a-week basis, with a perch in the Cabinet Office. There was a farewell dinner party at Number Ten to which the Prime Minister invited some sixty guests with most of whom Solly had been closely associated over the years. Solly, who was to be made a Peer, felt that the Prime Minister could not have been more gracious.

In the years that followed, Solly found himself unable to empty his mind of the problems which had occupied it when he was a full-time official; the encouragement of R&D, the protection of the environment and particularly the menace of nuclear weapons. In 1974 when Wilson again became Prime Minister, Solly wrote what was becoming his customary letter asking whether he wished him to continue, to which he received an affirmative reply. When in due course Jim Callaghan succeeded him, Solly wrote again. In the absence of a reply John Hunt, Trend's successor as Secretary to the Cabinet, advised him to carry on. In 1979 when Margaret Thatcher became Prime Minister, Solly asked her the same question as he had asked her predecessors. Robert Armstrong, when he became Cabinet Secretary, was evidently content with things as they were, and observed that Solly could be wheeled out for state occasions, as one would the oldest inhabitant of a village. Later, another Cabinet Secretary, Robin Butler, perhaps prompted from above, suggested to Solly that the time had come for him to go, adding that the Prime Minister would be giving a farewell lunch. More than a decade had passed since the Heath farewell dinner. In all ordinary circumstances the occupant of space in the Cabinet Office would, no matter how eminent, be eased out immediately he left the Civil Service. To have stayed, as Solly did, for some fifteen years was unprecedented and most unlikely to be repeated.

From those closest to him, the different and changing aspects of Solly, both as husband and father, demanded degrees of under-standing and patience, which he could not be counted on to show in return. Joan, without fighting pitched battles, somehow strug-gled through the attrition that living with Solly must have been. At one point, upset almost beyond endurance, she decided to leave. She got as far as packing her bags and booking a room at a hotel, but was then held back by that pride and sense of duty which she derived from her Jewish faith. Israel Sieff, kindly and perceptive, acknowledged her feat. 'You had a domineering mother, a domi-neering step-grandmother and a domineering husband. Yet somehow you managed not to be ground down by them all, to remain yourself and free.'

Rabbi Alexandra Carr spoke of Joan at her funeral; of her extraordinary integrity, her sense of justice and her profound sense of what was right and wrong. 'There was never any malice, but a kind of naive openness and generosity that attracted even strangers who scarcely knew her. She engaged you with her simplicity and humour, she touched you by her intuition and perception, she sur-prised you with her frank and shrewd insights.' It would indeed have been strange if the granddaughter of Rufus Isaacs and Alfred Mond had not been proud of her lineage, and Joan was intensely so. The word 'proud' has more than one meaning; it can be just conceit, or it can imply the possession of standards, bringing with them feelings of service, respect and even reverence. These last Joan had in abundance. For her they were a part of living, timeless and true, and not, as some seem to think, outdated and dispensable. Solly, short of self-assurance, moved by instinct towards those who could help him shine. He needed to be able to depend without being seen to do so. In that almost impossible assignment somehow she succeeded.

When Solly died, she felt at first a blend of relief, anticlimax and some bitterness. His seeming disregard hurt. So too did his failure to tell or warn her that in his Will he left most of his money to the University of East Anglia. Later, as time passed, the soreness went and perspective returned. She began to see how necessary she had been to this strange man of vision who understood so much about the world, but so little about himself. She had given him a stability and a poise which he would never have achieved without her. She seemed to surprise herself, explaining almost as an afterthought, 'Well, I suppose I loved him.' When the cauldron cools, it is possible that history taking shape, may show Solly as having been at least as large, as important, as entitled to the mantle of a prophet, as any of his more self-assured, more publicised contemporaries. If it does, it will be in no small measure due to Joan, who provided the anchor and who, with great generosity and wisdom, gave him a long chain. The chain may have rubbed a bit, but it held him. Of his story she was the undoubted heroine.

Stella was special; she nearly died as a baby and so was the more cherished by both her parents. Solly doted on her, without the worry that she might be a competitor, as Paul was from the beginning. Coming home from work he would sit down in the bathroom, drink in hand, and allow her to climb on to his lap and comb his fine curly hair into extraordinary hairstyles; he would look at them in the mirror and laugh and relax. He taught her the alphabet and the names of the bones in her hand, and told her stories. There was one about fairies; she always remembered them, as he first put them into her mind, dancing under the pear tree in the garden by the air raid shelter. Later, he would read to her the poetry of e e cummings. 'He read it with such joy and in such a way that these words which sometimes looked incomprehensible to me on paper, when spoken by my father took on a magic quality; they flowed and made perfect sense. It was like switching into another language. And a language which I have treasured ever since.'

Not long before her own death from cancer, she wrote a monograph, revealing both of her father and herself. She noted his obsession with privacy, 'the most over-developed sense of privacy imaginable . . . You couldn't go bounding into the bedroom whenever you felt like it. There was no question of going in without knocking and receiving an affirmative reply first.' She found it hard to understand his reluctance to talk even to his wife and children about South Africa and his youth. The most they could hope for were the odd, unconnected scraps of information that he handed out from time to time. She thought that perhaps, had he been prepared to look back a bit more, he might have developed 'a more realistic insight into the stuff he was made of, even if it didn't quite stretch to enlightenment on the stuff that those close to him were made of'.

His study too was his exclusive territory; it was 'a room of quiet and intellectual pursuit; it stimulated curiosity and inquiry. It emanated hard, hard, work and brilliance too, if a room can be said to emanate such things.' The cellar, too, was his domain; you only went there when he invited you to go with him. She and Paul spent hours down there arranging and rearranging the considerable variety of wines he always had in store. The numbers of bottles in the racks had to tally with those in the book he kept. If they did not, a huge search would take place, 'and as in all things with my father, you didn't stop until the mystery was solved'. 'They were happy times down in the cellar. My father wasn't the kind of man you could idly pass the time of day with, so unpacking wine was one way of spending time with him. And it was terribly important to be needed — and it was a great privilege to be a part of his team.'

Stella's account of her relations with her father reflects a great range of emotions — joy, admiration and love mingled with disappointment, anger and resentment at the ways of a parent who could not conceive of the possibility that he might be wrong. From time to time he was, and more seriously so within the immediate family circle than elsewhere. As time passed, the teenaged daughter who had expectations of guidance and warmth from her father, was hurt by his aloofness and obvious boredom, spiced from time to time with carping criticism. A weekend off from school, spent in a hotel in Swanage, was not to Solly's liking. Stella was left feeling that he was bored and that it would have been better if he hadn't come. She was pleased when he agreed to give a lecture at her school, but was astounded by his choice of subject – the pituitary gland. It was, she felt, unlikely that any of his teenage audience understood a word of what he said. It was at the same school that she learned for the first time that there was another whole side to life which was fun, frivolous and hedonistic. 'I felt angry with my father for having put so much emphasis on work to the exclusion of less serious things. More angry that he in no way denied himself.' The pressures to succeed were worse for Paul, but Stella still suffered, while the brother whom she adored was put through the mill of inquiry as to why he had not done better.

When not driven to fury by her father, Stella understood him well, and the reasons for his behaviour. There were times, however, when it became near to impossible. His sudden changes of mood, often precipitated by things quite unknown to those who felt their impact, made for misunderstanding. His worries as to how he was going to survive financially and his repeated suggestions that they would have to tighten their belts also made for difficulties, when he seemed to be living so well himself. His anxiety lest his small inner family should somehow shame him by not living up to expectations also made for tension. She realised that his behaviour towards them was an echo from the past which, real or imagined, seemed to haunt him. She could never fathom how Solly's father came to marry his mother. They were an unlikely, impossible mixture; his head had been as much in the air as her feet had been on the ground. With such a background, Solly must, she thought, have learned while still young to build 'an impenetrable cocoon round himself.' Inside it, 'he was safe and could go the way he wanted – and that is the way he lived most of his life ever since and, miraculously, got away with it'. She could not understand how her father, with his reiterated complaints about his mother, should, far from avoiding them, have repeated the errors he attributed to her. Added to those sources of friction was his total inability to understand that others were not like him; 'hence his intolerance, impatience, etc when people are not able to do everything at similarly supernatural speed'.

There were, however, other times when they were in harmony together, when they would talk about her work and he would give her advice and encouragement. 'The quality of his advice was always in a different league to that of my own teachers at university.' His always had something global about it, theirs was merely parochial. She was conscious that through her father she met many interesting people. She had a huge affection for Noel Annan, who was shocked at the way Solly, whom he loved and admired, behaved to his children. Hugh Gaitskell and Nye Bevan (an odd pairing) were her heroes. 'There was always much laughter when they came – separately of course – and much interesting discussion.'

She never thought of her father as belonging to any political party, and was indignant when someone told her very categorically that of course her father had always been a Socialist and surely she must have known it. He was a civil servant, and as such was not allowed to wear his political colours on his sleeve. Moreover, she did not feel he would have wanted to. A political definition would have detracted from the important business upon which he was engaged. She thought 'politics were an irrelevance to him. He didn't like labels. He never liked being identified with any particular group, for whatever reason. He was a truly independent man who liked to flit freely, and unobserved, wherever he chose.'

Her father's friendship with Victor Rothschild was based, so Stella thought, on 'deep affection mixed with enormous rivalry'. 'Victor', she wrote, 'had a daughter Emma in a different league of brightness from me. My father and he used to compete with Emma and me, rather as if we were greyhounds, to see which of us was the more intelligent and the more intellectually advanced.' It was a competition more to do with the fathers than the daughters. Solly's attitude towards any boyfriend of Stella's was anything but welcoming. To Andrew, her husband and his son-in-law, it was almost beyond reach of forgiveness; he never really gave him a chance. Even Solly's most devoted friends were shocked by his unkindness.

With that 'hostile, cold, ice cold and aggressive side' went 'an immensely loving and light-hearted side . . . Just occasionally, he would reach out to me and positively bubble over with a profusion of love and warmth. At these times he was so tender and gentle and . . . just plain ordinary.' Of one of their last meetings in 1990, not long before she died, Stella wrote:

It was a warming hour and a half. I felt he really wanted my company, whereas normally he would have been wanting to work. I asked him whether he was doing much work and he said he really didn't feel himself enough, he was just too woozy, either to do it or to worry about not doing it. We talked about a lot, and a little, but really it just seemed to be clearing things, making everything alright. For the first time ever he told me that he felt that what I was doing at the moment i.e. bringing up the children, was very important indeed – whereas before I always felt that he didn't place any importance on it and that he thought I'd given up because I no longer had a job. In fact, I'd always felt he'd given me up because I was no longer doing any-thing worthwhile in his eyes. He wanted to know how he could have been a better father – a difficult question to answer. So I laughed and said I had always regretted the fact that I hadn't done science. He laughed too, and said 'fuck you'.

Solly hated illness in himself or others; even a common cold was intolerable. That his daughter whom he loved had cancer was a fact he struggled to avoid. Her death from it suggested failure which he could not bear and he put it away from him.

Paul reflects his father in his warmer and more sensitive moods. Joan was unwavering in her belief that from the beginning Solly saw his young son as a likely competitor. If he did, it helps one to understand his contradictory attitudes of criticising without encouraging, of wanting Paul to be a source of pride and credit, without allowing him to become too prominent. Paul could be forgiven for not being able himself to forgive the confusion which his father must have caused him when he was growing up, yet he has allowed pride in his father to come out on top of other feelings. He wondered how his father got over the endless hurdles he placed in front of himself, marvelled at his endlessly inquiring mind and at his early recognition of great artists, Henry Moore, Barbara Hepworth, Elisabeth Frink and others. He reflected on his discerning eye and taste. Paul's memories of his father are clear-cut; they point to a man communicating with baboons, searching for cornelians on the Norfolk shore, playing croquet and keen always to win. He used verse to bring them to life. There follow some lines which tell something of Solly – and of his son as well.

> A memory of him refusing to stop for lunch
> and asking to be fed while he drove.
> Cracking hard-boiled eggs on his knee,
> my mother panicked and picked a fresh one
> from the basket of food
> for the next day's breakfast,
> with a delightful end result
> for us children in the back!
>
> ———
>
> there was the playful side,
> hurling rotten apples across the lawn
> in a game of catch.
>
> ———
>
> And the more driven side
> that even showed itself in croquet
> which he loved to play but had to win.
>
> ———
>
> Growing older, though, the playful side got lost,
> often substituted by a level of frustration.
>
> ———
>
> The salt and pepper,
> the ever present two sides
> of this formidable man,
> gone now,
> resting in a biscuit tin
> in his Norfolk garden wall.

———

But ultimately there's a pride
that this man was my father.

Secretaries, who see a man in all weathers, all moods, in good
moments and bad, for the most part stayed with Solly and, even
when tormented by him, still mostly loved him. Deirdre Sharp,
now keeper of his archive at the University of East Anglia, said that
people who came to work for Lord Zuckerman either left in a
week or stayed a lifetime. He was thoughtful and generous when it
came to Christmas presents; on the other hand, the importance of
his work and his own convenience always came first. Gill Booth
was told that her reluctance to drive on frozen snowy country
roads, with a real risk of ending in the ditch, was simply feeble. An
injured leg which made it awkward to type his letters attracted no
sympathy: she should have been more careful and have anticipated
the inconvenience it would cause. Pam Warwick was, as has been
told in an earlier chapter, the bridge joining Solly's lives in
Birmingham and London. All those who accepted Solly's yoke
understood the range of his expectations. He himself was the top
of the pile; whatever engaged him was of the first importance. You
didn't have bad days, you didn't get colds – or allow him to. You
accepted a wide range of tasks such as the carriage of paving-stones
in the boot of your car or negotiating for the purchase of a redun-
dant public convenience made of Victorian ironwork. But this
above all, you made it clear that even if you did work like a slave, it
was by your choice, not his command. Unreasonable, selfish and
demanding, Solly was all of those things, but there was something
about him that made those who worked for him feel part of something important; they could not fail to meet the demands he made
on them; they couldn't let him down and they didn't.

As a scientist, Solly found the agnosticism of his earlier days
remained convenient. Whether he intended simply to warn off
intrusive questioners, or to deny the existence of a superior power,
is uncertain. He never forgot that he was a Jew and many of his
closest friends were Jews. Joan was uncertain as to whether he
objected or was pleased when she converted to Judaism. He was,

however, anxious that she should not take the children with her. 'It was', Stella wrote, 'as if he was fearful that somehow or other his Judaism would infect Paul and me.' Far from discouraging Stella, his attitude increased her fascination with their Jewishness. Within the family his position on religious matters was negative, even derisive. Talking to Stella, he scoffed at the belief of some people 'like your mother' that grass was green because God made it so. Outside the family he was more relaxed; he agreed, though with some wry comments about his unsuitability as an infidel, to act as a godfather to the Mountbattens' grandson.

As a scientist, Solly was accustomed to grappling with questions which were within the range of human knowledge and experience. He declined to be tempted into anthropology; he thought it too speculative, it wasn't possible to point to some creature which existed in a remote past and say there was the ancestor of *Homo sapiens*. Even less could he look back over a vast distance of time to some unprecedented undefined event and say that that was the beginning. As a scientist he did not, could not know; as a man he was reticent almost to the point of silence. In a speech in the House of Lords he was clear that, 'Science will never provide the answers to the ultimate questions; the question of what brought about what we call life and what it is that gives man his unique quality in the world of living organisms.' Bishop Peter Nott, who in his maiden speech quoted Solly's words, looked questioningly at his credentials as an agnostic. He thought him too interested in and too sympathetic to other people's faith to fit that role. He added, 'You could call him a holy agnostic if you wished.' Solly came to live somewhere between the scientist's world in which facts were sought and questions answered, and in that other one of politics, business, money, instant communication and muddle, in which facts are often overlaid by opinion and interest; in which questions are asked, but those who ask them, like Pilate, do not wait for an answer. It might be as well if, in pursuit of Mark Twain's advice, the scientists were encouraged to do some more finding out and the politicians to do less supposing.

A point which Stella made perceptively about her father, was that while he was much concerned with the opinions and reactions of those he thought important and to whom he particularly addressed himself, 'it never occurred to him to bother very much how he presented himself to the outside world'. She did not think that 'he could have cared less what they thought of him, he didn't need their approval or acclaim'. In matters where emphasis and clarity were essential, Solly was content, in her words, 'to impart a flavour, rarely the entirety'. She felt 'he was wrong in that kind of insularity; that if he had bothered to put his views across more simply and more directly to a much wider and more general audience, the world would have been a richer place for it.'

Solly was indeed a man out of the ordinary and seen to be so by those who, with very different backgrounds, worked closely with him from time to time. J.Z. Young, Professor of Anatomy at University College London, a friend from Oxford days, who was frequently an exterior examiner at Birmingham, said of Solly quite simply, 'To know him has been one of the great rewards of my life.' Adrian Cadbury, once head of the firm that bears his name, found it remarkable that 'Someone who had been closely involved with nuclear issues at world level should apply his great mind just as fruitfully to getting bubbles into fizzy drinks.' Jerome Wiesner, sometime Science Advisor to President Kennedy, wrote when Solly died of the forty years they had worked together and 'agreed on most every military and scientific situation, and together we often fought losing battles to make the world a more sensible place. But the fact we lost the battles together made us doubly sure that we were right.' These are three examples of how Solly left his stamp on the minds of his contemporaries, themselves not ordinary men. Yet memory clusters round the names of lesser, even by contrast trivial, characters, while those such as Rabi and Zuckerman are, if not forgotten, pushed aside in an age that wishes to consume and to be amused, without concern as to where it might end.

Solly died in hospital in April 1993, a month short of his 90th year. Discussing his situation on the previous day, he questioned the doctor's readings of his blood pressure and told him that he should take them again, since if they were correct, he was already dead. It showed a side of him, questioning, quizzical and never far from laughter both at life and himself.

Acknowledgements

I would not have attempted to write this book had it not been for Joan's concern that I should do so: nor without her help and encouragement could I have finished it. She passed on to me something of the interest, the joy and the hurt which life with Solly brought to her; also, after his death, of the pride she increasingly felt in her achievement.

Paul's understanding of his father and his pride in him have helped me to see things I might otherwise have missed. His response to my pleas for help during the time when I was attempting to get to grips with Solly were both lively and generous.

Roy Jenkins, as aware as anyone of Solly's stature and achievements, could not have been more helpful. He read every word in more than one version: in his comments he was perceptive and helpful and, in his commendation, generous.

The Wolfson Foundation, of which in his lifetime Solly was a Trustee, made my task easier with a generous contribution towards the costs of research.

I am hugely indebted to a host of people who knew Solly and who were prepared to talk to me about him. I hope they will accept my warm thanks and forgive me if, in order to avoid a long catalogue of names, I mention here only those who have given me many hours of their time, raked over their memories and contributed something which only they could provide.

I am most grateful to His Royal Highness The Duke of Edinburgh not only for allowing me to see and quote from the large correspondence which passed between him and Solly over many years, but also for his willingness to talk to me at length about Solly, whom he knew well and admired.

I also wish to thank: Geoffrey Allen, Chancellor of the University of East Anglia, who, with Keith Clayton, the first Dean of the School of Environmental Sciences, has helped me to understand the importance of the University to Solly and of his contribution to it; Noel Annan, who sadly died before I was able to thank him for his encouragement at an early stage when he helped me over what at the time seemed an impassable hump; Alun Chalfont, who as Minister for Disarmament worked closely with Solly and became a family friend; Frank Cooper, sometime Permanent Secretary, Ministry of Defence; Marcia Edwards, at the Zoo during many years of Solly's rule; Margaret Gardiner, whose memories stretch back over sixty years; Richard Garwin, physicist and long-time collaborator with Solly in nuclear weapons and international security; Martin Holdgate, sometime Deputy Secretary of the Department of the Environment; Peter Krohn and Anita Mandl, colleagues in Birmingham and friends over many years; Robert May, lately Chief Scientific Adviser to the Government and now President of the Royal Society; Patricia Mountbatten, who understands Solly's importance to her father; Andrew Norman, husband of Solly's daughter; Terry Price, scientist and civil servant and a member of Solly's small MOD staff; Crispin Tickell, whose concern for the environment is an echo of Solly's; Angele Vidal-Hall for her memories of Solly in the early years of the war; Philip Ziegler, author of *Mountbatten*, surely a model biography, who has been most generous with his time and advice; Arie Zuckerman, a one-time pupil of Solly's and until recently Dean of the Royal Free Hospital School of Medicine: all of them have seen different aspects of Solly and have been generous in sharing their recollections with me.

In a category of their own are Deirdre Sharpe, who worked for Solly and is now the keeper of the Zuckerman archive in the

Acknowledgements

Library of the University of East Anglia, who has been a tower of strength in locating and retrieving material from that overflowing resource, and who has compiled the splendid index; Pamela Spikes, whose memories of Solly in Birmingham show the good and the less good sides of him; Sarah Macnab, my own secretary, who deciphered my writing, understood my meaning and somehow got it into legible form; and Patrick Horsley, who has also read several versions and has advised.

Sources

Works by Solly Zuckerman

The Social Life of Monkeys and Apes (Kegan Paul, 1932)
Functional Affinities of Man, Monkeys and Apes (Kegan Paul, 1933)
From Apes to Warlords (Hamish Hamilton, 1978)
Monkeys, Men and Missiles (Collins, 1988)
Six Men Out of The Ordinary (Peter Owen, 1992)

Correspondence between HRH The Duke of Edinburgh and Solly Zuckerman.
Solly Zuckerman archive in the Library of the University of East Anglia. It consists of
    more than 900 boxes of papers and includes the typescript of a diary kept between
    October 1964 and February 1968.
Letters exchanged between Solly and Joan Zuckerman and shown to me by her.
Unpublished monograph on her father by Stella Norman (née Zuckerman).
Richard G. Davis, *Carl A. Spaatz and the Air War in Europe* (Center for Air Force History,
    Washington DC, 1993)
In Memoriam I.I. Rabi (privately published, 1988)
Lord Tedder, *With Prejudice* (Cassell, 1966)
Philip Ziegler, *Mountbatten* (Collins, 1985)

INDEX

Index

Index

Index